Theory and Practice of Technology-Based Music Instruction

THEORY AND PRACTICE OF TECHNOLOGY-BASED MUSIC INSTRUCTION

Jay Dorfman

OXFORD
UNIVERSITY PRESS

OXFORD
UNIVERSITY PRESS

Oxford University Press is a department of the University of Oxford.
It furthers the University's objective of excellence in research, scholarship,
and education by publishing worldwide.

Oxford   New York
Auckland   Cape Town   Dar es Salaam   Hong Kong   Karachi
Kuala Lumpur   Madrid   Melbourne   Mexico City   Nairobi
New Delhi   Shanghai   Taipei   Toronto

With offices in
Argentina   Austria   Brazil   Chile   Czech Republic   France   Greece
Guatemala   Hungary   Italy   Japan   Poland   Portugal   Singapore
South Korea   Switzerland   Thailand   Turkey   Ukraine   Vietnam

Oxford is a registered trade mark of Oxford University Press
in the UK and certain other countries.

Published in the United States of America by
Oxford University Press
198 Madison Avenue, New York, NY 10016

Library of Congress Cataloging-in-Publication Data
Dorfman, Jay.
Theory and practice of technology-based music instruction / Jay Dorfman.
pages cm
Includes bibliographical references and index.
ISBN 978-0-19-979558-1 (hardcover : alk. paper)—ISBN 978-0-19-979559-8 (pbk. : alk.
paper)
1. Music—Instruction and study—Technological innovations.   2. Educational technology.
I. Title.
MT1.D666 2013
780.7—dc23
2012042404

9 8 7 6 5 4 3 2 1
Printed in the United States of America
on acid-free paper

CONTENTS

PREFACE

This book is intended primarily for practicing music teachers, though it is also applicable for people preparing to become music teachers. I assume of the reader a functional knowledge of music-related technologies including hardware (computers, mobile devices, electronic instruments) and software (for notation, audio/MIDI recording and editing, learning music fundamentals, and performance). There are several fine texts written with the intention of teaching readers to use those tools, but that is not the function of this book. This book is about learning the techniques of being a teacher who uses technology as a basis for music classes.

I also acknowledge that technologies for learning music have existed for many years. Using technology to teach music is not a new idea. The current rise of technology in K–12 music settings, however, has created demand for pedagogy, based on musical-philosophical beliefs that account for students' differences. Encouraging this type of considered, reflective teaching is the goal of this book.

Thank you for reading.

ACKNOWLEDGMENTS

I would like to thank my family—my parents, grandparents, brother, sister-in-law, niece, and in-laws—for their consistent support and encouragement through this project. My career is sometimes difficult to explain, and I appreciate their open-mindedness, willingness to listen, and the pride that they take in me and in my work.

This book would not have been possible without the teacher participants who gave willingly and enthusiastically of their time and expertise. Each of them facilitated obtaining consent from their principal, their students, and their students' parents, then voluntarily let me into their classrooms. They also contributed their insights to the final chapter of the text—some of the speculations about the future of technology-based music instruction came from suggestions about what they feel will be important in years to come. I appreciate their openness, honesty, and willingness to give up an occasional lunch period for the cause. I am unfortunately required to keep most of their names confidential, but these talented teachers were essential to the development of my theories. I hope we all have teachers like them at some time in our lives.

I wish to thank Norm Hirschy and the staff of Oxford University Press for their support through the process. I appreciate OUP for lending its prestigious name to my work. Matthew Koehler and Punya Mishra (TPACK), Tina Wells (ISTE), and Amy Burns (TI:ME) authorized the use of their organizations' models and standards, and I am grateful for their generosity.

My professors, from and with whom I have learned so much, were invaluable in the process of formulating the ideas in this book. Many of the strands of thought come out of work I did in their classes. Nicholas DeCarbo and Joyce Jordan inspired me to think, to become a teacher who worked in service of his students' musical and personal growth, and to understand the connections between theoretical constructs and good ways to teach music. The faculty I worked with at the Northwestern University Center for the Study of Education and the Musical Experience—Peter Webster, Janet Barrett, Maud Hickey, Scott Lipscomb, Carlos Abril, Bennett Reimer, and Bernie Dobroski—are mentors in the truest sense of the term. Thank you for providing me inspiration, and freedom to pursue my interests in logical and meaningful ways. I also value the friends I made who were CSEME fellows, and thank them for their support.

My music education colleagues at Boston University are simply the best group of people I have ever worked with. Some departments' members work very hard, other departments' members work very well together—few departments do both as well as we do. I am so thankful for your support of this project and for helping me to develop into a better music teacher educator every day.

I would like to acknowledge the support of my friends and colleagues in music technology organizations such as TI:ME and ATMI. These individuals number too many to name, but a quick glance at the organizations' websites will show the active, productive, innovative people I have come to know. I value your input and feedback, and sharing time together in meetings and at conferences. I look forward to many years of continued friendship with you and to seeing how our field will develop.

Teachers cannot accomplish anything without students to teach. I am fortunate to have taught hundreds of students at Flanagan High School, Kent State University, Boston University, and in many workshop experiences who have challenged me and have come with me on incredible musical and technological journeys. A great point of pride in my life is to see my former students become successful in their lives, and especially when their lives involve music or education.

Finally, my wife Janna provided me with unending support throughout the process of writing this book. She was a patient listener, an enthusiastic participant, and a source of great encouragement. Janna, I love you and could not have done this without you.

Theory and Practice of Technology-Based Music Instruction

CHAPTER 1

Introducing Technology-Based Music Instruction

PROFILE OF PRACTICE 1.1

Mrs. Jones has 14 years of teaching under her belt. She received her music education degree from an excellent state university program and completed a master's in music education early in her career during the summers. After teaching at several levels, she has settled in a good junior high school position in an upper middle-class neighborhood. The music department—she and two other teachers—is a collaborative group that consistently turns out strong performances for the school and community.

About five years ago, Mrs. Jones noticed that technology was becoming an increasingly important part of many of the school music programs she considered to be on par with her own. She had introduced some technology in her orchestra class—she used notation software to create warm-up exercises and often played listening examples for the students that she stored on her iPod. So, with the same enthusiasm that she approaches most of the parts of her job, she approached her principal about funding a computer lab for the music department. Her request was met with excitement. The principal agreed to set up a lab dedicated to the music department and to schedule a class for Mrs. Jones to teach called Music Technology for the following fall. There was no established curriculum for the class, but Mrs. Jones would have the summer to assemble the curriculum and lesson plans, in consultation with the principal and the other music teachers. They all recognized that starting this class would bring new students to their excellent music department and could only draw more public attention to their good work.

The lab would have 15 student stations and an additional station for the teacher. None of the music teachers or the school's administrators had any expertise in designing computer labs, so they left that task up to the district's architects. The information technology (IT) department was enlisted to set up all of the hardware and software and to make appropriate network and server connections, with enough time for Mrs. Jones to get used to the lab before the school year would begin.

The class's enrollment filled up quickly. Mrs. Jones examined the roster and did not recognize any of the students' names, which meant most of them were not involved in the school's musical ensembles. She knew it would be a challenge to teach music to students who were not necessarily trained in reading notation or performing in the traditional sense. Mrs. Jones spent her summer diligently working on her curriculum and lesson plans. Despite her best efforts, and the training she received in the use of technology applications during her studies at both the undergraduate and graduate levels, she was not sure she was approaching the class in the way that would provide greatest benefit for her students. Still, she was willing to consider the design of the class, and the daily lessons once the school year began, as a grand experiment. She was willing to be confused sometimes, and she was willing to learn. She was particularly interested in giving students musical opportunities that were more personally creative than she felt she could do in her ensemble classes, and she was not afraid to ask for help if she needed it. She definitely did not feel she was "in her comfort zone" and occasionally wondered if she had taken on something she could not handle.

When the school year began, Mrs. Jones had prepared units for her class that would focus on recording original compositions with sequencing software, composing with notation software, making soundtracks for videos, and other projects. She had gotten ideas for projects by talking with friends and doing research on the Internet. The class would last for half of the year, and Mrs. Jones's focus would be on helping the students become musically proficient while producing interesting, creative projects.

Mrs. Jones completed the first iteration of her Music Technology class successfully, but she knew there were parts of the class that she could improve. She had been thinking a lot about how she felt more comfortable sequencing instruction in her choirs and orchestras than she did in the Music Technology class. She felt she could see the "end-game" of the ensemble classes better than she could in the new environment. While she understood and felt comfortable with the skills she wanted her students to develop, she really felt no connection to any theoretical or pedagogical basis for those decisions.

INTRODUCTION

Mrs. Jones is not alone in dealing with the issues she faced in Profile 1.1. Every day in classrooms throughout the United States, teachers excitedly open the packaging surrounding the latest technological breakthrough. Teachers eagerly dive in to the technology—maybe a new piece of software, maybe a hardware component, maybe a compact, handheld device. Their minds swarm with ideas of how they might integrate this technology into their teaching, and into their students' learning.

Undoubtedly, questions abound. They wonder: Did I ask for the right technology? Will it help me accomplish what I want it to do in the way I hope to do it? Will it support the learning goals I hold for my students? Do I know how to use it well and to take advantage of all it affords?

Teachers who are in a position to integrate technologies into their classrooms are fortunate. Anecdotally, I have witnessed the power that technology has to engage students in the learning process. Also, most of my students are sophisticated technology users *outside* of the classroom so making use of technology *in* the classroom makes sense. While some schools and districts are certainly more advantaged than others, there is a general consensus from the last two decades that schools have a genuine interest in investing in technology that students and teachers can use to promote better—more effective, more efficient, longer lasting—learning experiences.

The socioeconomic diversity of American schools practically dictates that some schools will be able to provide more technological exposure for students than will others. However, the setting of schools is no longer a significant predictor of their access to technology; that is, schools in urban, suburban, and rural schools are equally likely to have access to technologies such as high-speed Internet connections (Bakia, Means, Gallagher, Chen, & Jones, 2009), which is a typical measure of technology access for schools. The promise of sophisticated technology integration is on the rise. Many more teachers have access to professional development opportunities than they ever have before, the gap in access across many subjects is closing, and many states are even conducting assessments of student technology literacy in order to promote achievement in skill areas that will be needed in the mid-21-st-century workforce (Bakia et al., 2009). Specific to technology-based music courses, Dammers (2010b) recently found in a random sample of schools in the United States that the socioeconomic status of school districts did not imply a significant difference in availability of these types of classes.

These are great strides in the cause of advancing technology use in schools. Music teachers should be proud of our work toward making technology integration a priority for students, and proud of seeking training to learn to use technology. Music teachers should recognize, however, that the advancements in professional development for teachers and the integration of technology into our classrooms are relatively specialized. The data that support the positive steps measure almost exclusively the integration of technology into English, math, and science curricula. Teachers who receive training in technology integration are most often the ones who teach those subjects, so students' exposure to technology is occurring primarily in the contexts of those disciplines. Naturally, this excludes the "non-core" subject areas, where music typically falls.

To be included in the "technology wave," music teachers have to raise our collective voices and assert our interest in using technology to benefit our own teaching and our students' learning. Music and other non-core subjects are not, and might never be, the focus of technology integration in education. However, if music teachers can understand and implement good practices for promoting quality learning of music through technological means, then our profession is far less likely to be left behind, in a cloud of silicon dust. We must understand that technology is not just a set of toys, nor is it just a set of teaching tools. Rather, technology is an important means by which we can teach music—introduce its concepts, reinforce them, provide experience, provide practice, assess and evaluate achievement, structure aesthetic interactions, and do all the educational activities that make learning music a distinct, artful pursuit.

PROFILE OF PRACTICE 1.1 CONTINUED

Mrs. Jones had several other concerns. First, she had left many of the choices about software, hardware, and lab design up to other people in the district. Those people made choices based more on economics than on pedagogy. Second, she still felt out of place teaching from her computer station, speaking to her students through a headphone audio system, as compared to standing in front of her ensemble on a podium or at the piano. The assignments she gave to her students were very different from anything she had ever asked her ensemble students to do, which made her feel uncomfortable about how to grade them. Finally, a few weeks into the school year, the principal came to observe Mrs. Jones teaching in her new lab. The principal had questions about how she had structured the class and whether she was taking full advantage of the capabilities of the lab that had cost the school so much money.

While this account of Mrs. Jones is fictional, the other Profiles of Practice in this text are real, and they reflect similar themes. Although

Mrs. Jones was teaching in a setting with excellent support and enthusiasm for the subject of music being taught through technology, she still felt frustrations and had problems to work through.

THE STATE OF TECHNOLOGY IN THE K–12 CLASSROOM

The idea of using technology to aid music instruction has existed for several decades and has proven successful in many ways. But early efforts at technology integration emphasized substitution of technology for the teacher (Williams & Webster, 2006; Rudolph, 2004). Technology-based music instruction (TBMI), the kind of teaching examined in this book, updates the notion of "technology *or* teacher" to one of "technology *with* teacher." Music teachers invest their time and intellectual energy in technology to varying degrees. The degree to which they invest is not always their choice—it can be dictated by a variety of factors including training, access, and need.

THE TOPOGRAPHY OF TECHNOLOGY INTEGRATION

Through my own observations, I developed a model for categorizing the extent to which teachers engage with technology as part of their teaching, which I now call the Topography of Technology Integration (Dorfman, 2006). I use the word *topography* for three reasons: (1) Topographical features do not exist in isolation. They are surrounded by additional structures that combine to form a broader landscape. (2) While it may be difficult to traverse from one topographical feature to another because there are obstacles in the way (geographically, perhaps a mountain range), it is not impossible. (3) Certain features in a large landscape are generally regarded as more desirable than others. Most people would rather find themselves on a beach than in a field.

The Technical Basin

The technical basin of technology refers to the position when teachers learn to use available technologies and when they acquire fluency with those technologies. For example, budding technologists might learn how to record an instrument or their voice using Audacity, or to create a simple score in Finale. Classes in technology for music educators are often designed to expose them to the tools currently considered useful for music teaching and learning and to provide practical instruction about their use. If those classes focus exclusively on the acquisition of technical facility, then they fail to serve the needs of teachers to learn to apply technology in educational settings.

At this level, music educators study technology for its own sake rather than as a means for learning music. Mastery of technical skills is necessary to advance to more sophisticated levels of technology integration and to a place in which teachers can *base* their teaching on technology as the major medium for music learning. The difficulty is that many classes about technology for current and future music teachers fail to address pedagogical uses of technology, instead focusing on procedures.

The type of learning that takes place in the technical basin is not detrimental; on the contrary, it is important for teachers to learn to use technology. For some, this is the chasm that stands in the way of sophisticated technology integration. At this time, when all music teacher preparation programs are required to expose students to pedagogically appropriate technologies, we owe it to ourselves to be critical of the ways we do so. While we strive to meet the needs of P-12 students, teacher educators miss the boat when we fail to prepare teachers adequately for using technology as a fundamental pedagogical instrument.

The Practical Plane

At this next level of technological integration, teachers put their technology knowledge into practice. This includes using technology as a tool for preparing lessons. Popular examples include using software for creating worksheets and handouts, managing aspects of ensemble organization, and recording rehearsals or performances for review.

While these and others are all valid and acceptable uses of technology to enhance music teaching, they are largely teacher-centered pursuits. The examples given are missing a key element of my concept of technology-based music instruction—the idea that *students can and should interact directly with technology*. While the use of a database program for tracking attendance, instrument and uniform inventories, and students' biographical information may be extremely valuable to busy teachers, the benefit of doing so does not often impact student learning directly. Uses of technology such as these are therefore relegated to the practical label because they do not necessarily address directly the delivery of instruction or enhancement of an educational objective.

Practical technology uses can be extremely valuable. They undoubtedly improve the quality of life and work for teachers. The concern is that teachers on the practical plane may claim that they are using technology to enhance their teaching and their students' learning, when in fact they are simply taking advantage of administrative tools. It is possible that teachers fail to make the transition into the use of technology for teaching because they are not prepared to do so.

The Pedagogical Summit

In the most sophisticated level of educational technology, teachers use technology to introduce, explain, reinforce, and provide practice with concepts and skills, and to assess student learning. Rather than reserving technology for their own uses, teachers design experiences in which students engage directly in activities with hardware and software. This practice requires a different kind of pedagogy than teaching without computer technology does. Teachers who have climbed to the pedagogical summit are able to apply educational theory and learning environment design, and employ technology tools while maintaining the integrity of musical content.

The three sections are not impermeable. On the contrary, new and experienced teachers can naturally progress from one phase to the next, perhaps even bypassing the practical plane en route to the pedagogical summit. The point is to realize that using technology as the major means for teaching music is a *learned skill*. Though teachers may demonstrate a proclivity toward using technology, it is unlikely that teachers will be able to do so naturally. Several reasons for this may exist:

1. While using technology to learn music is not new, technological pedagogy is. Current teachers have few models from their own education of people who do this skillfully.
2. Teacher training (both pre-service and in-service) models to support music technology pedagogy are not fully developed.
3. Opportunities for improving skills as a technology-based music teacher are rare, and can be difficult to find.

The research and practice communities are yet to fully explore the ways in which students interact with technology and therefore are severely disadvantaged when we attempt to design practical, sequential, educationally sound curriculum for music in technologically based settings.

This is precisely why a guide for music technology pedagogy is needed. The methods described in this book generally assume that teachers have a functional knowledge of technology and applications (as in the pedestrian basin) and are able to transfer that knowledge to uses that support their work (as in the practical plane). But the pedagogical summit is still largely unexplored terrain. We must examine it in terms of its philosophical grounding, the choices it implies that teachers make, and the cyclical assessment for which it calls. The following Profile of Practice includes an example of a teacher who struggled with some typical obstacles. Perhaps you can identify with some of these circumstances.

PROFILE OF PRACTICE 1.2

Mrs. U is a middle school music teacher with more than 25 years of experience in the classroom. She expressed ideas about priorities similar to those of many music teachers—she wants her students to be active and engaged, and she wants varied activities in her classroom to encourage that engagement. Her technology experiences are limited: in addition to a one-day in-service workshop several years ago, she has done some exploration on her own. She feels fortunate to have attended several sessions about technology at her state's annual music teacher conference.

I watched Mrs. U teach middle school general music classes into which she was infusing computer technologies. Many of the musical concepts her students encountered were introduced through lectures enhanced with PowerPoint presentations. She makes interesting uses of technology for preparing the lesson material—she uses YouTube to download music and videos, and iTunes to organize and play back media—but she faces limitations in her school because websites such as YouTube, which might contain explicit material, are blocked from use. So, she goes the extra mile and downloads media at home, then brings it to school on a laptop or a flash drive.

Despite Mrs. U's interest in using technology, she faces some real challenges. First, because technology is relatively new to her, she was concerned that sometimes her lessons feel like they flow poorly. This is a particular contrast to the way she feels in front of her band classes, where she is natural and hardly has to think to make lessons smooth. She said, "I grew up in the band environment, and it is kind of in my blood. I didn't have general music when I was in school because I was always in band." Second, in her current teaching job, she does not have a dedicated space in which to teach a technology-based music class. Her shared general music classroom has four workstations at one end of the room, and when she puts her students at them, usually in groups, the space gets very crowded. Her only other option is to reserve a cart of laptops in advance.

I observed Mrs. U teach lessons on concepts of theme and variation, and on elements of musicals and operas. Each of the lessons was enhanced through a technology-based activity. In the unit on theme and variation, the students used Audacity to manipulate recordings to demonstrate variation techniques. Mrs. U confessed that if the students were asked what type of lesson it was, they would probably identify it as an Audacity lesson rather than a theme-and-variation lesson. Students were directly interacting with technology, but the limitations of the physical environment and the teacher's limited experience with technology may cause this perception.

Mrs. U's integration of technology into her teaching is admirable, and her students enjoy the fact that they are engaged technologically. They take to the activities enthusiastically. But I get a sense from talking to Mrs. U that she would love to take her technology-based teaching to the next level.

TEACHERS' CONCERNS

Most teachers feel discomfort toward implementing technology in their music teaching (Dorfman, 2008; Taylor & Deal, 2003), and therefore students' needs may be less adequately met than in traditional music learning settings. In this section I will describe some specific concerns that teachers have expressed.

Preparedness

Many teachers say they do not feel prepared to integrate technology into their teaching, so they avoid doing so. This is most likely because they *are* underprepared to use technology in sophisticated ways and want to avoid teaching in ways that make them uncomfortable. This lack of preparedness may result from (1) inadequate training in undergraduate or graduate teacher education curricula, (2) insufficient time to plan for deep technology uses, (3) the ever-changing landscape of available technologies, and/or (4) an inflexible attitude that prevents teachers from feeling successful with technology.

Curriculum Development

It is difficult to teach what we do not know. When called upon to write curriculum that involves technology—which, as seen in the opening Profile of Practice, may include daily lesson plans, large-scale frameworks, or anything in between—teachers balk because they feel inadequate in creating lessons that use tools with which they are not entirely familiar. This is not unlike a biologist teaching a chemistry class, or a woodwind player teaching a group violin lesson—it is a difficult, often uncomfortable process that can only be learned with practice and a willingness to let go of insecurities.

Supporting and Evaluating Creativity

It is easy to think that what we do in traditional music classes inspires creativity. But consider this: The majority of the creativity that happens in a traditional ensemble class (a band, chorus, or orchestra) comes from the director, not the students. The director typically makes musical decisions, listens critically, evaluates, and modifies performance based on her judgments. In fact, we could say that the music production in those classes is largely *re*-creative, indicating a reproduction of music that a composer has already written, rather than creative, indicating the birthing of something novel.

Educational contexts in which students are free to create new work, typically within specified guidelines, are unusual. This type of freedom, and the unstructured time that it implies, is difficult for music teachers who are so accustomed to carefully planning every precious moment of rehearsal time. Allowing students to explore, evaluate their own work, help each other, and *revise* their creative output takes a commitment of time that might make teachers feel uncomfortable.

There is good news: this type of discomfort is a treatable condition. Learning the technology and engaging with it at a comfortable-yet-aggressive pace can help to address teachers' concerns. Throughout this book, you will encounter stories of teachers who were trained in traditional ways to be music teachers and to instruct in traditional contexts. They have accepted the challenge of making meaningful music learning experiences for their students that are based on technology. They have acknowledged the formation of this new strand of music teaching, and they will serve as examples of how to do so.

DIFFERENTIATING BETWEEN TECHNOLOGY INTEGRATION AND TECHNOLOGY-BASED MUSIC INSTRUCTION

Historical Integration of Technology

Technology integration is such a broad term that it is difficult to pin down a point in history when teachers started to integrate technology into their classrooms. Generously, every tool or device that we use for teaching (or any other task, for that matter) could be considered technology. Tools such as chalk and erasers could be viewed as technological in that they advance the ease with which teachers and students can do their work.

Let us narrow the discussion, then, to the early uses of *computer-based* technology. Though technological devices that predate the computer made substantial contributions to music education practice—one needs to think only of the phonograph—the computer as a mediating tool for shaping creative experiences stands as a unique device. In addition, new devices such as tablets and smartphones are making incredible contributions to technological advancement; however, we will assume for now that those kinds of devices are essentially derivatives or extensions of computers.

Though sporadic uses of computers certainly existed throughout the world in the mid-20th century, universities were the predominant setting for computer technology integration into music teaching. In 1975, a group of university professors formed the National Consortium for Computer-Based Music Instruction (NCCBMI). There are few historical records of the group's formation, but interviews with its founders (Dorfman, 2003) have helped to document the names and institutional affiliations of the people who started this group. In 1985, the group changed its name to the Association for Technology in Music Instruction, which is still a thriving organization.

Early technology integration into music instruction was mostly centered on work in music theory and aural skills, and the major players in the formation of NCCBMI were predominantly music theorists. Efforts such as the PLATO platform at the University of Illinois, and programs written for it such as GUIDO (at the University of Delaware), were used to enhance instruction in aural skills. Important contributions to technology-based music instruction came from music technology centers at Florida State University, Northwestern University, Pennsylvania State University, and Indiana University, among others.

The basis for much of the computer-based learning found in early efforts could be viewed as *programmed instruction*. This type of software (which, in the early days, was very much tied to hardware) was designed so that students followed a sequential set of tasks, and they were not allowed to advance to a new task until they had mastered the one before them. Software was designed as a teacher replacement; that is, students could use the software for drill and practice, essentially doing so in lieu of interaction with a teacher or other students.

Most of the contributions discussed so far were severely limited by a common factor: They were confined to hardware that was expensive and immovable. The advent of the powerful personal computer in the early 1980s changed the landscape of technology integration into primary and secondary levels of music education. No longer was technology-based music instruction the exclusive domain of universities. The early 1980s also saw the birth of the Musical Instrument Digital Interface (MIDI) specification, a protocol that allowed music software and hardware devices to interface with one another. This made sound production via computer attainable and brought music technology to the masses. Computer sound generation and the concurrent appearance of hypertext as a protocol for navigation gave rise to important multimedia aritfacts and learning tools for primary and secondary students.

The 1990s and early 2000s brought recognition that technology was here to stay. Teacher training became a priority so that teachers would be able to implement the uses of technology in their classrooms. Teacher training remains an emphasis in technological circles, and teacher educators have begun to recognize the weaknesses in the ways we train music teachers to integrate technology. A major effort that has advanced the cause of teacher training in technology integration was the founding of TI:ME (Technology Institute for Music Educators) in 1995. This organization emphasizes teacher training through organizing workshops and professional conferences that focus on technology in music instruction.

Recent Technological and Pedagogical Advances

Historical efforts toward technology integration such as some of those described previously have been focused on the uses of technology to replace the work of teachers. In the past decade or so, several influences have begun to change the nature of technological integration:

1. In contrast to the computers of the mid-20th century, modern computers are fast, portable, and relatively inexpensive. All of the major computer platforms (Macintosh, Windows, Linux, etc.) perform sophisticated processing with graphical user interfaces and support robust sound capabilities.

Also, the integration of wireless connectivity, as well as extensible media support (for storage devices such as CDs, DVDs, and USB drives) allows for the use of massive quantities of data, making the computing experience very rich.

2. Software for learning has undergone decades of scrutiny. The design of software has improved the learning experience by appealing to the natural and dynamic states of human behavior and cognition.

3. Educational philosophy, though not stable, has undergone something of a shift. New thinking about music teaching has encouraged teachers to take on a role that matches well with creative technologies. As such, technologies that support student creativeness have become increasingly popular.

4. Educational thinkers have recognized the changing nature of students. Computers and technology are not unfamiliar to the current, digital generation.

Technology integration in current educational practice has morphed to accommodate the changing landscape of teaching and learning. And yet, many music teachers still view technology integration in relatively simplistic ways.

TECHNOLOGY INTEGRATION VERSUS PEDAGOGY UNDER TBMI

In this section, I will describe the types of technology use that I advocate through this book. Recall the Topography of Technology described earlier in this chapter. Most of what most teachers feel comfortable doing fits into the Technical and Practical areas of the model. Practical uses of technology include preparing materials for students to use such as worksheets or listening guides; using recordings that have been edited; or recording students performing and having them evaluate those recordings. These are all important and valuable uses of technology, and in no way do I discourage these types of uses.

Technology-based music instruction (TBMI), the type of pedagogy described herein, refers to music teaching where technology is the major medium by which music concepts and skills are introduced, reinforced, and assessed. Technology-based music instruction also implies that students are directly engaged with technology rather than simply with the products of technology work that the teacher has prepared. TBMI can take place in many music learning environments, including traditional ensembles and general music classes, but the focus of this text is the music computer lab and the intricacies it presents.

To illustrate further the differences between simple technology integration and the more sophisticated, experiential teaching and learning advocated in this text, consider how a teacher's approach to a learning goal might change based on these two perspectives. Let us assume that Mrs. Brown wants her students to understand the concepts of theme and variation in composition—a long-term goal. In this particular lesson, she wants the students to recognize that one way to vary material is by modifying instrumentation—a short-term objective.

In the traditional model of technology *integration*, which does not necessarily insist on direct student interaction with technology, Mrs. Brown might use part of her planning time to prepare some artifacts for her students to listen to. These might include excerpts of recordings that she extracts from CDs. They might even be her own simple melodic compositions—she can use technology to modify instrumentation so students can hear the different tone colors produced by changing instruments. She could then play these artifacts for her students. The examples she prepares make admirable use of her own technology skills; however, to students, they are just additional material to be absorbed at a surface level during Mrs. Brown's lecture.

Technology-based music instruction, the approach explained in this book, takes this lesson to another level. Rather than learning passively as Mrs. Brown's students might do in a lecture, a TBMI lesson would involve students directly with exploring theme and variation concepts and examples. Her students might extract excerpts of pre-selected recordings that demonstrate instrumentation changes. They might use recording software to record voiceovers on top of those excerpts explaining what the composer did to achieve the desired effect. Additionally, Mrs. Brown might have her students compose a short melody using software such as GarageBand, then experiment with applying instrument changes so that they can decide which timbres they like for their own compositions.

While the traditional method just described might still accomplish the long-term goal, the TBMI version could succeed more effectively in several ways. With traditional methods,

1. Deep student engagement is much less likely to occur; if engagement does occur, it will probably be superficial.
2. Although evidence of this claim is only anecdotal, we might see less retention of concepts.
3. There is little opportunity for student creativity and higher order cognitive tasks such as analysis, synthesis, and evaluation.

While this illustration is quite simplified, it is an example of the type of direct interaction with technology supported by TBMI and the types of experiences teachers might design for students. The distinction between the two types of teaching contributes to the foundation of the approach described in this book. And because this is a new way of thinking, most of the remainder of this book is dedicated to examining elements of pedagogy that might take place based on the approach.

GOALS OF TEACHING IN A TBMI CONTEXT

The music teaching profession has been loosely guided by the National Standards for Music Education since their publication in 1994. Though many interpretations and arguments surrounding the standards exist, they are generally accepted as guidelines for the type of content on which music teachers focus. The question that naturally arises, then, is this: How does technology change the ways we help our students achieve the standards?

The answer is at the same time simple and complex. Simply, it does not. From a bird's-eye view, the long-term goals (as articulated in the National Standards) of music teaching are the same no matter how we approach them. Though the means by which we teach music may change from one classroom to the next, or from one period in the school day to the next, ultimately, the goal is to teach music. If the content were to change for technology-based music instruction, then logically, those focused on choral or instrumental instruction would have grounds to argue for modified standards for their areas as well. The goal of TBMI, just as in other kinds of music teaching, is to help students be able to perform, compose, improvise, listen, and understand music's connections to culture, history, and other subject areas.

In a more complex sense, specific objectives may be different in TBMI contexts than they are in traditional music teaching and learning contexts. Throughout the book you will read about teachers who practice TBMI in very sophisticated ways. Often, these teachers will address the "types" of students they find in their classes, and those students may be very different from the students who register for band, chorus, or orchestra, especially at the secondary level. As we prepare students to become productive members of society, we owe it to them to consider how the content of our classes will be useful beyond the school walls. We need to consider the possibility that the music students of today may not be the classically trained performers of tomorrow; rather, they might be the engineers, producers, game music composers, mash-up artists, DJs, or music software developers of tomorrow.

These developing lines of work may force us to change the ways we emphasize our long-term goals. For example, some teachers interviewed for this text have realized that critical listening should play a strong part in their curriculum and daily activities because it is an essential skill for technological musicians. Some teachers try to focus on reading and writing traditional notation as little as possible, instead emphasizing alternative forms of notation such as waveforms and MIDI editing displays. Still other teachers expressed the idea that performing in groups is a difficult goal to achieve, so they choose to de-emphasize it. As you read this book, keep in mind that while the immediate goal of teaching music comprehensively and thoroughly does not change in the TBMI context, the service we provide for our students may cause us to finesse and rebalance the ways we approach those goals and their outcomes.

PURPOSES OF THE BOOK

The purpose of this book may be most clearly explained by stating what it is not: This is not a book that will help its readers learn how to use all of the functions of music technology software and hardware. This book assumes knowledge of the types of music technology that are available and an understanding of how to use them. One of the obstacles to integration of technology into music teaching is a simple lack of awareness on the part of the teacher regarding available technologies, their affordances and barriers, and how to make those technologies do what is needed. If you are looking for a text that explains all of the functions of the menus in a particular piece of software, you will not find that information here. There is no shame in needing to seek out those kinds of guides in the form of another text or a workshop with a qualified professional, and I encourage you to do so.

This book assumes that its readers are "sold" on the impact that technology can have in the music classroom. The purposes of this book are these:

1. To examine some of the *theoretical underpinnings* that influence an approach to technology-based music instruction. While teachers may certainly impose their own philosophical beliefs on their teaching (and thus, on their students' learning), it is important to establish a tradition from which the TBMI approach is derived.

2. To present some guidelines for the *selection of materials* to be used in technology-based music instruction. This necessarily includes selection of both musical materials (music for listening, music for performance, music for learning software) and technological materials (hardware, and software for various types of learning activities). This book will examine some guidelines, but it remains technologically neutral because technology will surely change.

3. To investigate *the ways teachers plan for and act in* technology-based music instruction. It stands to reason that if the materials and goals are different, then the ways that teachers design lessons, and the behaviors that teachers display, will be different. This book will examine pedagogical techniques prior to implementation, and in action.

4. To present ideas about *assessment* in TBMI. New types of teaching and learning require revision to methods of assessment. In TBMI, we are obligated to evaluate not only our students' work, but also our work as teachers and the programs that make use of technology.

5. To show *profiles of practice*. Throughout the text, you will read vignettes about teachers who base their music teaching on technology. While most of the featured teachers are included because of their refined skills, vast knowledge, and diverse experiences, you will recognize that these model teachers still struggle with issues surrounding TBMI. They think constantly about balancing innovation with tradition, about engaging their students in meaningful ways, about adhering to external expectations, and about maintaining the rewarding nature of their profession.

6. *To generate*, through organic means, *an approach that guides technology-based music instruction*. As will be discussed later, this is a major hole in the thinking that guides current music education. We have several recognized methods for teaching elementary general music (Orff, Kodály, Dalcroze, Gordon's MLT) and recognized pedagogical guides for teaching band, choir, orchestra, and other types of ensembles, but we have none for TBMI. By calling on insights collected through interactions with excellent teachers, this book will represent perhaps the first method for teaching music with technology as the major medium.

Finally, this text will look to the future. The closing chapters will consider the possibilities for innovative lesson design based on the model that will be established throughout the book and will also imagine the impact of educational policies such as standardized testing. In addition, the book will include an examination of some established models of teacher training in technology-based music instruction.

There are teachers in the field who do extraordinary things with technology in their music classrooms. In striving to generate an approach toward technology-based music instruction that was worth its own weight, I thought it was necessary to call on those teachers to contribute to its development.

I contacted teachers who have established outstanding reputations for their solid music instruction through technology. I received permission from the teachers, their supervisors, the students in each class I would observe, and those students' parents, in order to protect them as participants in my observations. I also received approval from my university's Institutional Review Board to conduct these observations. Some of the teachers I have known for many years; others were new acquaintances. Some teachers I contacted after hearing about their innovative uses of technology, while others approached me after conference presentations or informal conversations. Recruitment of participants was ongoing throughout the course of the project, and participants often referred me to other participants in a type of "snowballing" recruitment process. In situations in which I interacted with students, in order to avoid identifying them, teacher participants were promised confidentiality, so the names used in this text are pseudonyms. In several cases, however, the research involved only interviews with teachers, so some real names appear. I observed 21 teachers, all of whom made use of technology in their music classrooms during my visits.

I visited, either physically or through distance technologies such as Skype or iChat, each of the teachers, most on three to five occasions, to conduct observations of their teaching. I took steps to be as unobtrusive as possible. If I visited the classroom in person, I sat in an out-of-the-way location with a camera on a tripod and tried not to interrupt the class. When students were working on their own I would occasionally walk around the lab and look at their individual screens, but I only did so with the permission of the teacher. In cases where I was observing via distance technology, the teacher and I worked together to position the webcam so that it captured as much of the classroom as possible. In most circumstances I observed for an entire class period, usually with my sound muted and my image turned off.

Soon after each observation, I watched the video recording with the teacher as time permitted. I conducted an interview with the teachers while the videos were rolling. I posed some questions that related directly to the elements of the TBMI method. The teachers were also free to comment about any aspect they wished. Recordings of the interviews were transcribed and were examined for themes that relate directly to the theory presented in this text.

The profiles that appear in this text are, in most cases, composite accounts of the interviews and observations described. Within a particular profile, there may be quotations from several different interviews with one teacher. In most cases, it became clear to me that each teacher displayed qualities that were most closely related to one of the segments of the approach I have developed. In most cases, the profiles are intended to be examples of teachers who are doing exceptional work and, in fact, all of the teachers I observed and interviewed were very skilled. In some cases, however, it seemed appropriate to document some of the teachers' struggles with TBMI, particularly in the confining contexts of their schools. This is not intended to belittle the outstanding work that those teachers do; rather, it is meant to demonstrate that even great teachers deal with difficulties.

This book represents a view of current practices in American educational settings. Certainly curricula in countries outside of the United States include extensive integration of technology in music and the arts. In some senses, other areas of the world—particularly the United Kingdom and Australia—are more advanced than the United States in terms of technology integration into the arts. A document that extends the British Music National Curriculum (Kirkman, 2009) contains suggestions for activities and learning sequences related to mobile systems, computer-based tools, user interfaces, and web-based services. However, since this book is rooted in observations of classrooms, and the classrooms chosen for study were all within the United States, it would be improper to assume that the principles explained in this book apply directly to educational practices in other parts of the world.

SUMMARY OF CHAPTER 1

In chapter 1, we examined a model that describes the levels of proficiency at which music teachers have been observed to integrate technology into their classrooms, and explored some of the typical hesitations that teachers express toward that integration. We explored a distinction between integration and instruction that is based upon technology. In chapter 2, we will examine some of the traditional ways that music is taught, and consider how those traditional models can influence a new pedagogy of technology-based music instruction.

ITEMS FOR DISCUSSION

1. What are some of your favorite resources for information on music technology products? Where would you turn to find out about the latest software or hardware, and what is right for your teaching situation?
2. It is important to assess your own level of comfort with technology. Think about Mrs. U, who was fairly new to the idea of technology-based music instruction. Do you relate to her circumstances? How prepared would you feel if asked to integrate technology into your teaching? Into which of the three topographical groups do you fall in your own technology-based music teaching?
3. Can you think of examples from your own time as a student when teachers have integrated technology at each of the three levels of the Topography of Technology Integration? How effective were they in doing so?
4. What are your greatest concerns about integrating technology into your own teaching?

CHAPTER 2

Models of Music Pedagogy and Their Influences on Technology-Based Music Instruction

EXISTING MODELS OF MUSIC PEDAGOGY

Pedagogical approaches to teaching music have developed into mature curricular structures. The most prominent music pedagogies have features in common that can inform the new pedagogy of TBMI, and we should learn from the success of these approaches as we develop technology-based methods that will lead students to musical ends.

In the section that follows, I will briefly summarize some of the major pedagogical approaches that are in use in today's music classrooms. Then, I will offer lessons that we can learn from examining traditional music teaching that apply to the development of the TBMI approach.

Orff-Schulwerk

Saliba (1991) described the Orff-Schulwerk approach to music education as "pedagogy to organize elements of music for children through speaking, singing, playing, and dancing" (p. vii). This approach, which dates to early 19th-century Germany, combines basic musical elements into small forms such as songs and patterns in order to make musical material manageable for young children (Saliba, 1991). Carl Orff's approach to music education was based on his personal experiences and his belief that integrating music and movement was fundamental to music learning processes (Frazee & Kreuter, 1987; Frazee, 2006).

Performing, listening, improvising, and analyzing music are all characteristic activities of Orff-Schulwerk music lessons. An important trait of this approach is its emphasis on children *feeling* musical elements (through active experience) prior to conceptualizing their *understanding* of the elements. Other distinguishing characteristics of the Orff pedagogy include the use of *ostinati* as accompaniment for singing and movement at varying levels of complexity and the use of simple instruments as a means for children's immediate expression (Wheeler & Raebeck, 1977).

Creativity is central to the original Orff-Schulwerk model of music pedagogy, as is the teacher's role in facilitating that creativity. "[Orff's] instructional plan includes provisions for several kinds of original work....The teacher should be prepared to help children notate their musical ideas, evaluate the music they produce, and relate their creative efforts to the study of musical form and style" (Landis & Carder, 1990, p. 110). Some have criticized the Orff-Schulwerk approach for a lack of structure, but the open, flexible nature of Orff-Schulwerk aligns reasonably well with TBMI in the sense that it acknowledges the need for understanding musical elements without attempting to overrun students' musical experiences with procedural knowledge. As Saliba (1991) stated, "A precise structure, if defined by step-by-step procedures, could be destructive to the nurturing of creative elements" (p. viii).

Kodály

The method of music education created by Hungarian composer Zoltán Kodály is based on several practical assumptions about young children's musical capacities: (1) children's voices have limited ranges, (2) children sing descending passages more easily than they sing ascending passages, (3) children sing small interval skips more easily than they sing large interval skips, and (4) children's vocal ranges are similar to one another (Choksy, 1999a). Kodály's method differs from the Orff-Schulwerk approach in that the Kodály approach is sequential, and it leads to the goal of children being able to read and write standard music notation (Wheeler & Raebeck, 1977).

Kodály employed a system of syllable singing based on movable *do*, hand symbols, and easily identifiable rhythmic language. Kodály lessons share with lessons based on other music pedagogies the goals of performing, listening, analyzing, and creating (Choksy, 1999b), emphasizing students' abilities to develop *inner hearing* (Shehan Campbell & Scott-Kassner, 1995). A characteristic of Kodály's approach that has influenced many teachers is its "insistence that the quality of the music used in teaching is of paramount importance, that only authentic folk music and great art music are good enough for children" (Choksy, 1999a, p. 16). Modern scholars have linked Kodály-based teaching to the popular cognitive-psychological ideas of Jerome Bruner, stating that Kodály's emphasis on children's experiencing sound prior to being introduced to symbolic representation meshes well with what we know about how students learn abstract concepts (Houlahan & Tacka, 2008). Experience in sound without over-emphasizing traditional visual representations in the form of music notation meshes well with technology-based music instruction; in TBMI, students may not have the need for traditional music notation.

Suzuki

Shinichi Suzuki believed that children are born with the potential to be musical and that adults can nurture that potential through a process known as *talent education*. The Suzuki method is based on several principles: (1) starting music education very early with listening activities, (2) situating music learning in a variety of settings including private and group lessons, and (3) removing competition from the music learning process (Shehan Campbell & Scott-Kassner, 1995). As Kendall (1966) noted, the method is based on

> ways of learning which go back far into Japanese tradition: the atmosphere of sharing in the education of children by members of the family, an environment that encourages naturally the kind of development desired by the group, the virtues of review and repetition until mastery and security are firmly gained...[and] that satisfaction of the young child's need for imitation through providing desirable models. (p. 4)

In the Suzkui method, standard music notation is withheld for quite a long time in favor of student imitation of the teacher. In contrast to the two methods discussed earlier, all materials are dictated by the methodolgy, and "all students, regardless of ability, follow the same sequence of materials" (Kendall, 1978, p. 9). An important element of the Suzuki approach is the involvement of parents. In particular, mothers are encouraged to attend lessons and ensemble learning experiences and to learn the instrument along with the child.

Music Learning Theory

The foundation of Music Learning Theory (MLT), created by music psychologist, researcher, and educator Edwin Gordon, is *audiation*, or the ability to hear inwardly music that may not be physically or aurally present. The ability to *audiate* allows people to make sense of music they hear and to give meaning to it. To explain the usefulness of *audiation*, Gordon presented an analogy:

> Linguists suggest that knowing the alphabet, or even reading phonetically by recognizing letters in print, has little to do with reading comprehension. The alphabet serves only as an explanation of aspects of the basic theoretical structure of a language to one who can already read that language with meaning.... The letter names and time value names of notes represent the alphabet of the music language. To be able to recite or identify the letter names and time value names of notes does not indicate a readiness to read music.... One gives meaning to the pattern one reads in music because one can audiate notation. As a result of being familiar with the *sound* of the pattern through basic audiation (as one is familiar with the *sight* of the object which the word symbolizes in language), one can read that pattern with meaning through notational audiation. (Gordon, 1980, p. 4)

Music Learning Theory is based on a series of empirical studies and tests of musical aptitude and achievement that Gordon and his colleagues developed. The structure of the method contains stages of music learning through which students progress, with each stage adding complexity to its associated tasks. The materials of the MLT approach are not wholly dictated; rather, Gordon prescribed content of rhythmic and tonal patterns that may be found in and applied to music used in classrooms. Among the most complex stages of the theory are Creativity/Improvisation, which "requires knowledge of content" (Gordon, 1980, p. 33) and Theoretical Understanding, which "is to music what grammar and linguistics are to a spoken language" (p. 36).

Dalcroze and Eurhythmics

The pedagogical approach formulated by Émile Jaques-Dalcroze in early 20th-century Switzerland is perhaps most closely associated with movement for embodiment of sound.

> The Dalcroze approach contributes to self-understanding by helping individuals to become aware of the expressive possibilities of their bodies.... [S]tudents recognize and develop the range of feeling inspired by music, sharpen their mental processes, coordinate them with physical and emotional processes, and cultivate a new expressive dimension that goes beyond the usual verbal one. (Landis & Carder, 1990, p. 8)

Typical movement activities in a Dalcroze-based classroom allow for free body response as much as possible and integrate structured movements (as dictated by the teacher) to reflect particular elements of the music in use (Mead, 1994).

The Dalcroze approach is commonly misconceived as solely focused on movement as the mechanism for musical training. In fact, the approach is designed to teach musical fundamentals, similar to the other methods described earlier in this chapter. In addition to the special kind of movement associated with Dalcroze's approach, which is known as *eurhythmics*, Dalcroze developed methods of teaching music through ear training and improvisation. Similar to Gordon's notion of *audiation*, Dalcroze, a music theory and aural skills professor, believed in the importance of *inner hearing*. Musical objectives are accomplished through the use of children's songs and folk music, as well as simple, elemental music patterns.

SHARED FEATURES OF THE EXISTING PEDAGOGIES

As stated in chapter 1, the goals of TBMI teaching are almost entirely the same as music teaching in any other context; the variation is in the methods that teachers use to reach those goals. To be clear, I am not suggesting that we should adapt Orff's method, Suzuki's method, or any of these to teaching music technologically. While certain elements of the methods described may prove beneficial when coupled with technology-based music instruction, the types of music, the techniques for creating it, and the characteristics of the students demand that we consider a new approach to music instruction, using these tried-and-true methods as a compass. The principles of TBMI, although most frequently applied in the computer lab setting, are usable in traditional ensembles and general music classrooms and can aid in teaching diverse types of music. The urge to examine these traditional pedagogies stems from two needs: (1) that of music teachers in ensembles and traditional general music classes to more effectively use technology in those settings (some examples of which are provided in the Profiles of Practice), and (2) that of guidance for music teachers in the computer lab setting. The second of these needs is the main focus of this book, but the first one is no less important.

The music pedagogies described earlier serve as guides in the formation of technology-based music pedagogy. Battles rage in the world of music education scholarship about the merits of each pedagogical approach, but the ideas presented here are not designed to influence opinions about the traditional approaches to teaching music. The point is to examine these methods and establish a set of common features that can serve as a point of departure for establishing the TBMI pedagogy.

While some teachers are irrationally devoted to a particular method and do not consider the benefits of using eclectic approaches to teach a diverse student body, I acknowledge the benefit of teaching according to a consistent, established set of beliefs. All of the methods discussed here, if conducted well, lead children to a state of musical literacy and, perhaps, musical expressiveness. They all value music education and acknowledge the importance of music for all students in school and outside of school. TBMI teachers should share in these values.

Each of the methods discussed mandates that the materials used for music instruction are of the highest possible quality. While there is variance in the degree to which each method dictates the materials that teachers use, there is certainly a notion attached to each method that expects high quality musical and instructional materials—materials that clearly demonstrate musical concepts, that are developmentally appropriate, and that allow students to experience authentic music-making activities. Selecting musical and technological materials is equally important in TBMI environments, as will be discussed in chapter 4.

The traditional methods suggest that music instruction should be sequential and should be carefully planned to meet students' needs at a particular time in their musical and intellectual development. The extent and validity of the psychometric foundations of the methods vary greatly, but each recognizes that simple, fundamental musical experiences are best for the start of music education. The methods also include suggestions for increasing difficulty as students develop greater musical sophistication, physical ability, and cognitive ability. While perhaps not as detailed as some of the well-established methods, TBMI should also be designed to account for students' abilities, and it can support students at various stages of their development.

Each method also contains suggestions for assessment. Part of any pedagogical model is the realization that students must be held accountable for their musical and non-musical behaviors. As we establish the elements of TBMI through the examinations in this book, we will see that assessment of students' work is often difficult, even for experienced teachers. The traditional methods dictate that assessment is necessary so that teachers can check student learning against objectives and adjust instruction to suit students' needs.

Assessment and accountability may also be related to classroom management. Management of music classes, and especially those that involve technology, can be particularly difficult when students are producing creative, open-ended projects. Chapter 7 will address some ideas and strategies related to assessment and TBMI.

PROFILE OF PRACTICE 2.1

All teachers, using all different kinds of teaching methods, have to deal with issues of classroom management. The music lab presents management circumstances that are, in some ways, similar to other types of music teaching/learning environments, and in other ways are very different. I talked with Mr. M, a relatively young teacher, about the issues of management in his class. He teaches Music and Technology I and II classes in an affluent suburban high school. The lab where he teaches is unique in that, while it has recent equipment, the room itself is very small, with space for eight student workstations and one teacher station. I observed the Music and Technology II class, with seven boys and one girl, all of whom had taken the level I class, and most of whom had taken the school's Advanced Placement Music Theory class.

I asked Mr. M about his perceptions of managing this class, especially as compared to his other teaching experiences such as his freshman band class. In his band teaching, Mr. M is able to employ traditional teaching methods, and his classes are designed around managing students' behavior. "I think we find that there are some similarities.... They all have *stuff* at their disposal. Whether it's an instrument, or a mallet, or a mouthpiece, or something in their hand, they've got all this technology right in front of them. They have a hard time not playing around with the keyboards or the computer.... In this class in particular, there is one group of four of the boys who are, I don't want to use the word 'trouble makers' because they're ultimately good kids, but the four of them together in the same room, in such small quarters, is challenging to deal with. That's why [there are] exchanges from kids from one corner of the room to the other. So what I try and do is to be as sequential as possible, and I try and stay in the middle of the room so that I can see what each of them [is] doing on their stations."

Late in their semester, I saw this same class engaged in an activity in which the students were watching each other's movie trailer soundtracks. This kind of feedback session aligns with a goal of the music department—the teachers consciously provide their students opportunities to develop their musical vocabularies and to work on providing constructive criticism.

Of the students' performance in this type of activity, Mr. M said, "At least half the class [does] those types of things very well. They are very intelligent, and they provide good feedback. But then there are several students who feel the need to make jokes and laugh at just about everything. I feel it's like a very fine line between keeping the decorum of the room, and still wanting to elicit responses and engage in a discussion. I felt that they were, particularly one or two students, making stupid jokes and laughing at just about anything and everything that happened, and that's their personalities. I try to minimize what they do, and it's really only two or three students in a group of eight."

In contrast to this high school situation, I observed Mrs. R, a veteran music teacher who is also the technology coordinator for her elementary school. In the first lesson I observed, she was instructing an entire fifth grade class somewhat traditionally, using a projection screen to show a video and then leading them through an activity about the video. In this lesson she used MindMeister—a web-based tool for idea mapping—to help keep the class organized. I asked her about her uses of this tool, and similar Web 2.0-style tools, and why she chooses to integrate many of them into her teaching: "I try to give my students the tools to organize...tools that they're going to use outside of my classroom, that they take away that it crosses the curriculum into other areas."

Still, the students demonstrated difficult behavioral issues that may have been influenced by the fact that their music class was based on technology. In the second lesson I observed, the students were engaged in a composition project for which they were working in groups of three or four. They were to create an original piece of music, then record it using GarageBand on an iPad. The catch was that there was only one iPad available, so the groups who were not actually using the iPad at the moment were left to do "offline" planning and practicing. I asked Mrs. R about techniques for maintaining order with the rest of the students who were not immediately involved in recording. She expressed some reservation about the whole arrangement: "I'm the kind of teacher [who] like[s] things extremely organized and extremely focused. So a lesson like this really stretches me because I like to be much more in control of my classroom than I allow in these real creative, just-let-it-flow [situations]."

In circumstances where there is only one computer or device available for student use, teachers appeal to all kinds of techniques for maintaining good student behavior. Mrs. R has her students practice in groups, then act as good audience members when a group is recording. She also has them journal about their group's participation and accomplishments, and she has them conduct self- and peer assessments. She facilitates overall management of her classroom by assigning, and periodically rotating, student roles as helpers who distribute materials, clean up the room, and take responsibility for various aspects of running the class.

Existing music pedagogies offer common features as explained previously. While their approaches are distinct, if employed correctly, they should all lead students to be musically skilled, knowledgeable, literate, and independent in the sense that they can continue to be musical away from the environment of the music classroom and the teacher. They should also guide the teacher through the methods by which students can reach those goals. While the methods related to Technology-Based Music Instruction are necessarily different from those of the traditional music pedagogies, the ultimate goals of musical skill, knowledge, literacy, and independence are the same.

Similar to the pedagogies discussed earlier in this chapter, TBMI can be examined in terms of its philosophical foundations, the materials teachers and students use, teaching methods, and the implied assessments. TBMI is influenced by selection of software and devices, and by the need for teachers to have technological content knowledge. Although it is, and will probably always be, in development, the framework through which TBMI will be examined is shown in the graphic in Figure 2.1.

Technology-Based Music Instruction has four major components, each of which contributes to the formulation of the pedagogy. Brief descriptions are provided here; each of the components will be explored in depth throughout the remainder of this book.

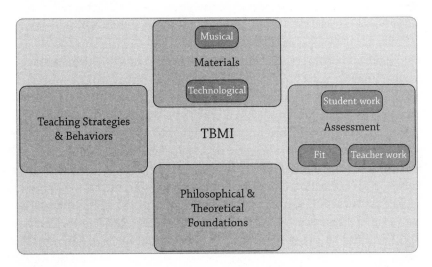

Figure 2.1
Framework for Examining Technology-Based Music Instruction

Chapter 3 will examine the *philosophical and theoretical foundations* of TBMI, stemming from several pre-existing expressions of educational philosophies and theories. Among the questions to be addressed as we explore philosophical and theoretical considerations are these:

- What is the value of activity and experience in music instruction, and how can teachers capitalize on technology to enhance experiences?
- How can teachers use educational and developmental theories to address students at levels of complexity that align with their readiness to learn?
- How can teachers balance guidance with student independence?
- How can we characterize teacher knowledge and its relationship to TBMI?
- Do certain forms of technologically-enhanced learning work better than others for students, and how do students' individual characteristics influence technology's effectiveness?

While these may not all seem like directly *philosophical* questions, they can be addressed by appealing to theoretical work of prior researchers.

The *materials* of TBMI, examined in chapter 4, represent important choices on the part of the teacher. As in other types of music teaching, the materials we use can have a tremendous impact on what students experience and what they learn. Musical materials are listening examples, composition examples, or examples of technological techniques applied in musical settings. Technological materials are the software and hardware used in teaching and learning, both by students and teachers. Teachers must be well versed in both musical materials and technological materials to make good choices for their students.

Chapter 5 addresses *teaching strategies and behaviors*, which are necessarily different in a TBMI environment than in a traditional music classroom. While the content of lessons and the desired end-states may not change, the means do. And because the ways that students and teachers move through content are drastically different in a computer lab from what they are in a rehearsal room, it is important to examine how teachers act. I have differentiated here between teaching *strategies* and teaching *behaviors*; the intention is to distinguish between *strategizing*, which can be viewed as the act of planning what one will do, and *behaving*, which is the act of doing. Experienced teachers move so seamlessly between planning and acting that it is possible to neglect the fact that these are different. The discussion of teaching *behaviors* will also examine the special physicality of TBMI teachers, and how computer labs can influence that physicality.

Chapter 6 contains theoretical notions regarding the delicate design balance of lessons in TBMI classrooms, as well as models, developed through observation, that depict the ways in which students work in those classrooms. Chapter 6 also includes a series of sample lessons collected through observations, and analyses of those lessons. These will serve as examples of how teachers plan, what they do with their students, and how those decisions reflect many of the theoretical ideas explained in sections leading to chapter 6.

Assessment, addressed in chapter 7, is an essential component of any pedagogical approach. In TBMI, there are three major components to assessment: student work, teacher work, and fit. Assessment of student work is important so that teachers can monitor students' learning, so that they can examine students' progress relative to learning objectives, and so that students can see their own progress. In music education, particularly in traditional performance and ensemble environments, teachers often do an excellent job of assessing student work formatively; that is, they listen to performances and help students to make corrections. TBMI offers us opportunities to assess student work both through those same types of formative experiences and through formal, summative opportunities.

The importance of assessing teachers' work is dictated by the relative youth of music instruction that is based on technology. Because early integration of technology most frequently substituted computer drill-and-practice for human teachers, and because most of these attempts took place on the collegiate level, such assessment, as is typical of teachers in K–12 classrooms, was not necessarily applicable. Even though many teachers who implement music technology are veterans in the field, the methods and content are still new. In order to improve TBMI, teachers must take a reflective disposition toward it, examine their own practice, and help guide those who are charged with formally evaluating their work to do so logically and responsibly.

Finally, the question of *fit* remains. Fit refers to the idea that in some circumstances, technology-based instruction may not be the best choice. The introduction of technology into the music curriculum is a usually a conscious choice that is made by one or more teachers. Those teachers have the right to make the choice *not* to use technology if indeed they think it is not the best fit for their students, their environment, or themselves. Teachers can use their knowledge of and experiences from their own classrooms to determine when technology-based learning will be effective in helping their students to achieve learning objectives.

SUMMARY OF CHAPTER 2

In chapter 2 we explored some of the tried-and-true approaches to music instruction and recognized that there are common features among them that can influence the formation of a new pedagogy called Technology-Based Music Instruction. We were introduced to elements that contribute to TBMI pedagogy. In chapter 3, we will begin to explore each of those elements, beginning with some theoretical underpinnings.

ITEMS FOR DISCUSSION

1. Many music teachers are trained to teach according to the principles of the methods (Orff, Music Learning Theory, etc.) described in this chapter. Think about your own music teachers from elementary school, middle school, and high school. Do you recognize any of the characteristics of these methods in their teaching? Which ones in particular?
2. Again think of your own music teachers from elementary, middle, and high school. What types of technologies did they integrate into their teaching? Were those technologies effective? Did they complement the music teaching and music making happening in their classrooms?
3. In the Profile of Practice in this chapter, the teachers were experiencing some behavior management issues with their students. What types of techniques might you recommend to help alleviate those problems? Can you think of ways to use technology to change the behavioral environment?
4. One of the assessment issues mentioned in the framework is that of *fit*. Describe any educational experiences you have had in which the use of technology felt particularly *unnatural*. Why was technology inappropriate in those moments? What were the effects of the technology uses in the short term or long term?

CHAPTER 3

Philosophical and Theoretical Foundations

Many authors have explored the ideas of philosophy and educational theory and how those ideas can serve as a foundation for teaching practices. Philosophy is a broad subject, and it is not the purpose of this book to create a new philosophy of music teaching and learning; however, we can beneficially draw on philosophical and theoretical works of others to form some foundations. By necessity, a theory of technology-based music instruction begins with a theory of music education. To deviate from this would be to neglect the important theoretical work that forms the guiding foundation of teaching in our chosen art form.

The critical role of theory in this new method of teaching is to help technology-based music instructors develop dispositions that make this type of teaching less forced, more natural than it might otherwise be. The most successful technology-based music teachers are those who recognize the capacities of their students to engage with technology, to be creative, and who are willing to modify some beliefs—possibly long-held ones—to allow their students the freedom to explore and construct their musical skills and knowledge. These are difficult dispositions to develop. Understanding some important theoretical and philosophical work can help in treading that path by helping teachers acknowledge findings that have come before, and by letting us make critical decisions about the ways we teach and our students learn.

The teacher in the following Profile of Practice has developed trust in his students and himself, assurance that he can promote students' creativity, and confidence in his TBMI abilities. He knows that students come to his classes with unique worldviews, and with experiences, both musical and otherwise, accumulated over each of their lifetimes. While he does not place great emphasis on theoretical models of creativity or on articulating his own music teaching philosophy, his teaching reflects some of the most important philosophical dispositions found in effective TBMI teachers.

PROFILE OF PRACTICE 3.1

Mr. E teaches middle school music in a relatively affluent suburb. He is fortunate to have experiences teaching music at many levels and has a wealth of formal training in music technology from both his undergraduate and graduate degree work. While his classes are not listed as music technology per se, he goes to great lengths to provide his general music students with experiences in technology. He elaborated, "I think that if kids are really going to get anything out of music, they need to do it by creating it themselves. It makes it less abstract for them, makes it more real."

Mr. E was very interested in providing his students with means of expressing themselves and being creative. As with many teachers, however, he struggled with exactly what *creativity* means, and he agonized over the balance between guiding his students to be creative and placing parameters and expectations on their work. He admitted that he does not think too much about theoretical ideas of creativity, although he was familiar with some of the prevailing models. He added, "I just want them to take chances. I want them to try something brand new, something they haven't decided before. And some of them aren't used to doing that.... They're used to having step 1, step 2, and I just don't want them to do that. I want them to be able to think on their own and really listen and adjust." It was evident that Mr. E was interested in encouraging students' divergent thinking by promoting open-ended, experiential learning.

The prominent technological tool in use in Mr. E's classes is HyperScore, a composition program based on drawing shapes that are then interpreted as sounds. Students got ample opportunity to create new material; however, time dedicated to going back, reviewing their work, and making changes seemed sparse. Mr. E expressed some frustration about the program's pedagogical limitations: "In an English class they write their rough draft and then they have to go back and review it and check it. I wish [in] a program like HyperScore there was a way for me to make notes...to look at a kid's product and leave a little sticky note on it or something. To say, 'hey, watch the beats here or try changing this.' Just like a teacher would mark up a student's rough draft so they could go back and make those changes. But then again, a lot of the changes are just subjective. It's not like a spelling error where there's one way to do it."

Mr. E's students know that he is an expert in the content of music and technology, and his mastery of communicating technological techniques was evident. He moves fluidly between presentation topics, and can sense the moment when his students understand the techniques he has demonstrated. Given the power of a tool like HyperScore, and Mr. E's desire to have students be their own critics, to learn by doing, I asked him about his own role in the lab: "More as kind of a guide. Not as much as a teacher, but more as a mentor. Just to show them things that have worked for other people in the past that they might want to try. But I would never demand them to do this or to do [that]. . . . I'm going to be looking for songs that have repeated sections, maybe like an ABA song or something like that. I'm not necessarily going to come out and tell them that's exactly what I want. But, at the same time, when we listen to examples, they'll see it through other people's work. This is what makes this song sound good, and this is what makes this song sound kind of boring. And so, I'm hoping they'll come up with those ideas on their own. They'll develop them."

THE BASIS OF THE TBMI IN CONSTRUCTIVISM

Much of the early technology-based instruction that took place both in music classrooms and in classrooms embedded in other disciplines was intended to find substitutions for drill-and-practice that might otherwise be provided by teachers. Early attempts at using technology to teach musical content were prescriptive; that is, the content was programmed so that students could not advance to a new level until they had demonstrated mastery over the content of a particular unit. Overviews of these types of behaviorist efforts are available elsewhere (e.g., Bransford, Brown, & Cocking, 2000). Essential to the development of a TBMI disposition is the acknowledgment that technology-based music teaching is *different* from traditional music teaching; teachers should not simply be looking for substitute methods for what they might do in traditional ways without technology. On the contrary, TBMI dispositions are accepting of the idea that students can be, at least in large part, responsible for their own learning by building on prior knowledge through experiences that the teacher designs. This is reflective of the *constructivist* approach to education.

Some teachers are familiar with the idea of pedagogy that guides students to *construct* knowledge through activity and to build upon prior experiences to develop new knowledge. Still, a clearly defined understanding of constructivism tends to escape most practicing music teachers. Webster (2011) has provided perhaps the most extensive review of music-related research based in constructivism and has offered definitions that may prove helpful in understanding the nature of constructivist learning. From his review of the theoretical literature, the following characteristics of constructivism became most apparent:

- Knowledge is formed as part of the learner's active interaction with the world.
- Knowledge exists less as abstract entities outside the learner and absorbed by the learner; rather, it is constructed anew through action.
- Meaning is constructed with this knowledge.
- Learning is, in large part, a social activity. (Webster, 2011, p. 36)

Webster further defined constructivist learning as follows: "Constructivism holds that all knowledge and meaning are constructed by the individual either personally or through social-cultural interaction. Information is interpreted by the mind, and the world is perceived and constructed by individuals in different ways" (2011, p. 38). This tendency toward individualism in learning, and developing new knowledge as a way to experience the world, is a hallmark of technology-based music instruction that emphasizes individual (or small group) production of creative work.

Constructivism is about changing the ways in which we view the world based on developing new knowledge. The difficulty with constructivist-based music teaching is that some of the knowledge associated with music in schools is abstract; that is, only some of what we expect students to learn is a fixed set of definitions, facts, and operations, while the rest is open-ended and oriented toward individuals or performing groups. Of this conundrum, Webster wrote:

> Most scholars assume, quite incorrectly, that educators in arts and humanities deal with constructivism routinely in their teaching. After all, meaning making, particularly in the arts is a very personal affair by nature—actively constructed. Far better to concentrate on the sciences and mathematics to make the case for constructivism, since the content of these disciplines is so strongly based in what some believe as unchallengeable truth that the discourse will be more controversial and perhaps more compelling a case if made well. . . . The field of music education practice has for years been dominated by directed instruction that is top-down in nature, often with little regard for student-constructed knowledge. (2011, pp. 45–46)

When experienced, constructivist learning in music is quite powerful; it can lead to students' serendipitous discoveries of new knowledge and connections within and between disciplines. They might be difficult to recognize, but the characteristics of constructivism lend themselves well to design of experiences in TBMI, as will be evidenced in sample lessons discussed later in this text. Open-ended, teacher-designed experiences with music software can allow students to discover novel approaches to solving musical problems, thereby developing new knowledge based on what they already know. Constructivism forms a foundation for pedagogical skill in TBMI, especially when considered in conjunction with several other theoretical approaches to learning.

PROFILE OF PRACTICE 3.2

Every so often I receive emails or stumble across Facebook posts from friends who share my interests, and those communications often contain links to online videos that feature people doing interesting things with music technology. A recent one really caught my attention, and no sooner had it done so than it achieved viral status. It was a video of a young British musician, Neil Johnston, who expressed this curiosity: "We had to see … how cool would it be to get 24 iPads in a classroom, get a group of enthusiastic learners? Let's see how this works."[a]

I tracked down Neil through the company he owns in the United Kingdom, Store Van Music. The main business for Neil's company is writing and recording music for commercial purposes such as television and film. But Neil was clearly passionate about music education. He is an experienced music educator, who also holds a degree in music business, and understands that there are deficiencies in the ways we teach music, especially in technology contexts. Store Van Music acts as an agency that supplies schools with private music tutors, and they often make school visits to create experiences like the one in the YouTube video. He said, "When we go into schools, it's always about rock and roll.... that's the cool element that we bring to the kids. So the kids are engaged because we're not teachers. We don't dress like teachers. We come with loud music. That road trip atmosphere that you can bring to a school visit is what makes a visit worthwhile. A lot of the criticisms we get are, 'How on earth do you expect this to work all the time?' We don't. This is a visit. I'm not saying that this is how music should be taught all the time. We're doing a visit to enthuse and to encourage, and that is it. So we're always trying to find a way to make it relevant, make it engaging."

Neil and his colleagues face challenges when they pop in, give an experience, and pop out, because in a sense, they perpetuate a privatization model of music teaching. About this he said, "Certainly from the response

a. The video can be seen on YouTube at http://youtu.be/2W9z-nrTQD4, or at the website for Neil's company, www.storevanmusic.com. As of this writing, the video had been viewed nearly 148,000 times.

we've had in America, it's a new thing, and it's something [Americans are] very much interested in. It's common here; there [are] lots of drama workshops or dance workshops, and they'll work their way around schools, going in and teaching. But I think it's something that education needs to be looking more towards. It just brings up this [idea of] using professionals to encourage and inspire. I think it's something that is beneficial. It brings a bit of reality to subjects where it might be lacking somewhat, because there's only so much teachers can bring. And that's no fault of the teacher. But seeing someone who really does it is always going to be much more inspiring than seeing someone who talks about doing it."

Engagement was a persistent theme throughout our conversation. Neil said, "The biggest thing that schools are longing for here in the UK is learner engagement. There's not one classroom in the entire world where there's 100% learner engagement yet.... The method [teachers are] using now is that there's an individual learning plan for every single learner in a classroom. Now my wife [an English teacher], her biggest class is 32 kids. How on earth can you work your way around to 32 kids individually in a lesson? Whereas, if you can use technology as the thing that keeps them engaged, they can all be working on something, and it can all be customized."

Since the iPad ensemble video went viral, Neil has been inundated with requests from all over the world to come to schools and create similar experiences. I asked him about the origin of the idea, about what drove him to make this happen. Neil took note of a particularly powerful device and piece of software—the iPad and GarageBand—and recognized that it could help him accomplish musical goals he held for students in the United Kingdom: "I'd been waiting for something like the iPad to come out.... With the launch of the iPad 2, lo and behold, GarageBand ...they bring out GarageBand and I'm like, 'Yes, this is exactly what I've been waiting for. This is perfect.' Straight away, my mind was whirling around with ideas. What can we do with this?"

Neil Johnston is an expert composer and music technologist, and he specializes in bringing engaging experiences to schoolchildren using the art forms that he loves. While he has experience as a secondary school music teacher, he does not rely on the traditional means of teaching music, nor does he really pay much intentional mind to traditional expectations. Principles such as active engagement, multimedia design, knowledge construction, and creativity theory underlie the activities that he designs for students, and students construct new knowledge through the experiences he facilitates. It is because of Neil's charisma and enthusiasm, coupled with his practical application of pedagogical technique, that he has created a lasting impression that may become a prevalent model for technology-based music instruction.

DEWEY AND ACTIVE LEARNING

Among the important thinkers to shape the constructivist philosophy is John Dewey. His ideas and work have had a relatively direct influence on thinking about teaching students and how to integrate technology into teaching. In *Experience and Education* (1938/1969), Dewey asserted that experience is the driving force of education—that students learn best by doing. His idea led to the development of practices of informal learning and to the inception of schools as communities of working learners.

In the late 19th century, Dewey founded a laboratory elementary school in Chicago, designed to connect the experiences children had at home to those they had in school.

> Classroom work in Dewey's school was a carefully designed extension of the child's familiar life in the home. Rote exercises were minimized. Projects resembling those of a traditional household–crafts and cooking, for example–were used as ways to teach practical lessons of reading and arithmetic. (Harms & DePencier, 1996, p. 2)

Dewey soon established a set of principles that would continue to develop in the school and would guide his philosophy:

- Students begin learning by experimentation and develop interests in traditional subjects to help them gather information.
- Students are part of a social group in which everyone learns to help each other.
- Students should be challenged to use their creativity to arrive at individual solutions to problems.
- The child, not the lesson, is the center of the teacher's attention; each student has individual strengths that should be cultivated and grown. (Harms & DePencier, 1996, p. 4)

To Dewey, experiences were moving forces that aroused curiosity, strengthened initiative, and set up desires and purposes. Experiences go on inside a person but also change the conditions under which future experiences occur. He wrote, "In a certain sense every experience should do something to prepare a person for later experiences of a deeper and more expansive quality. This is the very meaning of growth, continuity, reconstruction of experience" (Dewey, 1938/1969, p. 47). Though Dewey probably did not envision computers in education, direct interactions between students and music software are experiences that help prepare them for more sophisticated interactions, such as inventing a creative solution to an instrumentation issue or finding the best quantizing settings.

Many ideas that underlie the constructivist philosophy can be traced to Dewey's focus on experience. An application of this idea can be seen clearly in the work of Seymour Papert. In Papert's (1980) book *Mindstorms: Children, Computers, and Powerful Ideas*, he demonstrated how students interacting directly with technology can create complex geometric work. Papert is known for his programming language called LOGO, which allows even very young students to manipulate a figure on screen and create drawn patterns.

Constructivist educators believe strongly in these types of direct interactions and manipulative (in a positive sense) experiences, ones that allow students to build on what they already know and grow from experiences that also prepare them for more sophisticated experiences in the future. Constructivist educators conceive of technology as a supporting mechanism for learning experiences. Technology helps students because it can "provide direction, save time, help avoid wasted energy, and provide the benefit of others' experiences" (Adamy, 2001, p. 204).

In developing a disposition as a technology-based music instructor, it is critical that one keeps the tenets of constructivism and Deweyan philosophy in mind. Technology-based music teachers must focus on providing experiences that engage their students with technology and music and that push students to develop increasingly sophisticated approaches to their own learning.

PIAGET AND STAGE THEORY

Swiss psychologist Jean Piaget is credited with a "stage" theory of child development. Based on his observations of young children, Piaget claimed that humans pass through a series of somewhat discrete stages of abilities to learn. The distinctions between the stages reflect the ways in which children can process the sensory input they receive. The theory helps us analyze how children learn to think.

Piagetian scholars claim that by placing children within a developmental stage, it is possible to predict with reasonable accuracy how a child will respond to a particular intellectual challenge (Labinowicz, 1980). Piaget can be firmly placed in the group of psychologists known as constructivists; he claimed that along with acquiring developmental *knowledge* through learning experiences, children are able to create *meaning* out of their learning experiences, and that those *meanings* are based on *assimilation* of prior experiences. Thus, in Piagetian stage theory, students construct their own knowledge (Phillips, 1981). Piaget's work also became the basis for much research regarding the ways in which young children perceive sound and other sensory input (Bransford, Brown, & Cocking, 2000).

As with many educational theories, criticisms of Piaget's stage model have arisen. Primarily, the idea of child development existing in discrete stages may be a difficult structure to accept. Secondarily, although it is an educational theory, Piaget's model does not offer any particular pedagogical implications; though not impossible, it is difficult for teachers to design lesson plans based on the Piagetian stage model (Smith, 2009).

We have seen quite a bit of research that attempts to place music into the context of Piagetian stage theory. Serafine (1980) reminded us that "Piaget's primary purpose is not simply to study the child, but rather to study the issue of how the mind gradually comes to be capable of thought, language, and knowledge" (p. 1). The advantage of thinking about music students and their abilities from the perspective of Piaget's stage theory is that it reminds us to consider complexity of materials and tasks, and how that complexity relates to students' readiness. Selection of materials for education, and for TBMI, is a natural extension of Piagetian principles.

BLOOM AND THE TAXONOMY OF EDUCATIONAL OBJECTIVES

Among the most iconic and often-referenced educational theories we find the Taxonomy of Educational Objectives, credited to Benjamin S. Bloom and pictured in Figure 3.1. Ironically, though we often refer to the taxonomy to place critical thinking and creativity at the forefront of educational activities, the original intention of the taxonomy was to facilitate the development and exchange of standardized testing materials (Bloom, 1984). In addition, the perception that the taxonomy values certain educational objectives more than others lies contrary to its original aim; in fact, the developers of the model—Bloom and his colleagues—"agreed that in constructing the taxonomy every effort should be made to avoid value judgments about objectives and behaviors" (Bloom, 1984, p. 6).

Perhaps the most useful aspect of Bloom's Taxonomy is that it allows teachers to focus on specific types of educational objectives, and therefore on students' responses and behaviors. In doing so we are able to vary the educational objectives in our lessons and the expectations we have for our students' participation. Lesson planning and teaching with an eye toward the levels of the taxonomy force teachers to distribute students' activities over more or less complex forms of learning. Bloom (1984) pointed out

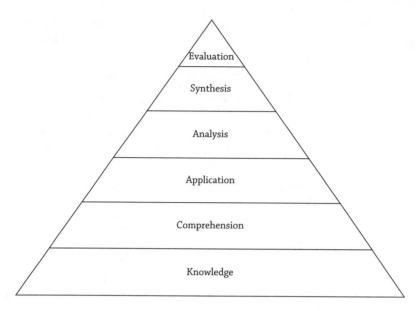

Figure 3.1
Bloom's Taxonomy of Educational Objectives

that the levels of the taxonomy are not distinct; that is, the less cognitively demanding layers at one end of the taxonomy (knowledge, comprehension, application) are simpler components of the complex layers at the other (analysis, synthesis, evaluation). In this sense the model is linear, and each stage builds upon those that have come before it.

In the years since its development, retrospective views of Bloom's Taxonomy have developed that cause concern. The linearity referred to in the previous paragraph is a point of criticism because, in truth, teaching and learning are rarely linear. Next, the relationship of the *behavioral* goals suggested by the taxonomy to the kinds of demonstrable learning that occur in music classes is questionable. In more general terms, Furst (1994) wrote that "A ... difficulty ... arising from the use of behavioral-specified goals ... is the neglect of important goals that do not yield readily to precise specification" (p. 29). In other words, some educational achievement, particularly in the arts, is difficult to measure. The taxonomy, over many years of its application to educational design and testing, has become increasingly controversial due to a vast amount of research suggesting that its order was incorrect, and due to its utility in the classroom in the face of mounting economic challenges.

Efforts to revise Bloom's Taxonomy began in 1965 with a call from Bloom to other interested parties (Krathwohl, 1994). One result of these revision efforts is a reconceptualized version of the taxonomy model described by Anderson and Krathwohl (2001), who recognized that "different types of objectives require different instructional approaches, that is, learning activities, different curricular materials, and different teacher and student roles" (p. 8). This is particularly salient for the new type of pedagogy embedded in TBMI because it suggests that a new type of music teaching (technology-based) requires learning activities, materials, and teacher/student functions that differ from those that would be found in traditional music learning environments.

The revised model of educational objectives (see Figure 3.2), first, modifies the language and, therefore, the implications of the six levels of the original model into these cognitive processes: (1) Remember, (2) Understand, (3) Apply, (4) Analyze, (5) Evaluate, and (6) Create. Notice that these levels now appear as verbs (rather than nouns), indicating that these are activities that students actually *do*.

A second dimension was added to the model, which Anderson and Krathwohl refer to as the "Knowledge Dimension." Four types of knowledge comprise this new construct: (1) factual knowledge, (2) conceptual knowledge, (3) procedural knowledge, and (4) metacognitive knowledge. The two dimensions of the model are arranged in a table, suggesting that each objective teachers use to plan lessons will most closely appeal to a single cognitive process and a single component of the knowledge dimension.

As it relates to TBMI, Bloom's original taxonomy and its revised form focus teachers' planning on the fact that we can expects students to do varied types of activities, and still those activities qualify as learning. Demonstration of

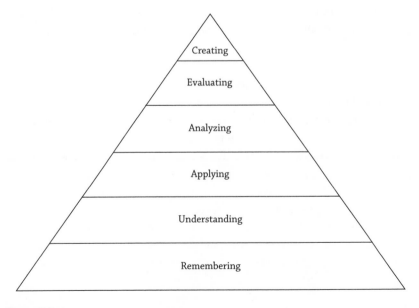

Figure 3.2
Revised Taxonomy of Educational Objectives

creativity—of development of original ideas based on prior experiences of remembering, understanding, analyzing, and so on—is a valid and desirable type of learning. The linearity of the model, although the source of some criticism, suggests that there are some educational circumstances in which students must develop skills and procedural understanding before they are able to appropriately apply those skills to creative tasks. This may be the case in situations in which students are using software tools for creative purposes.

KOEHLER AND MISHRA'S TPACK MODEL

An important, prevailing model of technology-based instruction has emerged from the interesting work of Matthew Koehler and Punya Mishra, and many of their colleagues. This model, known as TPACK,[1] encompasses the ideas of technological knowledge, pedagogical knowledge, and content knowledge, all of which intersect to form Technological-Pedagogical-and-Content Knowledge, which is the foundation that allows teachers to teach effectively in technology-enhanced environments. It is necessary to note that the TPACK model was not designed as a music-specific idea; rather, it was intended as a model that cuts across many (perhaps all) disciplines. Roblyer and Doering (2010) describe the TPACK model as "a metacognitive tool teachers can use to enhance technology integration into their classrooms by helping them visualize how their technology knowledge and skills work in tandem with their other knowledge domains about teaching and learning" (p. 50). Music researchers and teachers are beginning to adopt the model as a description of teacher training and practice in our discipline.

The TPACK model is based on the earlier work of Shulman (1986), who introduced the idea of Pedagogical Content Knowledge. All teachers must, of course, be well versed in the content of their subject area—in our case, music. Shulman wrote that pedagogical knowledge extends what teachers need to know beyond just the facts and figures of their field. Shulman defined pedagogical knowledge as knowledge that "embodies the aspects of content most germane to its teachability" (1986, p. 9). Shulman wrote:

> Within the category of pedagogical content knowledge I include ...the most useful forms of representation of those ideas, the most powerful analogies, illustrations, examples, explanations, and demonstrations—in a word, the ways of representing and formulating the subject that makes it comprehensible to others. (1986, p. 9)

1. The model was originally referred to as TPCK. The "A" was added later so that the term could be pronounced as a word, rather than spelled out.

Shulman also indicated that those with sophisticated pedagogical knowledge have a sense of what it is about the content of a subject that makes it difficult or easy for students to grasp.

The TPACK Model (Mishra & Koehler, 2006; Koehler & Mishra, 2008) was an extension of Shulman's model of Pedagogical Content Knowledge. The addition of Technological Knowledge to the model adds a level of substantial sophistication. The representation of the model is seen Figure 3.3.

The TPACK model[2] is a Venn diagram that illustrates the intersection of the three distinct types of knowledge (technological, pedagogical, and content). Pedagogical knowledge and content knowledge were defined earlier, so the remaining component is technological knowledge; this refers to the special knowledge of the operation of technology and its applications. In addition, technological knowledge is related to proper and informed selection of technological tools that can help students learn effectively. Koehler and Mishra (2008) indicate that keeping up with the rapid pace of technological change can be overwhelmingly time-consuming. Music teachers should seek to understand the tools that will help us and our students accomplish musical goals.

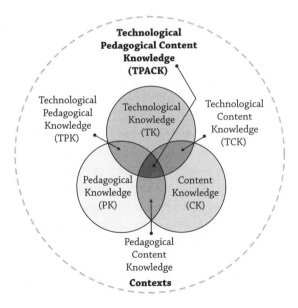

Figure 3.3
TPACK Model

2.   The TPACK image is used with the permission of its creators; further information, including a bibliography of research conducted in exploration of TPACK, can be found at http://tpack.org/.

The remaining overlapping elements of the model are these:

- Technological Pedagogical Knowledge—the ways in which technology impacts our teaching and our students' learning, and how we can best use technology to enhance teaching and learning;
- Technological Content Knowledge—our understanding of the influence of technology on the content of our subject area (music). TCK involves the selection and combination of tools, and matching the affordances of those tools to educational objectives.

The result of the intersection of all of the elements of the model gives us TPACK, or in the context of music instruction, *an understanding of the influence of technology on the ways we can teach and our students can learn music.* The model also indicates that the three distinct types of basic knowledge and their intersecting complex knowledges are impacted by the context in which teaching and learning take place. Bauer (2010) wrote that the TPACK model "has the potential to take the focus off technology itself and place it on ways in which technology might assist students in achieving curricular goals" (p. 428).

The importance of the TPACK model in the context of TBMI lies in the recognition that TBMI is a complex set of activities that requires expertise in several areas: (1) technology and its permutations; (2) musical content; and (3) the ways in which students may learn musical and technological content well. These are all complicated domains, but they intersect to form a foundation for technology-based music instruction. It is of critical importance that the *content* component of the TPACK model receive a great deal of attention. Without its inclusion in the model, the focus of TBMI may be lost, and music teachers run the risk of becoming technology teachers. This is not the goal of TBMI. In fact, the point is to keep music at the core of the experience. In recognizing the equality of content, the TPACK model provides us with a strong foundation to maintain our focus on musical experience.

TPACK, as both a theoretical lens and a way to examine teachers' abilities to teach with technology, is an important foundation for TBMI. Consider Figure 2.1 in chapter 2 that depicts the elements of TBMI. Reasonably direct relationships can be drawn between the domains of this figure and Figure 3.3, that shows the TPACK model. For example, the philosophical and theoretical bases of TBMI can be most directly correlated with what would, in other disciplines, be considered foundational knowledge of how students learn (pedagogical knowledge/PK). Teaching strategies and behaviors in TBMI equate with pedagogical knowledge but also draw on elements of pedagogical content knowledge and other domains of the TPACK model. These relationships are further delineated in Table 3.1.

Table 3.1. ALIGNMENT OF TBMI AND TPACK DOMAINS

TBMI Domain	TBMI Subdomain	Applicable TPACK Domain(s)
Philosophical & theoretical foundations	(none)	PK
Teaching strategies & behaviors	(none)	PK, PCK, TPK, TPCK
Materials	Musical	CK, PCK
	Technological	TK, TPK
Assessment	Student work	PK, CK, PCK, TPK, TPCK
	Teacher work	PK, TK, CK
	Fit	PK

A criticism of the TPACK model is that it assumes, to an extent, that content is bounded, that there is a defined set of knowledge that makes up the content of a discipline. This is complicated by the push in recent years for music teaching to be interdisciplinary. As music teachers, it is important that we have realistic expectations about our ability to master content outside of the music domain. Our teacher education programs are typically focused on musical content so that academic subjects outside of music are relegated to the status of "liberal arts requirement." In addition, the content of music is so vast that it is impractical to expect music teachers to be experts in math, science, history, or other academic areas. Barrett, McCoy, and Veblen (1997) wrote about the need for music teachers to approach interdisciplinary units with an eye toward the integrity of the musical components of our lessons:

> Educational experiences in music have integrity when students and teachers are engaged in processes of producing, perceiving, representing, and reflecting on sound, while attending to the elements of sound that make musical works expressive and give them significance in our lives. (p. 41)

While it is important that we recognize the value of disciplines outside of music, TBMI teachers should maintain a relatively strict focus on musical elements as the core, the foundation of their lesson designs, instruction, and assessment models.

MAYER AND MULTIMEDIA LEARNING

Very little research or theoretical work has been done about the interconnections between cognitive science and children's learning in technology-based music. We have substantial evidence about the relationships between music learning and memory (both long-term and working memory), cognitive load, attention, and distribution[3], but the particular context of the music lab presents interactions that researchers are yet to explore. In addition, the complexities of music-learning software, in which sound is often represented visually and is often coupled with auditory feedback, provides a context that is ripe for investigation.

To begin to understand the ways students interact with music software from a cognitive perspective, we can turn to the work of Richard Mayer and his colleagues, who have explored ideas of Multimedia Learning. Mayer provides a detailed explanation of delineated phenomena, derived from observations, of the ways students interact with computer-based multimedia. Mayer's Multimedia Principle suggests that people can learn better through multimedia—presentation of some combination of words, pictures, animations, and sound simultaneously—than they might with only one of those forms of media. Mayer wrote:

> The case for multimedia is based on the idea that instructional messages should be designed in light of how the human mind works. Let's assume that humans have two information-processing systems—one for verbal material and one for visual.... Let's also acknowledge that the major format for presenting instructional material is verbal. The rationale for multimedia presentations—that is, presenting material in words and pictures—is that is takes advantage of the full capacity of humans for processing information. When we present material only in the verbal mode, we are ignoring the potential contribution of our capacity to also process material in the visual mode. (Mayer, 2005, p. 4)

In addition to the Multimedia Principle, several subtheories are also described in Mayer's work, and other researchers have elaborated on these subtheories. The Modality Principle states that "under certain ... conditions, presenting some information in visual mode and other information in auditory mode can expand effective working memory capacity and so reduce the effects of an excessive cognitive load" (Low & Sweller, 2005, p. 147). The Redundancy Principle suggests that presenting redundant information in multimedia form can unnecessarily tax the learner's ability to tease apart information (Sweller, 2005).

---

3. A discussion of the relationships between music and cognition, though a rich and expanding area of research, is beyond the scope of this book. For overviews of concepts related to music cognition, see Colwell (2006) or Part IV of Colwell and Richardson (2002).

While much of the work of these researchers is focused on learning environments other than music classrooms, we can certainly extrapolate valuable lessons from them. Music software with which students in TBMI contexts often interact is essentially a combination of complex multimedia environments. Notation programs, for example, typically combine musical staves or systems with tool palettes, dialog boxes, and playback—thus, they are an example of software that uses visual and auditory cues. Music software for learning, or CAI (computer-assisted instruction), makes abundant use of redundant visual and auditory presentation of information. Many types of music software employ feedback techniques—both in terms of acknowledging right or wrong answers, or feedback in the form of roll-over help text. We should recognize that well-designed software is as important in technology-based music learning as it is in in other disciplines. TBMI materials should capitalize on the ways in which students best learn music and should allow the flexibility and adaptability that multimedia learning theorists suggest can enhance the power of technology-based learning.

SUMMARY OF CHAPTER 3

In chapter 3, we examined some of the underlying theoretical and philosophical foundations of the new TBMI pedagogy. These examinations are by necessity brief, and complete references to their original sources are provided so that you can pursue more detailed information. TBMI is informed by theories—constructivism, active learning, developmental stages, and others—that emphasize educational design that meets students on their individual level, allowing them to build new knowledge through experimentation and discovery. Other theories that inform TBMI, such as TPACK and Mayer's multimedia learning theories, relate more directly to technology and its influence on general education. TBMI is important, particularly right now, because teachers need concrete guidance, based on theory and rooted in exemplary practice, that will propel the profession into the next phase of technology-based teaching. Whether consciously or subconsciously, the ideas that come from these philosophies are present in the work of many TBMI teachers. As we continue to explore the components of the TBMI framework, in chapter 4 we will examine the process of selecting materials for TBMI.

ITEMS FOR DISCUSSION

1. Profile of Practice 3.1 provided an example of a teacher with a particularly evolved attitude about his students' creativity. Have you ever had or do you know of a teacher who demonstrated the opposite kind of attitude? What impact does this have on students?
2. Active learning, and constructing knowledge through experiences, can change students' worldview. Think about a time when you learned something through active experience. How has that experience affected the way you viewed yourself and your surroundings?
3. How good is your TPACK? A group of researchers have created an assessment tool for measuring teachers' technological and pedagogical content knowledge. The measurement instruments appear at the end of the article they published about this study. Take one of these tests (such as the one by Schmidt, Baran, Thompson, Mishra, Koehler, and Shin, 2009, which is available at tpack.org), then, if possible, compare your responses with those of classmates, colleagues, or others. Does knowing about your own TPACK influence your thinking about technology in your future teaching?

CHAPTER 4

Materials for Technology-Based Music Instruction

Nearly all forms of education make use of materials to support student learning. In the case of traditional music education, the type of material that comes to mind most readily is composed music. Since the dominant form of music education in the United States is the traditional ensemble, composed music is a justifiable representation of what most teachers think of as musical material.

In this chapter, we will look at a couple of examples of established criteria for selecting musical materials for various types of teaching scenarios. Then, we will imagine how those criteria might be applied to TBMI and address the crossover between the music we use in traditional music teaching and the music that might be used in technology-based music instruction. We will then examine the types of materials that are specifically related to technology (software and hardware) and sort through some processes for evaluating and selecting those materials.

MUSIC SELECTION

Though most teachers do not articulate any kind of formula for music selection, there are certainly criteria by which music can be chosen for the classroom. A well-known treatise on criteria for wind band music selection is a dissertation by Ostling (1978) in which the author spelled out several guidelines for selecting music with "serious artistic merit." Among Ostling's suggestions were the following:

- The composition has form—not "a form" but form—and reflects a proper balance between repetition and contrast.

- The composition reflects craftsmanship in orchestration, demonstrating a proper balance between transparent and *tutti* scoring, and also between solo and group colors.
- The composition is sufficiently unpredictable to preclude an immediate grasp of its musical meaning.
- The route through which the composition travels in initiating its musical tendencies and probable musical goals is not completely direct and obvious. The composition is consistent in quality throughout its length and in its various sections.
- The composition is consistent in its style, reflecting a complete grasp of technical details, clearly conceived ideas, and avoids lapses into trivial, futile, or unsuitable passages.
- The composition is genuine in idiom, and is not pretentious.
- The composition reflects a musical validity [that] transcends factors of historical importance, or factors of pedagogical usefulness. (Ostling, 1978, pp. 21–30)

Taken with a grain of salt, these suggestions can serve as reasonable guidelines for selecting music for performance. Others have more recently suggested additional criteria such as musicality, difficulty, completeness, contribution to aesthetic growth, social representation, and transcendence (Del Borgo, 1988; Gaines, 1988; Hughes, 1990; Mayhall, 1994; Pearson, 2000; Fonder, 2003; O'Toole, 2003).

Other types of considerations should be applied when selecting music method books, such as those that might be used in a beginning orchestra or band, or elementary general music:

- How is the book sequenced? Does it follow a logical order and appeal to educational psychology appropriately?
- What is the focus of the musical content of the book? Is it based on notation? What kinds of literature are used?
- How varied are the activities that the book suggests? Does it appeal to several appropriate standards?
- Is it visually appealing?
- Does the book help you to assess your students' progress?

Music teachers must weigh these variables against each other to determine what is best for their environment. Unfortunately, teachers often find themselves in a situation in which, despite careful examination of the materials based on the listed criteria, they do not get to choose. This may be a result of the economic factor outweighing all others, it may be based on tradition (the school/district continues to use what it has always used), or myriad other factors may force the teacher's hand.

Thus far, the discussion of selection of musical materials has centered mostly on *printed* material. But music is not a print medium; it is an aural one. It exists in time and in sound. Notation is simply one way to capture music so that it can be reproduced. Still other criteria are necessary when selecting aural material. Teachers use aural musical material to provide students with listening examples so they can practice critical listening skills. Aural musical material may also be for performance; some would argue that authentic performance of ethnic and indigenous music can only be achieved through listening to a performance of the music by persons embedded in the culture from which the music comes. Notation may, in fact, be unable to reflect the nuance of performance of music that is unfamiliar to Western students and teachers.

It is difficult to separate criteria for music to be experienced aurally from music experienced in performance or other types of study. Similar to the stated criteria for selecting printed music for performance, we can draw on criteria for selecting aural examples. Hoffer (1993) provided a general list of guidelines for music selection that seems appropriate here as we consider the types of music teachers might choose for their students' listening activities. Hoffer wrote that music should be

- Educational—music should allow students to "gain information, skills or attitudes" (p. 74) that they might not otherwise have the chance to gain if they were not to receive instruction that involved this music.
- Valid—the music that teachers select should be a recognized part of the field of music and should contribute something distinct to the learning experience.
- Fundamental—the music that teachers select for listening should be examples of elemental, important ideas.
- Representative—music selected for listening should showcase the vast types, genres, time periods, and demographics from which music comes.
- Contemporary—music should represent both the past and the present, in order to show students that music progresses, or at least changes, over time.
- Relevant—the relevance of a particular piece of music a teacher selects for listening is established by the teacher. If teachers cannot establish relevance of a selection, then the piece is probably not worthy of being selected.
- Learnable—this criterion refers to accessibility of the music to the students for whom it has been selected, or at least the majority of those students. This could be interpreted as developmental appropriateness.

It is important to consider how we select music for listening and to consider what we *do* with our musical selections in the classroom. The presentation and intake of music is just as important, if not more important, than the process by which it is selected. Hoffer's list of guidelines for selecting musical material may not be comprehensive, but it is an excellent starting point for considering the issues that surround music selection in the general music curriculum. Since TBMI can be viewed as an extension of general music (rather than as an extension of the performing ensemble curriculum), it is fair to use Hoffer's list as a basis for selecting musical materials that may be appropriate for technology-based teaching and learning.

CRITERIA FOR SELECTING MUSICAL MATERIAL FOR TBMI

The nature of teaching in a TBMI environment dictates that musical materials are somewhat different than they are in traditional music teaching. Just as musical materials in traditional music teaching environments should serve to expose students to examples of musical elements and to promote guided listening experiences, musical materials in TBMI environments should help students gain exposure to certain elements that are idiomatic to technology-based music. Musical materials for TBMI should relate as directly as possible to the goals the teacher establishes.

Selecting Music for Listening in TBMI

It is critical that students in technology-based music classes are provided with ample opportunity to listen to music. Among the reasons for the importance of listening in TBMI are these:

1. Students who enroll in TBMI classes are frequently not the same students who enroll in music performance classes. Only a small percentage of students regularly engage in in-school music performance in traditional ensembles, and alternative classes such as music technology may reach a different group of students. Since these students come to our classes with a relatively narrow, limited aural view of music, it is our responsibility to "stretch their ears"—to bring them listening experiences that they might not otherwise have.
2. Technology-based music classes must involve some type of music production (composition, performance, etc.). Students need to listen to music that has been produced in this idiom to understand the sonic possibilities of electronic instruments and devices. For example, the effects

of a vocoder, or the sounds of a Theremin, are very difficult to understand unless one *hears* them. They defy explanation, and are therefore best understood through the experience of listening.

3. TBMI is interrelated with composition. Students' creativity needs to be "fed," and perhaps the best way to do so is through listening. This is akin to the tradition of jazz pedagogy in which students learn to improvise by listening to the improvisations of masters, and sometimes transcribing solos so they can fully understand them. Teachers find that using listening examples that emphasize particular elements of music allows students to understand those elements better. This is a type of experiential learning that appeals to the philosophical foundation of TBMI. Music listening can be the fodder for musical creativity. And in return, creating music can lead to more sophisticated listening; that is, students will approach further listening activities with a more acute awareness of the happenings within the music.

Selecting music for listening in the TBMI environment is very similar to selecting music for listening in any other type of music class. In fact, the guidelines that Hoffer (1993) suggested are completely applicable to TBMI. The responsibility of the teacher in technology-based music classes is to provide listening experiences that take on some more nuanced characteristics. I suggest the following guidelines:

• Relevant—Music selections in TBMI should be even more diverse than they might be in traditional music learning environments. Selections should include even the most recent music of many styles and substyles.
• Compelling—Selections should be more closely related to the types of music that students might produce in an electronic environment. For example, if students are being encouraged to explore synthesized sounds, then listening examples should feature synthesized sounds. Watson (2011) provided us with a justification for selecting "compelling" musical examples, writing that selecting the right music for use in creativity-based music classes "charges up [the students'] imagination" (p. 36). Offering students the chance to explore their imagination will surely lead to satisfying and memorable learning experiences.
• Motivational—Selections should reflect the kinds of music that students *want* to listen to. Allowing students to have input into listening activities can be a motivating factor. Teachers might also be surprised at the diverse tastes of their students; in fact, listening examples might even be more diverse if students drive the listening activities than they would be if the teacher were to make all of the decisions.

In the following Profile of Practice, we learn about a teacher who places tremendous importance on listening in his technology-based music classes, and about some of the reasons he has decided to do so.

PROFILE OF PRACTICE 4.1

Mr. Y is a relatively young teacher, and upon accepting his job in a middle-income community, he became the only music teacher in the large urban high school. Prior to his arrival, no music program really existed in the high school, so he set out to create one and has done so with admirable facility. Only a few years into his work, he has established guitar classes, piano classes, and music technology classes. All of these classes meet in his second-floor classroom that is configured as a music lab with modern student workstations, a projector and interactive whiteboard, and a teacher station with a group controller system. In the corner of his classroom, what was once a storage closet has been converted into an isolation booth for his Level 2 technology students to use for recording projects.

Mr. Y's classes are among the favorites in the school's curriculum, and he has even been featured in an article in the local newspaper about his efforts in reviving the program by focusing on technology. His students are diverse—based on some of the research in this field, a surprising number of female students take his class. The students seem to enjoy his class for several reasons, most obviously because of the creative outlet it provides, and because it allows them direct interaction with technology and music.

Another reason the students enjoy Mr. Y's class is that he dedicates a lot of time in class—almost 20 percent of class time—to listening activities. He allows the students to provide the listening examples so that they are relevant to the types of music they listen to. During the times I visited Mr. Y's class, I heard listening examples such as *This is How We Do It* by Montell Jordan, and *Keep Away* by Godsmack. He says that, especially in the urban district in which he teaches, "Kids need relevance. So I feel like it's OK that most examples are from the pop idiom—that's what most students know and it shows them that I am not out of touch with the music they listen to, and this is the music they want to play. It tends to be the reason why they signed up for the class."

Since Mr. Y designed the course himself, I wondered if there were external motivations to include such a substantial focus on listening, or if he had done this out of some innate sense of its importance:

"Looking at the state standards definitely was a big influence....I think I can hit most of the bullet points under that standard[a] with the listening journal, so that's one of the reasons why I do it.... Standards one through four are more about what the students are doing: singing, playing instruments, and the note reading. And I feel like the listening journal will take care of a lot of [standards] five through ten so then for the rest of class, I can focus more on one through four."

I asked Mr. Y if he feels comfortable knowing that so much of his class time is dedicated to listening:

"It takes a decent chunk of the class, but I feel like it's an important thing because first of all, it takes into account the students' preferences, so it makes them feel like they have more input and their own personality matters in the class, which I think is a big deal. Also, it shows them the things they are learning about music are universal and it doesn't matter that one day we hear rock, the next day we hear rap, and the next day we hear classical and jazz; no matter what the style of music, the things that we are learning in the class can be applied to the analysis of that music. So, it acknowledges the personality, it shows that I'm accepting all different styles of music and I'm not going to press one over another on them, and it shows that all these musical characteristics that we are talking about really apply to all styles of music, which keeps them more engaged than if every listening example was classical or jazz. I think they wouldn't have that connection because they think, 'This is school music! When I get home, my style of music doesn't do these things.'"

The students record their ideas about the listening examples in electronic journals that he reads every few weeks. Mr. Y uses this as an evaluative tool, and to help him guide the connections between the music students are listening to and the musical concepts he teaches. Listening is important to him, and he is glad that his students enjoy it, but he is most concerned about using listening as an influential factor toward his students' composing. He sees these activities as feeding off one another; that is, the compositions his students write get more sophisticated based on their listening experiences, and the listening gets more attentive based on the composition activities. He commented, "I feel like the students noticed a lot more [in the listening examples] once they started making music themselves which is why the lab helps so much.... They are able to really apply everything pretty immediately when they are consistently creating

a. The standard to which Mr. Y referred reads "Critical Response. Students will describe and analyze their own music and the music of others using appropriate vocabulary. When appropriate, students will connect their analysis to interpretation and evaluation." A full citation for this standard would reveal the location of Mr. Y, who was promised anonymity.

music. Other classroom situations would be more difficult to make [that] happen. If you didn't have a technology lab, you know, in a concert band situation, the students generally don't do much composing in there, if any. And so I feel like having students making their own music, especially in the classroom lab situation—it's just a great way to teach something that can be immediately applied and it will stick [with] them a lot longer than if you were treated just like a normal appreciation class where you are just talking and talking about things, and not really applying it."

I prompted him: "So it's kind of striking a balance between the analytical mind-set and the creative application kind of mind-set?"

He responded, "Yes, exactly. Before I had the lab, I felt like it was divided. I had a music appreciation class, where you just discuss the music and analyze the music all the time, but didn't get much music making. And then I had a guitar class, where the students [made] the music all the time. I just felt like the students [were] getting such different experiences ... because understanding is so much deeper when they actually apply over and over again."

Mr. W sees the benefit of providing his students with listening experiences and has astutely noticed the cyclical, mutually beneficial relationship between listening and creating.

Selecting Music for Performing

In addition to the guidance about selecting music for listening to enhance and support the goals of teaching in TBMI classes, consider that TBMI is not just for learning *about* music as listeners from the outside, but TBMI should also provide students with opportunities to learn *within* music as performers. The nature of the types of students who often populate technology-based music classes may steer teachers away from trying to facilitate performance; these students often do not read traditional music notation, they are not enthusiastic about performance, and the mind-set or logistics of the school environment may not be conducive to creating performance opportunities. Performance is at the core of musical activities, and TBMI teachers need to approach their classes with creative ways to get students performing within the idiom of technology-based music.

Part of technology-based music is capturing or recording music performance. Students understand that in order to practice recording, there must be sound to record. Performance can be embedded within a curricular unit about live sound amplification technology, including the uses of microphones, speakers, amplifiers, effects units, mixers and cables. In this sense, the music that might be selected for performance is virtually limitless. Some teachers have students prepare and perform "beat poetry" so that there is a sound source available for recording. Others encourage students to form laboratory rock bands, prepare a piece for performance, and capture it as a recording. Other teachers design "found sound" activities, relying on sounds that occur in nature. Although this is not performing in the purest sense, students are still involved in seeking out sounds that are appealing and making critical decisions about how to use technology to enhance them.

It is important for inexperienced performers to develop a sense of rhythm, and many teachers use the TBMI environment as a place to encourage this. Performing compositions using simple percussion instruments, or perhaps body percussion, can help encourage a sense of pulse and rhythm. For students to take ownership in these types of performances, they could be encouraged to compose their own percussion pieces.

Since TBMI is part of the school's *music* curriculum, teachers can, and often do, insist on the inclusion of traditional music performance as part of their classes. Typical practices include basic guitar skills or, more frequently, basic piano skills. Since many music labs have piano keyboards as a component of the students' workstations, it makes sense that students would be taught to use the keyboards. In addition to using keyboards for data entry in electronic composition, students can be taught to use the pianos as traditional instruments in keyboard ensemble music. This music for performance need not be particularly difficult or sophisticated. It is important, however, for budding music technologists to understand the role of performer in an ensemble. Only through performance experience can students feel the sense of responsibility of playing their part in time and correctly. Remember that students in TBMI classes may not read standard notation, so carefully approach the idea of how to notate music for performance—perhaps use alternate notation, or avoid notation completely.

A final possibility is the most sophisticated. Consider that the use of electronic instruments for performance is common and completely valid. Students who have some degree of accomplishment with electronic instruments may have an interest in forming an electronic music ensemble. Models of these types of ensembles will be examined in chapter 10.

SELECTING TECHNOLOGICAL MATERIALS

The emphasis in the approach to technology-based music instruction presented in this book is on the *music*. Music should always be kept at the core of all we do in TBMI. However, the material choices we make as technology-based music teachers reach beyond musical materials. Not only must we be intimately familiar with music, but we must also be well versed in the available technologies so that we can choose wisely for our students to use.

Some of these choices are dictated by financial concerns. When choosing a piece of software or hardware, it is rare to have unlimited financial resources. The best ways to overcome this restriction are to be aware of all possibilities and to be able to make the case to those who control the purse strings for your music program.

Here are a few practical suggestions for seeking funds for the hardware and software you choose:

1. While you should strive to keep music at the core, do not hesitate to reach beyond the music department for funding. The most obvious connection to make within your school or district is to the technology or media coordinator. People in these positions typically have access to funds for technology in many departments—it is your responsibility to express the needs of your program so that you have equal opportunity to use those funds. Quite often, technology coordinators do not consider the needs of music departments because they are simply unaware of the potential for technology in music. Make them aware.

2. In many schools/districts, a special pool of money is reserved for textbooks, which are the dominant type of materials in many academic classes. In music technology classes, computers and software are the essential materials. Therefore, it is possible that the money that has been allocated for textbooks could be spent on technology equipment. This may seem a stretch to some administrators, but it never hurts to ask!

3. Many technology labs are funded through grants. While it is beyond the scope of this book to examine the ways to obtain grant funding, there are several excellent resources that can help you do so.[1]

In the remaining sections of this chapter, we will examine processes of selecting hardware and software for a TBMI environment. I will use the term *lab* as a catchall to refer to the type of classroom in which technology-based music instruction typically takes place.

---

1. These resources include the Grants section of the website of the Technology Institute for Music Educators (www.ti-me.org) and the book *Finding Funds for Music Technology* by Rudolph (1999).

Mr. G has a lot of experience with music technology. He is well versed in many pieces of software and hardware. When he recently sat in a conference presentation in which the speakers were suggesting that 80 percent of students nationwide are not involved in music at the secondary level, and that technology might be a way to draw them in, he was inspired to start a music technology class at the school where he teaches. When the new class began, he had the opportunity to choose the software and hardware his students would be using. He chose to base most of his instruction on GarageBand, the pervasive music recording and sequencing program from Apple. He was not alone in this decision—the majority of classes I observed used GarageBand, or the teachers said they would like to be using it.

When I observed Mr. G's class, he was teaching a lesson about connectivity of electronic instruments and devices. He distributed a handout with pictures of various cables and ports and conducted a live demonstration of some of the possibilities for routing signals between devices. He described the lesson: "We looked a lot at live sound and microphones and putting it through a mixer, so I wanted to show them the difference between some of the cables used for MIDI [and] some of the ones they were already familiar with. The first sheet was just a reference of different cables and what they look like. And then I had three different setups using the controller keyboard that we use and the computer that we use. [I was] just trying to do some different diagrams of how you might connect them up.... So we kind of worked through three different scenarios."

Mr. G knew that, since GarageBand is a self-contained music-making environment, it would be difficult to draw the connections between the lesson and the software. He said, "Everything's kind of *in* GarageBand," expressing the notion that physical connections are not really at the cutting edge of technology. He sees this as an advantage of the program because it takes care of so much, but also as a disadvantage because it removes the knowledge of signal flow that is necessary in more sophisticated systems. He said, "What's interesting is that the setup that we have really doesn't involve much technical knowledge, so they haven't had to deal with it."

Every software package has features that afford opportunities. GarageBand is a relatively powerful sequencer, and it forms the foundation for entire yearlong courses in some schools. But teachers I spoke with, including Mr. G, recognize that the program has limitations. It is important to examine software choices critically and to keep in mind the limits that software imposes on students.

Selecting Software

Many practical and theoretical considerations enter into the decisions regarding software selection. At the forefront of this crucial decision, we must remember to frame software as what it really is—*just another material we select for our students*. No piece of software is the "magic bullet" that will make your planning and teaching, or your students' learning, easier or better. Every software package has its particular affordances and limitations, and thoughtful teachers make choices based on many criteria.

Elementary general music teachers choose songs for students to sing and study; band teachers choose literature for ensembles to play; jazz instructors choose chord progressions for their students to learn to improvise. The selection of software for a TBMI teacher is analogous to all of these choices because they impact, and may confine, learning experiences. Teachers should not be flippant about software choices because they might represent significant expense, investment of time to learn, and adherence to the protocols of one piece of software over another. However, teachers need to be willing to experiment with varied types of software and to expose students to many pieces of software that are designed to accomplish many tasks.

When selecting software, first consider the sources from which it can come. In general, software is *commercial, shareware, freeware*, or *open source*.

Commercial software is produced by a software manufacturer and sold to the consumer either on boxed media (CD or DVD), or downloaded. Software prices can run the gamut from a few dollars to hundreds of dollars. Commercial software can, in some cases, be purchased in volume or licensed for an entire school or business. Since commercial software is backed by its manufacturer, users can expect full technical support and fully featured software packages. These luxuries, however, often come at exorbitant prices.

Shareware is software that is often produced by smaller software development companies, or even individuals. It is called shareware because those developers are willing to share it with a community of users for a small fee, usually only a few dollars. Shareware often lacks the type of support and full feature set of commercial counterparts.

Similar to shareware is freeware, the cost of which is indicated by its name. Freeware programs usually have limited feature sets and generally lack any kind of technical support availability. In many cases, shareware is disguised as freeware; that is, programs are made usable for free with limited feature sets (such as disabled printing or saving) that are made available once the user pays.

Open source programs are similar to freeware with one special characteristic: in addition to the application itself, the programming code is available for download and editing, and the user community is responsible for developing the software. As such, very little technical support is available for open source software other than postings on community message boards. While these programs are typically free, and often very powerful (take, for example, Audacity, a cross-platform audio editor that fits in this category), bugs and technical glitches occur frequently because the programs themselves are always in development.

The lesson to be learned from these categories is that despite financial constraints, teachers can develop technology-based music labs on a budget; however, budget concerns are not the only consideration for software selection. Even though free software is available, the old adage "You get what you pay for" is one to be aware of when selecting freeware or open source software. Selecting software that is buggy or difficult, and expecting students to become fluid with its use, is comparable to asking a beginning trumpet player to produce a good sound with a bad instrument. Remember that software is *just another material we select for our students*, but we cannot expect our students to learn well with poor materials.

PROFILE OF PRACTICE 4.3

Many TBMI teachers do units on remixing with their students. Given the growing popularity of remixing and creating mash-ups outside of school, this type of project is appealing because of its cultural relevance. Mash-ups are compositions created by blending some of the elements of existing songs—perhaps using a drum groove from one and overlaying vocals from another. Of all the types of projects I saw students doing in TBMI classes, remix/mash-up units seemed to be the one that would be most transferrable to the kinds of things that they would do outside of school, and in many cases, beyond their K–12 years. Mr. N's class was engaged in this kind of project when I observed him.

Mr. N had a particularly challenging music technology class because he only had three computers for nine high school students. The computers were located in the back of a band room rather than in a dedicated space and were not particularly recent models. He thinks of the students, who sit in groups at the computers, as "drivers and passengers," and he periodically asks them to take turns "at the wheel." He moves from one station to the next and, rather than concentrating on the student who is at the computer at the moment, he engages the other two students by asking them questions about what the "driver" is doing.

Despite the physical and equipment challenges, he is able to run a robust curriculum that includes a unit on mash-ups. The students seem to enjoy this quite a bit. He instructs the students to find short clips of music on YouTube and use a simple audio recording program (in this case, Audacity) to capture the sound files. Then they use either the free version of Sony's Acid, or Acoustica's Mixcraft, to learn about beat mapping and matching, and to produce mash-ups. As we talked, however, Mr. N expressed some frustration over software selection as it relates to the mash-up project. While Mixcraft is a relatively full-function sequencer, he had not fully integrated it into his program yet. The version of Acid the students were using allowed only for manual beat matching, rather than the automatic functions of commercial versions.

As he wrestled with his thoughts, he recognized that I often deal with similar pedagogical choices and asked, "If you have software that does this automatically, would you just throw that at the kids first, or would you go through the process of some critical listening? We need to stretch this one, we need to shrink this one, they don't quite match. Have them go through that process and then say, 'OK, here's Mixcraft or the full version [of Acid] that does it automatically for you.'"

I wanted to know how Mr. N would resolve this dilemma, so I responded: "It's kind of a pedagogical choice, but because you're limited with the software that you have, it kind of dictates that choice for you. I don't know the answer to the question. I guess the answer is, if you can get something that does it for you, then maybe that progression that you're talking about is the way to go so that the students see what goes into the technique."

Mr. N was coming to grips with the affordances and limitations of certain software. We talked more about additional possibilities. I told him that Ableton's Live is quickly becoming the standard software in the mash-up artist community. He balked at that suggestion because he has heard that Live has a steep learning curve, one that he might not be willing to tackle. After some further discussion about the trade-offs of the software his students use, he came to the conclusion that some combination of manual exploration of beat matching technique and automatic features of software is probably the best way to go. This seemed to match well with his teaching style and pedagogical priorities. This was a thoughtful way to approach software selection, and his students will likely benefit from Mr. N's investment in choosing the right software for their learning.

Models and Criteria for Software Selection

There are many types of music software on the current market. They include titles that are designed for computer-based notation, music production (also known as sequencing), digital audio recording and editing, and music learning. Given that there are so many choices, teachers should have some means by which to select one piece of software over another, once they have focused on a particular purpose for that software.

Selecting software, however, should not be isolated from the curriculum. *The single most important factor in selecting software is the ability of that software to support the learning goals teachers establish for their students.* Some teachers in technology-based music classes allow the software they use to drive the curriculum and daily lesson planning. This practice should be avoided. The musical concepts and skills that students learn should be supported by the software, and those concepts and skills are the most important motivations in selecting software. Remember that software is *just another material we select for our students*, so, just like other materials, the software should support the objectives and goals.

Deubel (2002) provided some ideas for reviewing software for possible use in their classrooms. What follows is an adaptation of those ideas to technology-based music classes:

1. *Learning objectives.* Deubel wrote that software should have stated learning objectives. I suggest that rather than software having learning objectives, the software should support learning objectives that are established through our own curriculum design and lesson planning. However, when software itself is designed to develop specific skills or guide students to learning certain content, then the objectives should indeed be stated clearly, and they should be the guiding principles of all aspects of the software.
2. *Motivation.* Software should be interesting and help students concentrate on the tasks they are expected to accomplish. Interest in the topic can be developed in the classroom through the teacher's demeanor and presentation. Software can support students' motivation by providing feedback when students do things correctly or incorrectly.
3. *Individualized instruction and automatic adjustment.* Software can provide flexibility so that individual students, whose learning needs may differ drastically, can be accommodated in terms of speed of progress and difficulty of material. In many cases these adjustments happen automatically. In addition, software might make provisions for students with disabilities such as visual impairments or learning difficulties.

4. *Clear examples*. When using software to introduce concepts, teachers need to be sure that the examples provided in software are easy to understand, and make sense with the concept. This criterion also applies to music production and notation applications that include sample files. Those files should be usable to demonstrate musical concepts and skills within the software.

5. *Repetition*. Especially in computer-assisted instruction software, it is important that students receive ample repetition toward mastery of concepts or skills. In some software, the amount of repetition is selectable, so teachers should be aware of the available options within the software's controls.

6. *Multiple solution methods*. Music software should support students' creativity. Students will have moments of extreme satisfaction when they are able to "figure out" the solution to a music production problem in the software they are using to make music. Software that provides only one path toward any single task can be limiting and frustrating.

7. *Feedback*. As with traditional learning, it is important for students to have feedback, both positive and negative. Students need to know when they have accomplished a task correctly, and when they have been unsuccessful. Some computer-assisted learning software does this particularly well. Music creation software is less adept at providing feedback; oftentimes the feedback students receive is that the software works or doesn't work the way they expect it to. This can be frustrating and can stifle students' creative work. Look for software that offers on-screen support or help to overcome this problem.

Additional Criteria

We can further distill the criteria for selecting software for TBMI into five key areas: Design/User Interface, Media, Extensibility, Necessary Technical Knowledge, and Educational Applicability (Dorfman & Jacoby, 2006).

Design/User Interface—This category addresses the general ease of use of the application. Good design means that users can quickly recognize what the components of the software are capable of doing and what features may be excluded. We can all probably list a couple pieces of software that do not meet this criterion!

Included Media—Certain types of software provide an environment for music production or editing but are dependent upon the use of external media for them to perform these tasks. For example, loop-based music production software (such as GarageBand, FL Studio, or Acid) allow users to do many things, but at their core they are production software that use predefined chunks of audio or MIDI which can be looped, stretched, and truncated. If the software does not include a substantial amount of media, then students' creativity will be crippled. You will be forced to find media elsewhere, which can be expensive and time-consuming.

Extensibility—This category represents the question, "How well can the particular software package be extended beyond its factory-packaged features?" For use with younger students, you may not find it necessary to go beyond what the software can do upon its initial installation. But with older students, and for use in the professional world, it is essential that software "plays nicely" with other music applications and products. This category includes an evaluation of support for add-ons and plug-ins (both effects and instruments). Also, how well does the software support after-market products such as audio and MIDI interfaces? Does the software communicate well with other software via ReWire and similar resource sharing technologies?

Necessary Technical Knowledge—Students, especially younger students and those without formal performance training, must be able to use software without much instruction. What prior knowledge will the user need to use the software effectively?

Educational Applicability—Does the software address a broad range of age and skill levels? Given the economic hardships of many music programs, maximizing the uses of a particular software package could just be the deciding factor. The number of settings in which software could be used and the varieties of educational goals that it can help meet must be considered.

With criteria such as these in place, the TBMI community should consider actually *testing* music software to understand how well it is designed. Reeves et al. (2002) outlined a process called Heuristic Evaluation, which is designed to apply evaluation criteria to a software title. In their article, a group of testers examined software according to a list of criteria. Each time they encountered a problem, they rated it according to its severity and extensiveness. Gibbs, Graves, and Bernas (2001) conducted a similar study of a formal method of evaluating software.

While such formal evaluations may not be realistic for busy teachers, it is important to remember the significance of the selection of software. Just as the music we select for ensembles in many ways constitutes the curriculum, software can shape the ways we teach and the ways our students learn.

Selecting Hardware

Hardware selection is simple. It boils down to this: get the newest, fastest hardware you can afford with the money you have. Here are a few additional pointers:

1. Try not to "skimp" on the size of computer monitors. Almost all monitors on the current market are of the flat-screen or LCD variety, and most have excellent resolution and clarity. However, supplying your students (or yourself) with a small monitor can be detrimental in two ways: (a) staring at a small screen for many hours can be fatiguing on the eyes and body; (b) without having a large enough screen, many music applications will be difficult to use without constant scrolling. A monitor of at least 15" (measured diagonally) is recommended, but bigger is better.

2. Choose hardware that allows connectivity and upgrading. For music and media applications, it is essential that computers allow for several kinds of devices to be connected to them. Minimally, a computer should support USB connections. In fact, some software that you might use in your music class requires connecting an external USB device for the software to run. Computers should have at least two USB ports that are accessible for use in the lab. Firewire or other high-speed connections are often necessary to import video from tape-based video cameras.
Upgrading will probably not be necessary within the first few years of a computer's life; however, if we assume that funding is limited, it may be better to upgrade computers that are a few years old than to replace them completely. Upgrades might include adding memory; replacing hard drives with faster, larger capacity ones; or replacing sound or graphics cards.

3. Music technology can be done on a shoestring budget; however, to enhance your students' creative potential, provide them with a palette of tools that will not limit their workflow. In addition to a computer, each student workstation should have a MIDI keyboard or controller. Some teachers opt for additional outboard equipment such as MIDI or audio interfaces. If audio recording is to be part of the curriculum, consider external audio interfaces that accept microphones—these will result in much higher quality recordings than are possible with internal computer microphones.

4. Presentation hardware for the teacher is essential. A data projector capable of projecting the display of a computer revolutionizes teaching. Some teachers have completely changed the way they teach based on the ability to project a computer on a screen, as opposed to using a chalk or marker board. In addition, the employment of an interactive whiteboard can profoundly influence the ways we interact with technology as a group.

SUMMARY OF CHAPTER 4

In this chapter we have explored ideas related to selecting teaching materials for TBMI environments. First we examined selection of music for traditional music teaching and how those ideas can be transformed for technology-based classes. Then, we examined selection of software and hardware for TBMI. All of this should be understood in the context of software and hardware as *just materials*, which is the reason for placing all of this discussion in the same chapter. In the next chapter, we will look at how teachers use these materials and how they shape their practices in the classroom.

ITEMS FOR DISCUSSION

1. Locate a method book that might be used in a beginning band or orchestra class. Examine the book carefully. Are there references in the book to technology? How might the teacher infuse technology into lessons that are based on the book?
2. In the first Profile of Practice in this chapter, the teacher was very dedicated to including listening examples in his curriculum. Find a listening example that you might use with a TBMI class. What kinds of lessons can be learned from the example? How might a lesson plan design be based on the example?
3. In the second Profile of Practice in this chapter, the teacher was somewhat torn over whether or not it was important to teach his students about physical connection of music technology devices. Do you think this is important? Given the capabilities of software to do so many things internally, how might you go about teaching this content?
4. Choose a piece of music-related software. Use the criteria described in this chapter to evaluate the software. Try to articulate some of the characteristics of the software as they relate to each of the evaluative criteria. Try to establish a recommendation for whether the software is appropriate for use at the elementary school, middle school, or high school levels.

CHAPTER 5

Teaching Methods and Teacher Behaviors

TBMI differs from simple integration in that this type of teaching emphasizes *direct student engagement* with technology for introducing, reinforcing, and assessing learning experiences. While teachers' uses of technology are encouraged, the main idea associated with TBMI is that teachers design experiences during which *student engagement with music technologies is essential*; students are learning music by experiencing it from within. This encourages construction of new knowledge through creativity and builds on previous experiences.

In this chapter and the next, we will address several questions:

1. Why are new teaching methods associated with TBMI?
2. What are the dispositions of teachers as they develop teaching methods for TBMI?
3. How are these methods designed?
4. How do teachers function physically in the TBMI classroom?
5. How do teachers connect theory and practice in the act of teaching TBMI lessons?

Answering these questions will help you to understand exactly how TBMI lessons look and how to carry out lessons in a space designed for them.

JUSTIFYING NEW TEACHING METHODS

It makes sense that traditional music teaching uses traditional methods. When choir teachers, for example, direct an ensemble, they typically make use of techniques they saw their own teachers use or that they were taught to employ during their own teacher education programs. While they may be using new music, and the students are new from year to year, the techniques teachers use go essentially unchanged.

Teachers determine learning objectives for their students through a process of diagnosis, adherence to curriculum guidelines, and sometimes through input from the students themselves. But once those learning objectives are determined, in reality, the teaching methods that teachers employ are dictated by the demands of the material the students are to learn. When choir teachers encounter a passage in a piece of music that requires soft singing, they will employ the techniques they know to encourage their students to sing softly while maintaining proper breath support and diction. And so it is in other types of music instruction—the technique matches the content.

TBMI presents us with different content and therefore with a new set of techniques to convey material. While the musical content may not change— that is, students are still learning the same musical knowledge, concepts, and skills—the tools that are available for teachers to convey that content change dramatically. Since the tools and materials are different, it stands to reason that the techniques for teaching should be different.

PROFILE OF PRACTICE 5.1

Standards in music education suggest that by the time they graduate from high school, all students should develop proficiencies in many modes of musical experience—listening, responding, performing, improvising, and others. In reality, few schools and districts mandate music education beyond elementary school, and some do not even make elementary music a requisite part of the curriculum. So, reaching all students in a school is very difficult, if not impossible.

Mrs. H teaches in a high school where the performing ensembles are, she says, far more valued than her keyboard and music technology classes. Her students are non-traditional music students because they are not part of the performing ensembles. About teaching this group of students she said, "I feel it's a great service. I'm not sure my music department feels that same way. They want nothing to do with any of the kids that I think are outside of band or chorus. That's the mind-set. I feel like I want to reach as many as I can. And if it is making them come to school, then that's a great thing. I can [make] a positive difference, because I get on their backs about other classes. You know, 'Why didn't you make it to English first period?'"

Still, she admits that there are difficulties associated with teaching music to non-traditional music students, even in the technology-based environment. One particular challenge is that she cannot expect a great deal of musical background from her students because, even though they might play in bands outside of school, they are not involved in traditional performing ensembles. She said, "I know what they've had in middle school, generally. I'm not expecting very much. Even though there is a prerequisite on the course—they're supposed to have some kind of keyboard background—the counselors don't always pay attention to that. So I have to deal with going from a beginner all the way up to the one kid who's a pretty good percussionist." Another challenge is the general demeanor and academic performance of the students she gets. Despite her best efforts, some of the students in her classes are not succeeding in high school and may not graduate according to a normal plan.

As she has considered her students and the challenging circumstances they present, Mrs. H has come up with strategies that she thinks accommodate them as well as possible. Despite their difficulties, the students do a remarkably good job of attending to assignments and coming up with original, creative work. Among the strategies she calls upon most is active engagement. Rather than structure her class with a lot of talking and demonstration, she prefers to get her students involved and working as quickly as possible. She also recognizes that non-traditional music students cannot be taught using the same strategies as can traditional music students, and she avoids some of the pitfalls that might occur if she were to do so. She tries her best to avoid using standard music notation. "Some kids really struggle when I bring in the notation element. Some of them have really great ears and can do many, many things by ear. But if I give them something with notation and expect them to read it, it's usually a challenge."

While working with non-traditional, inexperienced music students might not be the absolute ideal circumstance, Mrs. H realizes the benefits of doing so. Teachers like Mrs. H are willing to struggle a bit with their students because they know that, in the end, beneficial experiences will occur. They blend the challenges into development of strategies and dispositions that help them and their students to be successful. In doing so, it is possible to bring more students into music study during school and to try to help them to meet the expectation of skillful music proficiency by the time they finish.

TBMI TEACHER DISPOSITIONS

Despite our academic pedigree and professional training, every teacher has individual ideas about the ways they interact with their students. In Profile of Practice 5.1, we learned about a teacher who has taken a particular stance toward working with non-traditional music students—an important population for TBMI teachers to consider. While individuality is key in developing one's teaching style, observations of the successful teachers featured in the Profiles of Practice have revealed several dispositions that may lead to successful technology-based music teaching, some of which are described in the following sections.

Willingness to Experiment/Be Lost

Effective technology-based music teachers are willing to do things in ways that are different from ways they may have used before, even if they are unsure of how successful the outcome will be. They realize that if a particular lesson does not go as planned, there are opportunities to learn new techniques and solutions and to make success out of apparent failure.

This is perhaps most clearly exhibited when technology itself does not respond as expected—a situation where all technologists find themselves eventually. In one observation conducted for this book, a teacher, who is widely known as an expert, experienced some technical breakdowns in his lab. The teacher asked his students to use a sequencing program, with which they all had substantial experience, to export MP3 files of their compositions. For several students, the export process failed. The teacher did not immediately recognize the underlying issue causing this problem. However, rather than derail his lesson, he made sure the majority of his students, who were able to achieve the task successfully, were on the right track. Then he was able to focus his time on resolving the errors that only a couple of his students were facing. Also, he involved those students in resolving the issues. This teacher demonstrated appropriate pedagogical technique because (1) he addressed the majority of his students first, rather than the small minority who might cause disruption to the flow of the lesson, and (2) he demonstrated calm and forged ahead to try to resolve the issues, while modeling for his students a logical path to do so.

Willingness to Ask for Help

Teachers cannot know everything. We should be as prepared as possible when class begins, but questions and problems will always arise to which we do not know the answers. Sources of answers may include professional organizations, online help, or even your students.

Focus on Musical Fundamentals

In traditional music teaching, many of our instructional decisions are based on the repertoire we choose for our students to perform. TBMI, by definition, is not typically focused on performance, though it can make up part of the curriculum. TBMI teachers are often predisposed to focusing on musical fundamentals such as rhythm and pulse, pitch, harmony, and form. Perhaps a weakness of TBMI is its lack of inherent ability to teach expressiveness.

Willingness to Listen to/Teach New Music

As discussed in the section on selecting musical materials, students who are engaged in TBMI may have a different perspective on music from that of students who participate in traditional ensembles. While TBMI teachers can assume the responsibility of exposing these students to the types of music they might miss by not being part of traditional school music experiences, we should not discount the legitimacy of the music that students bring to the TBMI environment. Good TBMI teachers should embrace the fact that music they do not consider *their* music might be more closely related to the techniques and skills of technology-based music creation.

TBMI teachers frequently listen to music that is new, different, and contemporary, and music that stretches their own experiences. Doing so accomplishes two valuable things. First, it will show students that while teachers may or may not *enjoy* certain types of music, they are willing to listen and honor the creativity that went into making it. Second, listening to contemporary music will expose teachers to new techniques of music production that they can, in turn, use in their curricula.

Desire to Teach Non-traditional Music Students

Recent research has shown us that only about 20 percent of American high school students who attend schools where traditional ensemble classes are available elect to participate in those classes.[1] This leaves 80 percent of the student body with no exposure to formal musical activity in their high school experiences. TBMI teachers recognize that this is a tremendous injustice, and they accept the responsibility of pulling those students into their classes. In many circumstances, high school music technology

---

1. See http://musiccreativity.org

elective classes become the most popular classes in the school, often leading to waiting lists to register for classes. TBMI teachers recognize that not all students want to learn music in the same ways and that technology is a draw for non-traditional music students.

While TBMI teachers accept that all students have the right to a strong musical education, we are presented with challenges when course enrollments reflect an extreme range of prior music experiences. Students who take technology-based music courses, especially at the middle school and high school levels, come to them with such varied musical exposure and training that it makes lesson planning and assessment very difficult. Teachers observed and interviewed for this book offered some interesting suggestions and strategies for dealing with this problematic, yet realistic circumstance. Some teachers require formal prerequisites in the form of prior music classes. For example, some teachers may require that students who take technology-based music classes have taken group piano class or have performed in a school ensemble. Other teachers offer students the chance to earn their place in the technology-based music class by taking a placement test, similar to those used in other academic areas. This is a problematic strategy because the profession does not currently have any standard set of knowledge that would be included in a placement test, but local versions of tests can address skills and knowledge expected in a particular school system or by an individual teacher.

The most frequently found scenario is that students take technology-based music classes regardless of their performance experiences, and those experiences may be extremely limited. In some schools, these classes are viewed as a place to put students who have nowhere else to go, as was the case in Profile of Practice 5.1. While many teachers express dismay over this situation, they often find that the students who "wind up" in their classes are among the most interested, creative, and enthusiastic members of their roster.

Students may or may not have the ability to read standard music notation; they may or may not understand the layout of a piano keyboard; they may or may not be able to recognize the sounds of orchestral instruments. But it is important to remember that, despite extremely rare cases, the vast majority of students bring a lifetime of music listening experience to the table. Students know what they like and what they dislike, they have strong preferences for particular genres, and they communicate in musical ways. The power of technology lies in its ability to help those students with non-traditional musical experiences—those who are not trained performers—to be musically creative, and to think in sound.

Willingness to Fight the Good Fight

Music education, in general, is expensive. Schools have limited resources, and administrators need to dedicate those resources to subjects for which they are held most accountable. That, however, is not an excuse that we should blindly accept. If a school's setting is appropriate for technology-based music classes, then the teacher must be willing to "go to bat" for the necessary equipment, time, and support. Anecdotally, many labs have been developed starting with a single computer, which provides opportunities to show administrators the value and benefit that students get from their experiences with music technologies. TBMI teachers are willing to push for their cause and to be persistent until they reach a point where their students can be successful.

Willingness to Relinquish Control

Great TBMI teachers are willing to take risks. Researchers have recognized that risk is associated very closely with the particular context of a school, and risk is a profound issue when viewed in light of technology integration (Howard, 2007). Despite the risks associated with technology integration, teachers must be willing to give up some of the autocratic control that is a part of traditional teaching, including directing ensembles. TBMI demands that, to an extent, students are allowed to determine the pace of their own learning. Musical decisions become the domain of the student rather than the all-knowing director. While the teacher can still be seen as an expert and can guide students toward good decisions and uses of their time, relationships between students and teachers are far more collaborative than they might be in a traditional classroom.

Knowing the Software and Hardware

The content of TBMI is complex. It should be assumed that music teachers in the classroom are qualified in terms of their musical content knowledge as a result of their lifetime of musical training before, during, and since their teacher preparation programs. In addition to musical knowledge, however, these teachers in technological contexts are expected to function well with music software and hardware—the Technological Knowledge component of the TPACK model.

This seems like a reasonable expectation, and one that is upheld by many sophisticated technology-based music teachers. However, there is still a widely held belief that teachers of music in technology-based contexts do not need to be experts or have advanced knowledge of music software and hardware. *A fundamental, underlying principle of this text and the methods of TBMI is that is that technology-based music teachers must have a sophisticated knowledge of music software and hardware.* It is not enough to "stay a day ahead" of the students. Teachers should invest time and intellectual capital into becoming skilled users of technology. There are two reasons for this. First, in all other areas of education, including traditional music teaching, teachers are expected to be experts in the content being learned and the associated pedagogical techniques. It is extremely difficult, for example, to teach a student to form a trumpet embouchure or a violin bow grip without having learned to do so oneself. We should expect the same level of experience from TBMI teachers. This is not to say that teachers should be the *exclusive* holders of knowledge, but they should have a mastery of the common and useful components of the software so that they can guide students through well-designed lessons with the software. Limited knowledge of the technological tools leads to learning designs that are creatively shortsighted.

The second reason for teachers to have advanced knowledge of technology is that without this knowledge, teachers may not have the ability to envision the end result of projects that students can do. Limited knowledge of software and hardware tools results in a limited perspective of their uses. An example of this conundrum lies in the use of interactive whiteboards.[2] These devices, which have become fairly commonplace in all levels of schooling, allow teachers to project the display of a computer onto a surface, and to interact with the display. Interactive whiteboards are capable of facilitating activities that students love because they are able to engage with digital media without being tethered to a computer. Interactive whiteboards, however, have a learning curve (shallow as it may be) for teachers. When teachers do not engage fully with these devices, they run the risk of using them as nothing more than glorified projector screens. Without a thorough knowledge of the capabilities of the interactive whiteboard, teachers are unable to envision the possible uses of the device in their classroom.

Students in today's schools live their lives in a "connected" world, and their social interactions, in many cases, are based on electronic communication. While teachers should be expected to attain a level of expertise with technology, we should also not discount the expertise that students bring. At times, students may be able to help with technological problems, and it is perfectly acceptable to capitalize on that help. For example, while not many teachers are engaged in the culture of DJ-ing, many students are. DJ-ing requires a

---

2. The term "smart board" is often used in reference to interactive whiteboards. Smart is a brand name that has become somewhat synonymous with these types of devices although, in reality, there are many more manufacturers of interactive whiteboards.

special set of skills for which many involved in that practice use sophisticated beat matching, sequencing, and editor-librarian software. If students know that software and understand its uses in particular contexts, teachers should not hesitate to engage them in demonstrating their special expertise.

Interest in Fostering Creativity

Technology-based music classes should be creative places. They should be settings that allow students the freedom to explore musical and technological ideas, to review and modify their ideas, to share their ideas with others, to receive critical and supportive feedback, and to be proud of their work. Teachers who can establish that kind of setting have a true interest in fostering students' creativity regardless of the cost in terms of time and energy.

Too often music teachers relate creativity to free, unstructured time for students to experiment, explore, and make new things from scratch. While that is occasionally appropriate and can be fruitful, models of musical creativity have emerged that show us the importance of certain aspects of the creative workflow. One important model about the creative process in music (Webster, 2002b) suggests the following:

- Creative thinking most often begins with the intention to make a product. Products can take several forms including compositions, performances, improvisations, and unique listening experiences.
- Thinking during the creative process is often an internal negotiation. People being creative move between thinking that develops new and different ideas, and thinking that brings those ideas into a recognizable, usable form.
- Constraints and conditions, both internal and external, can help people to be creative.
- Creative work is necessarily impacted by the skills people bring to the work.
- Creativity is a process that requires time for thinking, exploring, and revising.

While technology-based classes are linked to the purposeful and proper uses of technological tools, excellent TBMI teachers create scenarios in which the technology actually *complements* the process of creating while fostering students' creative thinking rather than hindering it if the students are not bogged down in procedural information. TBMI teachers should value the formal, procedural, structural knowledge that students can learn by using rich technology applications, along with the broad, less-structured thinking that students can do to create content using those applications. Beghetto and Kaufman (2010) wrote:

> Teachers who successfully support creativity in the classroom recognize the complementary (and necessary) relationship between creativity and curricular constraints. This recognition is underwritten by an understanding that in order for an idea, a product, or a behavior to be considered creative it must combine originality *and* appropriateness.... When teachers recognize that creativity is not simple unconstrained originality—but actually requires a combination of originality and task appropriateness—they can see the value of curricular standards and conventions. (p. 193)

While TBMI teachers can and should have expectations of their students in terms of the curricular knowledge gained from being in their classes, they can couch those expectations in experiences that afford students ample time and space to create their own knowledge through musical exploration. Watson (2011) agreed with the notion of providing appropriate parameters and limitations: "Well-crafted parameters define the task ahead, create a comfort level that helps break the creative ice, and provide the forward motion many kids need to be productive and creative" (pp. 45–47).

In well-structured TBMI classes, uses of technology actually encourage students to think more deeply about the musical constructs and tasks with which they are dealing, therefore adding value to the technology-based activities. Regarding this confluence of musical and technological knowledge, Baer and Garrett (2010) wrote, "Teaching for creativity and teaching specific content need not be in opposition, as is often feared by educators. Creative thinking actually *requires* significant content knowledge, and thinking creatively about a topic helps deepen one's knowledge of that topic" (p. 6).

Transitioning from the traditional model of music teaching, in which the teacher provides specific direction regarding performance of music that someone else has written, to a model that encourages students to be creative can be difficult for even the finest teacher. But encouraging creativity by allowing students the time and freedom to be creative is absolutely essential in a TBMI classroom.

As a starting point, Stokes (2010) offered an interesting set of considerations for fostering creativity in the classroom. Stokes wrote that by establishing constraints for given assignments or tasks, we can help students to focus their creative energies. Stokes offered several "basic principles" through which teachers can help students to follow creative paths, but do so in a controlled, achievable setting:

- Instructions matter. Make them as clear as possible. Young children are novices. Your instructions should make a problem relatively well structured, indicating appropriate task constraints and, of course, your goal criterion.
- Examples matter. Use them to communicate your criteria... the more ways information is presented and processed, the greater the number of neural connections made and the easier it becomes both to retrieve new information and build on it....
- Contexts matter. Instructions, examples, and consequences matter most when habitual variability levels are first acquired. However, since many skill areas will not be new, they can be used to create contexts that *temporarily increase* and sometimes even *sustain* variability. In the short-term (single) session, instructions and reward can create an immediate context for novelty in a different domain.... In the longer-term (multiple) sessions or lessons, they can create a continued context for novelty in the rewarded one....
- In art, materials matter. They matter for mature artists. In mid-career, Matisse eschewed color for black ink and concentrated on contours, outlines that altered the ways he subsequently organized color. They matter for fledgling artists. Children can only give shape to their ideas in ways that materials allow. (Stokes, 2010, pp. 106–107, emphasis in original)

What we can take away from these guidelines is that we should apply general techniques of *good teaching* to our work in TBMI. The ideas of offering clear directions, using good examples, and selecting good materials are certainly not new; however, they are magnified by the complex combination of technology and music.

Willingness to Fail

TBMI is a new idea, and not everyone does it well immediately. Experienced music teachers know that some days go better than others; sometimes ensemble rehearsals fail to meet expectations, and sometimes general music lessons just do not get the point across that we want to convey. Willingness to fail does not mean that we accept failure; it simply means that we can tolerate the possibility that some lessons, projects, and TBMI experiences will not be immediately successful. Failures might be caused by technological problems, poor planning, or simply not knowing a technique as well as might have been necessary. Regardless of the source of a failure, TBMI teachers, much like all good teachers, move on and try to succeed the next time.

Clearly, these descriptors do not apply in equal measure to all TBMI teachers. Individuality is important, and unique combinations of these characteristics, among many others, are what distinguish teachers from each other. It is safe to assume that teachers who do not possess some degree of each of these elements would experience tremendous frustration with TBMI.

PROFILE OF PRACTICE 5.2

Computer labs have a humbling way of removing the traditional physical characteristics of a music class. They can be configured in near infinite ways and so they offer many distractions for students. The physical setup of a lab can influence the pedagogical techniques that teachers employ. I observed two teachers demonstrate exceptional fluency in directing students' attention using technological infrastructure tools that are designed to help teachers manage classrooms.

I observed Mr. O teaching a mixed class of first- and second-year electronic music students. On this particular day, the students were finishing up a series of projects they had recorded in GarageBand and Logic, and they were learning about mastering their work and burning it to a class compilation CD. Mr. O had very specific steps that he wanted the students to follow so that they could produce the CDs—he had to have access to the files so that he could create a class playlist in iTunes. He had shown a PowerPoint presentation to delineate the steps, and he gave the students ample time to finish their work and follow the steps. There were students interrupting him occasionally because they had fallen behind by a step or two. This sparked our conversation about pedagogical technique.

Mr. O did most of his teaching standing by a projector screen, using a remote control to advance his PowerPoint slides. Regarding this technique he said, "This is the first time I can really do what I want to do. I've never had that mobility before. Just like in teaching band or orchestra, when you get down to sectional work, you've got to be closer to the people so that they are more on task. When you walk around the room, you're checking to make sure that they are following directions and they're on the right screen and things like that, so that they don't have problems later. If they follow us on the screen it's not a problem, but there's always somebody who's kind of lagging. So I think it's like when you teach a [band] lesson, you want to make sure the focus is where it's supposed to be. Your physical proximity to the student and the screen is important, to have that [ability to] walk around, double checking that everybody's getting the concept you want to teach."

Mr. O preferred to have the mobility that a remote control provided for him. He insisted, however, that the way he teaches, in terms of his physical placement and mobility, depends on the kind of lesson or activity the students are doing. "If I'm dealing with listening to projects or helping one-on-one, then I'll use the [group audio controller] over the headset, one-on-one, so that people keep on working. In a whole classroom situation, learning something for the first time, [the projection screen with the remote control] is the better way to do it because things go quicker, you can share with students, and they will share with each other to make sure everybody's on task. Otherwise it becomes one-on-one all the way, and that's time consuming."

Taking this idea a step further, some teachers use tools to focus students' attention on detailed elements of what they are presenting. Mr. I, also a high school teacher, exhibited outstanding skills in terms of directing students' attention toward the element he was trying to teach. The lesson I observed him teaching was about a specific component of Logic—the Ultrabeat drum machine module. In teaching a tool such as Ultrabeat, screen elements can be so small that it is difficult for students to pick out where he is pointing with his mouse on a projection screen.

I asked him about any tools that he finds particularly useful. "The two main tools I use to make sure that the students are following me on the screen are, I use a mouse locator...so that instead of the kids trying to find something on their screen and then looking up on my screen and not being able to find my itsy bitsy little pointer arrow, I use that. Then the other feature I use is the zoom feature on the Mac. Especially in a program like Logic with 8 million tiny little buttons that are going to be really hard to see from 20 feet away, I try to zoom the screen in so they can see exactly where I'm looking. I didn't use it in this presentation, but I've also used OmniDazzle. I'll use the pen feature so I can draw on the screen so maybe I'll circle something, like here's where you're supposed to look, and then they can see that staying on the screen while they're trying to find it on their screen."

Certainly the use of relatively simple tools such as remotes and mouse locators on projection screens is not the only reason that these two teachers are sophisticated professionals—years of training, practice, and experience lend credence to their qualifications. But they have recognized that by teaching in the physical environment of the computer lab, the traditions of the ensemble setup that function to draw students' attention to the teacher are thrown out the window. They are considered successful teachers largely because their students produce interesting work, but without the ability to communicate with their students, these teachers probably would not have the success that they have. Technological tools can facilitate communication, and infrastructure can be designed to support those tools.

CONTEXT OF TBMI

As you may have sensed from reading to this point in the book, many of the ideas that make up the TBMI framework are set in computer labs. Computer lab classrooms are the best context in which to demonstrate the concepts of TBMI because they are, by their nature, removed from traditional music teaching. In the lab, there is typically more emphasis on *creative* work, rather than *re-creative* work; there is more focus on independent exploration than on large-group productivity. These views align well with the philosophical and theoretical underpinnings of TBMI.

This is not to say that TBMI is *only* for students and teachers in a lab. Whenever teachers integrate technology into their teaching, they should think about the principles of TBMI. Integrating technology into a band, orchestra, chorus, or general music class presents challenges unique to those settings; however, technology should not be reserved for non-traditional students. The creative rewards and efficiency benefits should cross the boundaries of all types of music learning contexts.

For the sake of explaining TBMI, the lab remains the contextual focus. The scenarios of traditional music teaching are extensively studied and well documented; the difficult part is learning to teach in a new setting. So while technology should definitely make its way into all kinds of music learning contexts—and therefore influence all types of students—I focus on the lab environment because of the new challenges it presents. Technology can and should be used with traditional music students—those in ensembles, in classes such as music theory or music appreciation, in elective classes like guitar—and teachers should apply principles of good pedagogy no matter where technology uses are taking place.

LAB ARRANGEMENT AND TEACHER PHYSICALITY

In addition to personality characteristics as described earlier in this chapter, the physical environment can profoundly impact TBMI. Both the environment of the lab and the nature of interactions between members of a TBMI class have interesting and unusual interplay with the physical presence of teachers in the lab. In this section, we will examine the physical layout of some of the classrooms I observed in conducting observations for this book and examine their influence on the teachers' behaviors. I urge you to consider the characteristics of music teaching spaces—ensemble teachers and general music teachers often place a great deal of importance on the way their teaching spaces are arranged. TBMI classes should place similar emphasis on this idea, but with new variables introduced into the design equation.

Ultimately, the physical space in which a TBMI class takes place should be designed similarly to any classroom in that it supports learning, and makes learning activities comfortable and convenient. "A component of designing instruction must be a deliberate effort to ensure that the learning environment fosters positive, confident attitudes on the part of the learner" (Lever-Duffy, McDonald, & Mizell, 2005, p. 47). Many teachers do not have a choice about the ways in which their labs are set up, as was the case with Mrs. Jones in the Profile of Practice in chapter 1. If possible, teachers should insist that their labs are set up in ways that allow maximum flexibility, while accounting for their pedagogical needs.

For many TBMI situations, classes are held in a lab that is either for the exclusive use of the music program or is shared with other departments throughout the day. What follows are sketches of some of the labs in which observations for this book were conducted, and brief comments on their compatibility with the goals of the classes they contained.

In the lab depicted in Figure 5.1, 16 student stations were arranged in four rows, with the students seated so that they were facing the back of another station. The room in which this lab was built was a converted

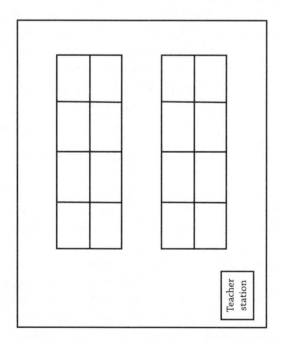

Figure 5.1
Lab with Stations Arranged in Rows

science lab, so it was particularly large. The aisle down the middle of the room, as well as the aisles on each side of the room, allowed the teacher plenty of space to traverse the classroom to observe and help students.

The main difficulty in this lab was not with the physical layout of the space but with the student station furniture itself. The furniture was outdated—not in the sense that it appeared old or worn, but that it was designed for computers from a different age. With the "all-in-one" design of today's desktop computers, the location of the screen on the top shelf of a large piece of furniture forced the students to strain their necks to look at the screen. The teacher was considering ways to remedy this. Clearly this observation was not the first of its kind. Badolato (1995) found the design of individual student workstations to be a tricky formula, especially in the music lab environment:

> An individual workspace in this situation will be configured to provide prac-
> tice in essential aural skills, tools for the creation of musical compositions, and
> perhaps *general* applications such as word processing and spreadsheets for per-
> sonal productivity.... Accommodating this range of activity can be a complex
> undertaking. In addition to a personal computer system, a workspace designed
> for this purpose usually includes an electronic music keyboard (synthesizer),
> audio recording equipment, headphones, a reading/writing surface, and per-
> haps other specialized peripherals as deemed appropriate.... Configuring
> this array of equipment and surfaces within a limited usable space is not as
> straightforward an effort as designing a simple word processing station and
> often results in a less than optimal positioning of equipment. Even when user
> comfort and convenience is an expressed design goal, it is difficult to achieve at
> every point. (pp. 5–6)

Figure 5.2 was a middle school classroom. It was brightly colored and decorated, which was not the case for most computer labs I observed, per-haps because many of the labs are shared spaces, so teachers hesitated to personalize them. The main benefit of this lab design was that it afforded the teacher the ability to observe all of her students' screens from the cen-ter of the room, or from her station. Most students were sharing stations during my observation, so the student stations (especially the ones in the corners) became cramped and crowded. However, the open middle of the room allowed the students to move freely about the room, and therefore to collaborate with new partners.

Figure 5.3, a lab in a small high school, made for a particularly interesting observation. The teacher told me that the space had been acquired through a hard-fought battle over where in the school the music lab should be located.

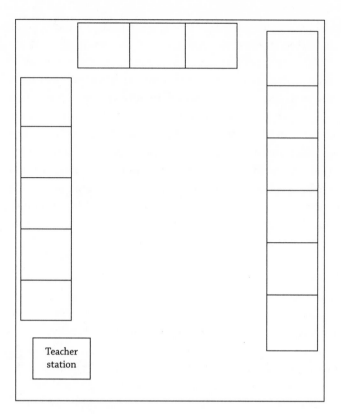

Figure 5.2
Lab with Stations around the Perimeter

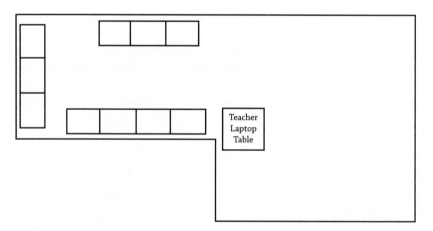

Figure 5.3
Lab with Divided Spaces

The space itself is used for several purposes. Ten student workstations were situated around an alcove on the left side of the diagram. The configuration of these stations has the same detriments and benefits of the layout in Figure 5.2. The larger open space on the right side of this diagram is just that—open space. The teacher often holds portions of class in this space that are lecture-based (as opposed to hands-on time), and he has a portable projection screen that he can wheel from one area to the other. The large space on the right also contains some musical instruments—a drum set and a synthesizer—as it is also used for jazz combos rehearsals. This allowed for clear delineation between lecture portions of the class, and time devoted to hands-on activity, helping to avoid the potential distractions that may occur when students are at workstations while the teacher lectures.

The lab in Figure 5.4 was another middle school classroom. The large object in the middle of the graphic is a table. The students in this teacher's

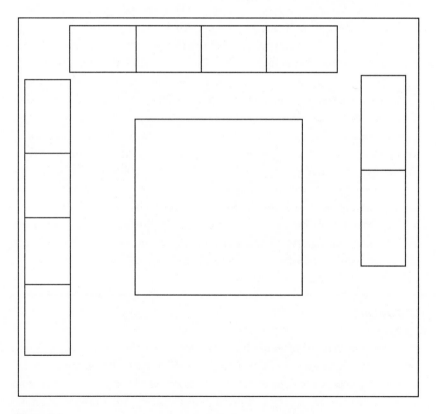

Figure 5.4
Lab with Perimeter Stations and Central Table

classes were provided with a routine: When they entered the class, they were to sit around the table first, unless otherwise instructed. The teacher led introductory activities while the students were all seated at the table and would then dismiss them to go to their workstations. This teacher found the routine worked particularly well for two reasons: (1) The students were used to having "entry routines" for their other classes, so this kept the environment in her class aligned with the rest of their school day, and (2) the arrangement of the workstations around the perimeter of the room forced students to be facing the walls rather than toward the center of the room. In order to instruct them as a large group, they would have to turn either their bodies or their chairs toward the center. Keeping them at a large table in the middle of the room, for the most part, eliminated this problem. In this classroom, two students shared every workstation. Once students were sent to their workstations, they quickly became cramped. The design of this lab tried to accommodate this problem by making each of the workstations a bit larger than typical ones.

Comments from the teachers who participated in my observations shed light on the negative and positive characteristics of their physical environments. The strongest conclusion from all of these observations is that there is no perfect design for a music lab. While some are better than others, they vary in terms of access/proximity to students, space, and many other characteristics.

Music teachers should think about physical arrangement of a lab similarly to the ways they think about setting up an ensemble rehearsal/performance space. Is there enough space in the room for students (and teachers) to be comfortable? Does the room allow the teacher and students to move freely when necessary? Does the room support collaboration between students? Does the infrastructure of the room support technological needs such as power and network connections? These questions and many more should be considered when arranging a lab.

ERGONOMICS

An extensive body of research has developed over the last decade or so in which researchers have examined the ergonomic variables of computer lab spaces. Ergonomics is defined as "The study of work performance with an emphasis on worker safety and productivity" (Berg Rice, 2007, p. 1); however, in common parlance, we often think of ergonomics as the study of comfort in a working environment. Among the most frequently studied aspects of ergonomics is the seated comfort of students, but ergonomics researchers also focus on elements such as vision, furniture design, back-pack health, and ergonomics education curricula (Erez, Shenkar, Jacobs, & Gilespie, 2007). Dockrell et al. (2007) determined, from a survey of more than 1,800 Irish teachers, that almost all of the schools represented had students using computers, but few of the teachers had been trained in any type of ergonomics. Several studies in this field have suggested that students who are not comfortable at a computer workstation are not likely to report this to their teacher and are also less likely to persist in their work. Straker et al. (2010) suggested that in order to achieve maximum comfort in the lab, teachers should encourage students to vary posture, vary activity types, and pay careful attention to issues such as chair selection, surface selection, and angle of gaze toward the monitor. The vast majority of the research into ergonomic characteristics is focused on students' comfort; thus, a relatively solid set of guidelines is available to teachers,[3] and technology equipment is manufactured with the best ergonomic interests of students in mind.

An observation I made while observing TBMI classes has to do with the physical strain teachers place on themselves. When we do traditional ensemble teaching, we tend to take our place in the front of the ensemble—sometimes on a podium, sometimes not, sometimes seated, sometimes standing. In the music lab, however, it is rare to see a teacher remain stationary. Teachers in labs instinctively move throughout the classroom and help individual students or perhaps make sure that students are remaining on task. When we work with individuals, we tend to twist and turn our bodies into awkward positions. We lean in and point at spots on a computer monitor, or we kneel next to a student, or we bend to help them with a specific task by taking control of the mouse. During my observations, I affectionately labeled this movement "lab lean." When I pointed it out to teachers during interviews, they suggested anecdotally that they often feel strain in their backs and knees after teaching in their computer labs.

Despite the extensive research into student comfort in the lab, the maneuverability of teachers in the computer lab is an area that is yet to be researched. The only research I located on *teachers'* uses of computers was conducted by Williams (2001), who found that teachers use computers in short spurts both at home and at school, and that many of them experience physical discomfort during and after computer use. This research did not,

3. Sets of recommendations and guidelines related to the ergonomics of computer workstations are published by groups such as the Human Factors and Ergonomics Society (www.hfes.org/), the International Ergonomics Association (www.iea.cc/), and Computer Ergonomics for Elementary School, a project of Oregon's Occupational Safety and Health Administration (www.orosha.org/cergos/index.html).

however, account for teachers' activities in a computer lab, where their use of computers is rarely in a comfortable position.

Teachers need to be careful of their physicality in the lab. This issue should be treated akin to that of hearing loss in ensemble directors as it may similarly inhibit teachers' ability to do their jobs in the near future. The profession should research the physicality of teachers in the lab and develop a set of guidelines in which the physical safety and comfort of the teacher is as important a consideration as that of the students.

The physical environment of the TBMI classroom is an important consideration and can profoundly impact the pedagogical choices that teachers make. Environmental factors, coupled with personality dispositions, lead to more, or less, successful teaching and learning experiences. In the next chapter, we will examine the theoretical bases for designing those learning experiences and look specifically at some lessons that, each in its own way, exemplify theory-driven practice.

COACHING METHOD

Students need individualized time with the teacher so that their specific needs can be addressed. In *Using Technology to Unlock Musical Creativity* (2011), Watson used the term "coaching" to describe this individual teaching. Watson referenced his own training as an instrumental musician in studio lessons as the basis for his belief in this type of teaching.

As you approach coaching, think about the training you received in musical performance from your own teachers (either in large ensembles or in a studio environment). Typically, teachers establish the routine of a lesson, sometimes with the input of the students. Studio teachers and ensemble directors provide exercises and etudes to develop specific skills. Then, in the core of a lesson, teachers listen to their students perform and provide critical feedback. It is this final component that is most closely related to what TBMI teachers do when coaching. Listening to your students' work, or to their difficulties in progressing through that work, will trigger you to offer your students advice about how to proceed.

Watson provided advice on several elements of coaching, as summarized below:

• Coaching experiences can be short and need not occur in every class. Although it may seem unnatural, try to provide coaching at the beginning of a project when students are making critical creative decisions.

- Consider involving students in coaching each other and try using alternative forms of coaching such as online discussion or virtual conversation. The teacher is not the only person able to offer coaching. Peer coaches and guest coaches may offer new perspectives that you may not consider.
- When providing coaching, focus commentary on one or two issues at a time so that students do not become confused or overwhelmed. Similar to good teaching in an ensemble setting, try to avoid misdirecting students' attention away from the most important corrections or procedures.

In summary, consider that teaching in the music lab can occur in many ways. Many teachers like to demonstrate techniques for all of their students at once. Others prefer to address specific skills with individual students. Most teachers blend these techniques throughout the course of a lesson.

TECHNOLOGY'S INFLUENCE ON LESSON/UNIT PACING

What factors influence the pacing of a lesson or unit? Answers to this question, though infinite, may include these:

- The type and difficulty of the content of the lesson;
- The students' readiness and preparation for the lesson;
- The amount of time allotted for the lesson; and
- The depth at which content needs to be mastered.

Pacing a lesson is an artistic balance between all of these factors and many more. Even the most experienced educators find themselves running out of time, or short on content, every now and then.

Pacing in music instruction has been shown to vary between novice and experienced teachers, and it is characterized by an alternation between teacher-centered activities, such as direct instruction and modeling, and student-centered activities, such as performing (Duke, Prickett, & Jellison, 1998). As we learned from examining the TPACK model, knowledge of musical content, of pedagogical practices, and of the sophisticated merger of those two types of knowledge is further complicated by the integration of technology. Pacing is similarly impacted by technology.

Tasks such as notating music can be accomplished with speed impossible without technology. Also, with the implementation of non-destructive editing techniques and infinite "undo" commands, the process of digitally creating and revising takes on a different structure from the one it would have under analog circumstances. Simply, things done in computers can happen very fast—in fact, faster than by human processes alone. Because of the speed of technology, we are tempted to increase the rate at which we teach. It is important to remember that while students may demonstrate a facility to accomplish musical things technologically, we cannot assume musical understanding based on technological evidence. Teachers can establish an environment of success by controlling the pacing of lessons. Outlined here will be several general principles for pacing technology-based music lessons. These principles are based on the author's experience as a technology-based music teacher in K–12 and university classrooms, and on observations of excellent teachers. These instructional techniques were seen consistently during the observations.

Principle #1: Check to make sure everyone is caught up

In the early part of each instructional cycle, much of the instruction may be direct. That is, teachers will show students how to use particular elements of a piece of software, often using a projected display and sample files that are designed to teach particular tasks. During direct instruction such as this, some students will inevitably miss a step, fall behind, or become confused about something the teacher has demonstrated. In time, teachers develop clarity of instructions and are able to articulate expectations so that fewer students lose their place, but losing a student here or there is inevitable.

Though it may seem to slow the pace of the lesson, I recommended that teachers make sure that students are all caught up and in the same place during direct instruction. The further students fall behind, the more difficult it becomes for the teacher to help them catch up. Teachers must circulate the room and observe the progress that students are making to ensure that they understand the processes that are being demonstrated.

To facilitate this component of pacing, many skilled TBMI teachers make use of technologies that allow them to present material more effectively. A large display of some sort is practically a requirement in a music lab. Most teachers use LCD projectors on a standard screen, though others use interactive whiteboards, large-screen televisions, or even a white wall on which they project their computer's image. Some teachers use presentation devices such as remotes and laser pointers to emphasize certain areas of the screen, while others use commands built into their computer's operating system to zoom in on particular elements. The teachers in Profile of Practice 5.2 demonstrated some of these tools.

Two technologies were reported as being particularly effective in the labs I observed. First, several teachers use lab management software such as

Apple's Remote Desktop, which allows them to observe students' activities from their teaching station. It also allows the teacher to "lock" or "freeze" the students' workstations to draw their attention elsewhere. The software contains other valuable tools for lab management, but observing students' stations and locking their computers were the two most commonly used tools. Second, many labs contained group controller audio systems. These systems allow teachers and students to communicate through headsets/microphones. The teacher has the ability to interact with an individual student or a user-definable group of students. Also, the students are able to listen to one another's work through their own headphones. Used in conjunction with lab management software, these technologies help to create an environment of communication and collaboration. They also contribute to a calm, quiet environment in which the teacher can communicate efficiently with a student or group of students without ever leaving her own station.

Principle #2: Allow plenty of exploratory/creative time

As suggested in Principle #1, early stages of a cycle may involve predominantly direct instruction. As students progress through cycle (a concept that will be discussed more in chapter 6), they need to be given time to explore, to put to use techniques they have been taught, and to encounter obstacles that they cannot overcome based on their limited knowledge. These obstacles are the moments that necessitate moves to greater sophistication and complexity. The teacher's responsibilities during this time are two-fold: (1) Allow the students ample time to put techniques to use and to encounter issues they have trouble overcoming. Teachers should offer creative assignments that encourage uses of techniques that students know and understand, and allow ample time for them to dive into those assignments. (2) Monitor students so that it is easy to tell when they have "hit a wall." While it is important to give students ample time to explore, avoid letting students become frustrated when they encounter tasks they cannot achieve at their current level of sophistication. This is an artful balance— one that even the most experienced teachers can sometimes miss.

Principle #3: Allow time for technological issues

Where there are computers, there are computer problems. Despite efforts to maintain them, computers in a lab will inevitably break down. The key is to try not to let technological breakdowns negatively impact the pacing of your lesson.

Some suggestions for dealing with computer crashes and technical difficulties are these:

- *Back up before it is too late*. Make sure you back up your own data, and encourage your students to do the same. Many schools use server-based storage so that students' work is saved on a remote file server rather than on local hard drives. Encourage your students to make backup copies of their data, perhaps on a removable flash drive.
- *When breakdowns occur, take them in stride*. Perhaps the worst thing a teacher can do when a technical glitch occurs is to appear rattled by it. The behavior you demonstrate when a malfunction occurs should be a model for how you want your students to react. Remain calm and collected.
- *Consider making technological issues an impromptu part of your lesson*. I have observed several teachers experience technical problems. Some of them have made these problems into learning opportunities for their students. In the best-case scenario, students will learn with you to approach computer problems systematically, and learn that it is a good idea to ask for help (perhaps from your school's IT administrator) when you do not have the answers you need.
- *Put it off until you can deal with it*. One excellent teacher I observed encountered a technical issue, but he was determined to cover a certain amount of material during the presentational portion of his lesson. When the student brought the malfunction to his attention, he acknowledged it, and told the student he would fix it when he was able. The student was satisfied that the problem would be investigated and solved.
- *It is OK for students to share computers*. Ideally, students should work at their own computer independently. This is how today's computers are designed to be used. However, if a circumstance occurs in which a computer breaks down and, as a result, students must share a computer, it is OK. Employ strategies so that students have ample time at the workstation, and so that they are all as engaged as possible.

Principle #4: Realize that creativity is never done, but someone must draw it to a close

As students grow more sophisticated with their uses of music technology, they will realize that creative possibilities are essentially limitless. The school environment imposes time limits. The teacher should maintain a careful eye on time both within a class period and throughout longer divisions of time (curricular units, weeks, marking periods, etc.). Given unlimited time, students can spend an inordinate amount of it making even the smallest of choices, such as the selection of an individual loop in a sequencing program or instrument sound in a notation program. Teachers simply must enforce clear time limits on these choices so that students continue to make progress. In most situations, choices are not final—they can be changed later if students are unhappy with their initial selections.

In some circumstances, students will want to continue crafting and refining their work infinitely. Teachers should provide students with regular updates regarding the amount of time allotted to a particular activity. Such limitations allow students to make creative decisions within a reasonable amount of time. At some point, creative projects must be concluded. Some teachers employ countdown clocks to keep their students aware of the time they have left to accomplish a task; I have observed this to be an effective method in some circumstances, though some students find it to be a distraction. In the Profile of Practice below, time is certainly a restriction, as are other educational realities.

PROFILE OF PRACTICE 5.3

A brightly colored poster on the wall of an otherwise institutionally decorated room reads: "Life is all about making mistakes and learning from them." This adage is reflective of how Mrs.V wants her students to understand learning, and how she views it herself.

Mrs. V is an experienced music educator who holds a master's degree in instructional technology. Along a spectrum from *digital immigrant* to *digital native* (Prensky, 2001), she describes herself as leaning further toward the digital native end. She is comfortable with integrating technology into her classes and does so enthusiastically and consistently. Her school district, despite recent budget cuts, has proven to be wonderfully supportive of technology across the curriculum. During two observations, in fact, an instructional technology specialist stayed in the room during the whole class so that she could monitor the Skype connection and reposition the laptop to allow for appropriate camera angles.

During the first two observations of Mrs. V's class, she was working with her students on a composition project in Sibelius notation software. The students' compositions were based on Greek mythology-related stories that they had constructed in other classes. The music curriculum in Mrs. V's school is somewhat bound to the idea of integrating content with other subject areas. There are also several curricular mandates that guide the activities in her classroom. Mrs. V is acutely aware that in her school district, budgetary concerns often drive the curriculum and lead to decisions about what stays and goes in her school. Although the curricular mandates may not be the best choice for her students, she is willing to sacrifice and adhere to models such as Guiding Questions. She makes it work.

Mrs. V's situation is interesting because she works under a curriculum that has been written expressly for the music technology classes. All of the music teachers in the district have been part of developing this curriculum and, as such, have had a hand in determining what the "contributions" of the music technology curriculum should be to the larger responsibilities of the music department. In that curriculum, which was guided by curricula from other districts and states, the students in the music department must be involved in four essential roles: creating, imagining, presenting, and critiquing. Mrs. V talks about where music technology class fits into this picture: "The performing groups—band, chorus, jazz band—there's not much creating time in there, it's more at the performing level. So because I have the only class that really does the creating piece of it, I have a lot more responsibility to cover more of the standards."

Shocked by the notion that creativity is, in the minds of the authors of the district's standards, limited only to the music technology lab and is not the responsibility of ensemble directors, I ask her about this: "For the most part it falls here because it is about composing." If TBMI teachers are to be saddled with only one area of music teaching and learning, creativity would be an appropriate one, but still some may find the notion disturbing.

She continues, "The standards that I'm working with, this is the first year I'm using them. This is what has actually been handed to me this year. So, I think it's a little early right now. Some of them I really appreciate because it sparks some new ideas with how I can get the kids to meet these standards. Do I think it closes in the box for creativity? Maybe a little bit. But . . . it's pretty much what I've been doing only kind of in writing."

I also wonder about the impact that the standards have on the students' experiences in music classes in this district. Do the students feel differently about music classes due to the fact that teachers have to adhere to standards? "I think, because I feel a little more pressure to get things covered, I think I, I don't want to say bombard them, but I really give them a lot of information in a very short amount of time and expect a lot more of them. It's hard when they're creating to have a box put around them. This time box. You have to get this done. I know when I'm creating music or when I'm doing anything creative, I need to have my time to really be allowed to create, and they're not given as much time as they need, I think."

Time is essential in TBMI classes. Music and technology are both complex, and taken together, they only multiply each other's complexity. While Mrs. V appreciates the structure of the curricular standards she has been provided with (and helped to create), she also recognizes that in a six-week middle school "wheel" structure, mounting expectations can hinder the richness of students' experiences. Many teachers wish their students had more time to be creative, but the realities of schooling make this difficult.

SUMMARY OF CHAPTER 5

In chapter 5 we examined some justifications for establishing new teaching techniques for TBMI and some characteristics often exhibited by those who do it well. We also looked at some physical characteristics of TBMI teaching spaces and the way those characteristics influence pedagogical behaviors. Finally, we explored some general principles of coaching students and pacing lessons. In chapter 6 we will see additional theoretical concepts about TBMI teaching, and how those concepts play out in real lessons.

ITEMS FOR DISCUSSIONS

1. TBMI classes might be populated with music students who are considered "non-traditional." These students do not necessarily participate in their school's performing ensembles, they may not read music proficiently, they may not have experience performing in public, and they may not have experience playing an instrument or singing at all. What are your attitudes about teaching these non-traditional students? How might your attitudes impact the way you teach?
2. Chapter 5 contains descriptions of dispositions that are often observable in successful TBMI teachers. Do you see these qualities in yourself? Which of the characteristics might be the most difficult for you to adopt?
3. In a Profile of Practice in this chapter, two teachers were profiled who used techniques to enhance their presentation of information and procedures. What other techniques have you seen teachers use that have made it easier for you to follow along? Also, what presentation techniques make it difficult for students to keep up with the teacher?
4. Consider some music computer lab spaces with which you are familiar. What characteristics made them good learning environments? What might be changed to make them better?
5. Describe the pacing of a lesson you have taught, have been a student in, or have observed. Was it too fast? Too slow? Just right? What evidence can you provide for characterizing the pacing? What might the teacher have done differently to improve pacing?
6. Use the Internet to find a music curriculum plan for a local school/district, or one from your home town. How is technology incorporated into the music curriculum? What role does technology play in the students' musical education?

CHAPTER 6

Lesson Design in Technology-Based Music Instruction

THE TBMI LESSON CONTENT SPECTRUM

The content of individual lessons and units in TBMI classrooms falls somewhere on a spectrum of content, as seen in Figure 6.1.

At the left end of the spectrum fall activities that are purely musical. Even in TBMI classes, we can occasionally design activities that we believe address long-term goals and short-term objectives that are purely musical. For example, when we ask our students to rehearse or perform a piece of music (although it may eventually be recorded, edited, mixed, etc.), we are addressing musical goals through musical activities without integrating technology.

At the right end of this spectrum fall activities that are purely technological. These activities may include procedures for digital file management, techniques within software, or hardware connectivity and maintenance. Even though the broader content of TBMI classes should be musical, the focus on technology in lessons that fall to the right side of the spectrum is one of the ideas that separate TBMI classes from traditional music classes. We include lessons that focus on technology because those are the tools in use to make music. It is important that students learn how to use them properly, and teachers should consider it their responsibility to include lessons that meet this description.

Purity of content is rare. In truth, longer-term sequences of TBMI might be categorized in one of two ways:

1. Lessons fall somewhere in the middle of the spectrum. This indicates that the lesson has some content that is musical and some that is technological. The teacher artfully blends them together so that students recognize the application of technology to music, and of music to technology.

Figure 6.1
Spectrum of TBMI Lesson Content

2. Lessons shift from one end of the spectrum to the other, perhaps exhibiting more than one shift within a class period. Sometimes it is necessary to explore a musical concept in non-technological ways, then shift to a technological technique that will further address that concept. So, when the activities associated with the two phases of the lesson are combined, we achieve "neutrality" along the spectrum.

Also, it should be acknowledged that this spectrum of lesson content depicts lessons under ideal circumstances. Certainly some lessons that might be planned or executed poorly will lack either a musical or a technological focus. Also, some lessons may break the mold of the spectrum and feature content that is both highly technological and highly musical. Analyzed in detail, however, lessons rarely focus on both musical and technological concepts at the same moment; rather, they move swiftly and adeptly between the ends of the spectrum.

Teachers are typically aware of the location of their lessons relative to the spectrum, both from their own perspective and from their students'. The student perspective is often different, as indicated in Figure 6.2. Technology-based music instructors should strive to land squarely in the middle of this spectrum. Perhaps the most often cited strategy is this: Some lessons will fall on the technological end of the spectrum, others will

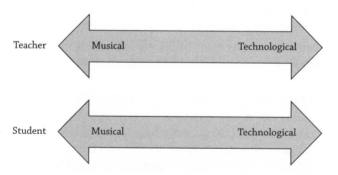

Figure 6.2
Spectrum of TBMI Lesson Content—Student and Teacher Perspectives

fall on the musical end of the spectrum, so try to balance your lessons so that there is an "average" near the middle. Doing so will ensure that students are working in technology but with a focus on musical content.

THE CYCLE OF MASTERY

Many of the teachers interviewed for this text expressed a desire for their students to gain a level of competence with musical-technological skills that would allow the students to make music independently at the conclusion of their class. This is similar to the commonly expressed notion of developing lifelong learners in ensemble teaching settings to the extent that students will continue to perform once they are no longer in the K–12 setting where such opportunities are more easily accessible. The observations conducted for this book made clear that students do depend on their teachers for guidance, and they do so in particular at a point when they reach a moment of mastery of a tool, concept, or skill that the teacher has previously introduced. This Cycle of Mastery might be depicted as in Figure 6.3.

Although the TBMI experience could truly begin at any point in this recursive model, for the sake of explanation, begin with the top and view the model moving clockwise as the arrows suggest.

In the first phase of this model, the teacher introduces a new technological or musical tool, concept, or skill. Note that lessons at any point in the musical-technological spectrum can be viewed on the cycle. Next, students explore this new tool, concept, or skill with substantial teacher guidance. In

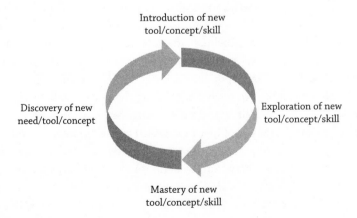

Introduction of new
tool/concept/skill

Exploration of new
tool/concept/skill

Mastery of new
tool/concept/skill

Discovery of new
need/tool/concept

Figure 6.3
TBMI Cycle of Mastery

this phase of the cycle, students are still highly dependent on the teacher for procedural instructions or clarification of conceptual information. Though difficult to account for in a model such as this, it should be noted that students naturally bring previous knowledge to TBMI learning experiences. New tools, concepts, and skills can and should be taught in the context of previous knowledge. For example, a skill that enables a student to record a melody into a sequencing program calls on previous knowledge about performing a melody. Each new introduction of a tool, concept, or skill serves in part to enhance prior knowledge and understanding, similar to the Deweyan notion of experiences as preparatory for further experiences explained in chapter 3.

Exploration of the tool, concept, or skill continues, and as the student approaches an understanding or mastery, the teachers' guidance becomes less crucial; that is, students are capable of integrating the tool, concept, or skill into their vocabulary of musical-technological functions without much teacher intervention. The tool, concept, or skill can be explored at a high level, with near complete independence.

Eventually, students will encounter a circumstance in which the tool or skill, or their knowledge of a concept, reaches a limitation. At this point it is appropriate for the teacher to intervene, making her presence and guidance again necessary, and restarting the cycle. It is also possible that, at this point in the cycle, students continue to explore the software on their own and discover a solution to the obstacle they have encountered. Progress to new cycles is not necessarily dependent on the involvement of the teacher; rather, students may move to further levels of sophistication by their own volition, similar to the notion of constructivism in which students develop new knowledge based on previous knowledge.

To further illustrate the applicability of this cycle, let us consider an example that occurs in many music labs, particularly at the middle and high school levels. Many teachers design units in which students learn to use notation software such as Sibelius, Finale, Noteflight, or some other music scoring software. In order to acquaint their students with the basic functionality of such software, a popular technique is to provide a printed musical score that students are to re-create using the software. Some teachers will provide a copy of their school's *alma mater* or fight song, for example, while others use scores to popular music with which students are familiar.

As students get acquainted with notation software, teachers may introduce a method of data entry that is useful for that software package, such as real-time entry with a MIDI keyboard (inputting notation data in time, usually with a metronome). Students may be asked to use the MIDI keyboard to enter a section of notation into the score, or perhaps even an entire score. Teachers might demonstrate techniques for slowing down entry tempo to improve accuracy and other idiomatic tricks and tips. Typically, teachers will allow students time to work on their own to experiment with these techniques. The teacher and students in a scenario such as this have moved from the beginning of the cycle, through the point of exploration. In time, students may become quite adept at data entry using a MIDI keyboard device.

While real-time entry technology has certainly improved in recent iterations of notation software packages, it still presents difficulties in accuracy and does not usually allow for complete entry of all musical symbols. For example, attempts to enter *staccato* or *legato* markings into a score may be misinterpreted by the software as variations in rhythm (*staccato* eighth notes may be interpreted as sixteenth notes, for example). At some point, students will "bump into" this problem. Despite their mastery of real-time entry techniques, it will be impossible to explore the full range of musical data entry possibilities with the knowledge that they have of the software tool. So, as one might expect, the teacher would intervene in order to reveal to the students some of the techniques for editing data entered in real time. It is also possible that students will discover the solution to this obstacle by "poking around" in the application until they find the symbol they need. Thus, the Cycle of Mastery begins anew.

Notice that in addition to working their way around the cycle, students are traversing the spectrum of musical-technological lessons, continually moving from one side to the other; in doing so, they are achieving a reasonable balance between musical tasks and technological tasks.

Layering Cycles

Part of the willingness to give up control that is characteristic of many successful TBMI teachers is acknowledging that not all students work at the same pace. As a result, students in TBMI classrooms may not all be working on the same task, project, or assignment at the same time. It is also likely that teachers will need to reteach particular technological concepts or skills as they relate to the software in use at the moment. Rather than viewing this as an obstacle, experienced TBMI teachers accept this opportunity to reinforce content and skills.

Since students in a TBMI class might be encouraged to work on individualized content, it is likely (and it has been observed) that two students, perhaps seated right next to each other, might be working on very different material, or on the same material at different stages. This is depicted in Figure 6.4.

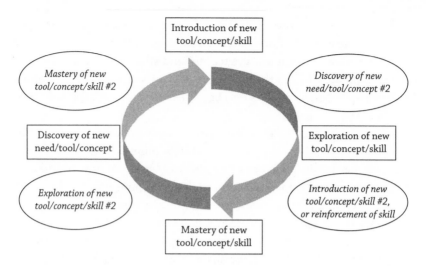

Figure 6.4
TBMI Cycle of Mastery (2 Students)

In this figure, note the distinction between parts of the cycle shown in rectangles, which indicate one cycle, and those shown in ovals, which indicate a second, simultaneous cycle. As shown, the cycle represented by rectangles is slightly behind the other. This indicates that the teacher would need to monitor progress for students who are doing diverse things within one classroom. Though only two cycles are indicated here, in reality, each student in a class might be in a slightly different place. In Figure 6.5, each

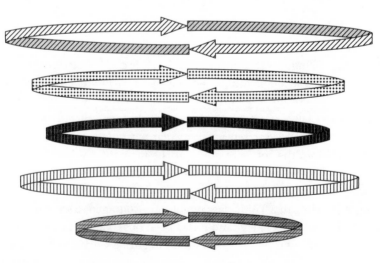

Figure 6.5
Stacked Cycles of Mastery

stacked cycle represents a student; notice that the flattened out cycles are all different widths, indicating that each student might take a different amount of time to complete a cycle.

Though not exactly the same, this model of repeating or reinforcing skills at appropriate times is analogous to Bruner's Spiral Curriculum. Bruner (1977) suggested, "The foundations of any subject may be taught to anybody at any age in some form" (p. 12). The words "in some form" from this quote suggest that the form in which material is introduced need not be the most complex form; rather, fundamental ideas can be presented in simplified ways so that they are attainable according to students' developmental state. Bruner's work is clearly and explicitly based on the stages of development outlined in Piaget's stage model, but Bruner acknowledges that development is also influenced by the environment in which a child matures, which includes the school environment.

The idea of the spiral curriculum is that while it is appropriate to introduce content and concepts to students at young ages, assuming this is done in developmentally appropriate ways, it is necessary to return to that content or concept in more sophisticated presentations as students mature. In its original form, Bruner related this idea to large-scale curricula; he referred frequently in his writing to "science" or "literature" as disciplines, as opposed to specific elements within those bodies of knowledge. The spiral curriculum can be related to the TBMI Cycle of Mastery in this way: similar to a "spiral" in the Bruner model, students experience a skill, concept, or tool in TBMI with a limited level of sophistication. Then, when that level of sophistication no longer affords them all that they need to make progress, they are forced to seek out more advanced and complicated skills, concepts, or tools. One important distinction between the two models is that in the Bruner spiral, it is suggested that the teacher is the one who recognizes the limitations of students and decides when to advance to more sophisticated levels. In the TBMI Cycle of Mastery, the students "bump into" limitations and seek out resolutions—perhaps from the teacher, or perhaps through experimentation.

Further Examples of the Cycle of Mastery

The previous example provided a set of procedures that refer to the use of a particular music technology tool—notation software—with a reasonable amount of expectation for notation experience. If applied to the simplified version of the model, the procedures might resemble Figure 6.6.

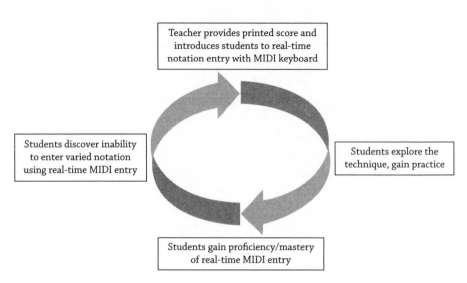

Figure 6.6
Cycle of Mastery with Notation Software

In further occurrences of the cycle during this lesson (or series of lessons), the teacher would use a new technique to allow students to experience notating music with a different method (such as using a mouse or a QWERTY keyboard).

This example shows students learning a technological tool; however, the model includes instances in which students are learning concepts and skills as well. We must also explore modified versions of the model that might be used in the classroom to allow students to learn musical skills and concepts.

A similar set of procedures can be applied when students are learning to compose with sequencing software. A student of mine recently designed a five-lesson unit for fifth graders, the goal of which was for the students to create a composition in GarageBand. In the first lesson of the unit, she introduced the students to techniques for creating loop-based percussion tracks. She did this with the students in a large group using an interactive whiteboard. For the second part of the cycle, students used their own computers to practice these techniques and create percussion tracks on their own. The indication of mastery of these techniques was the students' ability to create a sixteen-measure section of looped percussion sounds, which they shared with each other for peer assessment. The students recognized that their compositions were relatively simplistic, so the teacher introduced a second technique in the program—adding pre-recorded bass loops. The cycle started anew when they were shown this tool and given the opportunity to make their compositions more sophisticated. An additional cycle included the use of synthesized sounds that the students played, and they were permitted to leave blank space in these tracks.[1]

Another student created a set of lesson plans for exposing eighth grade students to world music genres in an international school setting. Following general study of several types of music from around the world, the teacher outlined a goal for the students to create a multimedia website that would demonstrate their general knowledge and understanding of a particular genre. In the first technology-based cycle, she instructed the students in creating a website using iWeb. She provide examples of how the website should look and function from her own work and from that of students who had done the assignment in previous classes. The students were given time to create the basic shell of the website. While working in iWeb, they discovered that the program does not afford functions for creating and editing videos that they needed to include in their website. In the second cycle, the teacher introduced iMovie as a tool that the students could use to edit video and include it in their web-based assignment.

Most of these lessons fall on the technological end of the spectrum of types of lessons; however, the lessons that came before it, which introduced the students to genres of world music, are firmly embedded in listening, performing, and analysis activities. Again, we approach a balance along the spectrum.

The lessons described herein did not simply appear out of thin air. In each case, the teacher who designed the lessons based them on a musical goal that they held for their students. These goals are derived from the particular ways in which students are able to be musical. Reimer (2003) described seven musical roles (what he referred to as "musical intelligences"), each of which suggests several kinds of outcomes. For the remainder of this chapter, I will refer frequently to Reimer's concept of musical roles and how they can be dissected to imply music learning activities. Of the seven roles, only the final one, music teaching, was deemed not applicable to the ideas in this book. Further comment on this particular quality appears at the end of the section.

Each of these activities is then matched to technological tools, and for some I demonstrate how the cycle might work for each scenario. For each lesson, I have also provided an analysis/commentary section that explains the elements of the lesson, the particular pedagogical choices the teacher made, and how they reflect educational theories described in the opening chapters.

Several observations regarding these lessons should be noted. First, you will see an unequal balance in this group of lessons toward those that

---

1. These lessons were contributed by Janine Slaga and Amy Keus, students in the Boston University Master of Music Education program.

are focused on students creating original compositions, performing, and analyzing music. This is, perhaps, a natural tendency. The software applications typically employed in school labs are those designed to facilitate composition in one form or another. Performance and analysis are the most common types of actitivtes of traditional music teaching. Recent scholarship on music activity types supported by technology lend credence to this observation (Bauer, Harris, & Hofer, 2012).

Many of the teachers I observed spoke passionately about their belief in developing students' musicianship through composition. Some of the musical roles are more difficult to address through technological means. At this point in the development of TBMI, composition is often the focus of lesson planning.

Second, some of the projects described herein actually cross the boundaries of each musical role. For the purposes of the organization of the text, I have chosen to locate each lesson within a particular role; however, I recognize that it is difficult to compose without listening or, in many cases, without employing some music theory constructs. Great lessons are those that address the multitude of ways students can engage in music. Therefore, teachers should certainly not shy away from lessons that are complex enough to achieve such esteem.

Finally, as I observed teachers teaching many of these lessons, it occurred to me that some of the lessons were more developed than others. Some of the teachers were simply experimenting with new technologies or new procedures while others were teaching lessons they had taught many times. Many of the lessons I describe are in need of further extension and refinement.

Role #1—Composing

Reimer (2003) defined composing as "the linking of sounds into meaningful configurations through a process of decision making, reflections about previously made decisions, and altering and adding to and deleting sounds previously decided upon" (p. 221). The lessons described in this section encouraged students to create original sounds through technological means.

Rap Beat Project

Level observed: high school
Suggested tools: listening examples, sequencing software (observed using GarageBand)

Observed procedures:

1. The teacher introduces the project by saying that the focus will be on the instrumental parts of a rap song.
2. The teacher plays two examples of rap songs for the students (the teacher observed used songs by Eminem). Students listen, focusing on the instrumental backing tracks of each song.
3. The teacher and students have a discussion about the characteristics of the instrumental backing tracks.
4. The teacher leads students through an example of developing a backing track for a rap song of their own creation.

Analysis/commentary:

Prior to this lesson, the teacher had established a culture in the classroom that emphasized two qualities: (1) that he (the teacher), despite his own leanings toward jazz and pop styles, was very open to other styles of music, and (2) that listening was one of the keys to successful composition. As the students listened to the examples, he focused their attention on the simplicity of the backing tracks. The selection of this particular Eminem recording as the "setup" listening for the project was particularly effective because it provided a perfect example of the type of work that the teacher hoped his students would produce.

The cycle model indicates that students "bump into obstacles" throughout the course of a project. In this lesson, and in the successive lessons, many of the students were less familiar with the rap style than others were. Although the teacher tried to circumvent this obstacle by providing an example in the beginning of the sequence of lessons, the teacher needed to be prepared with additional listening examples for those students who would need them. The simplicity of the backing track also created a potential moment of difficulty, as many students were tempted to make their compositions more complex than was necessary. The teacher, noticing this, should be prepared to help the students to reduce "clutter" in their compositions by demonstrating editing techniques within the software.

Another important element of this lesson, and one to strive to emulate, is that it sets reasonable limitations on composition, an idea related to Webster's creativity model described in chapter 5. Simply by choosing a genre-specific type of composition—here, rap—the teacher imposed a reasonable parameter on the project that helped students not to feel overwhelmed by the infinite possibilities of the software. While some students might not be as excited to compose a rap song as they might be to create another type of composition, this parameter provided a limitation on the project that facilitated success.

Free Composing with Hyperscore

Level observed: middle school
Suggested tools: Hyperscore composing software
Observed procedures (over the course of several lessons):

1. The teacher instructs students to compose a few melodies in Hyperscore. Students spend time on their own doing so.
2. The teacher circulates around the room helping students with technical issues and individual questions.
3. The teacher instructs students as a group regarding techniques within Hyperscore for aligning beginnings of notes and sections.
4. Students share work with each other using an electronic commenting (wiki) system.

Analysis/commentary:

Hyperscore is a composition environment based on the idea that students should be able to simply draw on the computer screen using the mouse and have their drawings converted into sound. It is a wonderfully open-ended environment that instantly engages students in composing, with very little instruction needed. In the beginning of this series of lessons, the teacher provided the students with ample time to work on their own within Hyperscore, a technique from which the students definitely benefited. Hyperscore is so easy to use that even teachers who are novices with technology integration can experience the Pedagogical Summit described in chapter 1, in which students are directly engaged with technology.

The students in this class experienced many obstacles to their composition. While the teacher did not impose any limits or restrictions on their work, the students clearly came to this task with some preconceptions about what they were "supposed to" create. In step two of the lesson, when the teacher circulated to deal with individual questions, students asked the teacher for guidance in accomplishing compositional tasks such as erasing individual notes, deleting entire groups of notes, and changing the (MIDI) sound associated with each melody. Since the teacher provided very minimal instruction prior to setting the students free to compose, these obstacles came quickly, and the teacher was called upon for help. Many cycles overlapped in this lesson, perhaps even a different cycle for each student.

In the third step of this lesson, the teacher noticed, based on his experience from teaching this project in previous years, that many of the students would benefit from learning how to align notes or sections of their compositions rhythmically. Based on this observation, he stopped the whole class and drew their attention back to a group lesson on how to accomplish these editing procedures. He realized that while coaching was appropriate for individuals' questions, it was not the most efficient way to deal with inconsistent understandings of the alignment technique.

Mythology Story Composition

Level observed: middle school
Suggested tools: notation software (observed with Sibelius)
Observed procedures (over the course of several lessons):

1. The teacher introduces students to several aspects of notation software, including score setup and basic note entry techniques.
2. Students begin working in pairs to create compositions based on themes from myth-stories they are studying and writing in their English classes.
3. The teacher circulates throughout the room focusing students' attention on the task and helping with technical issues.
4. The teacher reminds the class and several pairs of students to try to depict their myth-stories in the melodies and mood of their compositions.

Analysis/commentary:

In this series of lessons, the focus was on connecting the content of the TBMI class to the curriculum of the students' English class, in which they were studying mythology. In their English classes, the students had studied some well-known myths and had created their own stories similar to those they studied. The particular school in which this series of lessons was observed was heavily geared toward interdisciplinary connections, and the teacher took advantage of what she saw as a natural connection between the two subjects of music and literature.

The goal of this series of lessons was to have the students compose an original piece of music that somehow depicted the action of their original myth creation. In order to do so, the students needed some knowledge about how to operate the software. Therefore, the teacher chose to start her lesson by focusing the activity on the technological end of the lesson design spectrum, to expose students to the tools necessary to begin composing. This type of skill development is placed at the root levels of Bloom's Taxonomy—it involves simple knowledge of the software's tools and an understanding of what they do. The teacher introduced only the bare minimum set of procedures for the students to get started.

Another important observation about this set of lessons was the way in which the teacher employed routine in her classroom. Just as in every other class in their day, the students knew that when they entered the room, they were to sit at a central table (as shown in Figure 5.4). The teacher chose to do the bulk of her group instruction in that arrangement, then "release" the students to their workstations. This routinized practice brought a sense of academic formality to the classroom.

As the students worked in pairs on their compositions, they quickly ran into technological obstacles. The only techniques they had learned in the software were score setup and note entry. The initial introduction to the software did not include techniques as basic as deleting notes, or note entry through methods other than pointing and clicking with the mouse. The majority of questions the students asked of the teacher were about simple techniques to which they had not yet been exposed. This was a case in which students' desires to be creative had outpaced their knowledge of the software. Based on this lesson, teachers must find an appropriate balance between the amount of technical information they provide their students, what they expect their students to be able to do, and what they encourage their students to discover on their own. This lesson was effective, but in her desire to let her students be creative, the teacher may have neglected some of the practical considerations that are necessary if students are to use software effectively.

Melody Writing

Level observed: high school
Suggested tools: sequencing software (observed with GarageBand)
Observed procedures:

1. The teacher has pre-selected a small group of "loops"—pre-made chunks of audio or MIDI—for students to use during this project.

2. The teacher starts class by leading a discussion about what makes melodies memorable. (The students come up with answers such as repetition, variety, rhythmic interest, instrumentation, etc.)
3. The teacher instructs students to create a melody by selecting several loops (from the group that he pre-selected) and using the software's editing functions to create interest.
4. The students spend independent time creating their melodies.

Analysis/commentary:

By pre-selecting a group of loops for the students to use, the teacher imposed an appropriate limitation on the students' creativity. Similar to the limitation imposed in the "rap beat" project described earlier, this pre-selection allowed the students to have *some* creative freedom, but it avoided a common pitfall associated with loop-based software: that students spend an inordinate amount of time selecting loops while neglecting the actual heart of the assignment. The students in this observation seemed accustomed to such a procedure, so they were not bothered by the limitation of their choices. The teacher considered the materials for this lesson carefully, as suggested in the TBMI framework.

The method by which the students composed their own melodies was, perhaps, less effective. The students used the pre-selected loops to do so. All of the loops the teacher had selected were audio samples—as opposed to MIDI clips—making their manipulation difficult in GarageBand because of its limited set of audio editing tools. Many of the resulting melodies did not adhere to the characteristics the students and teacher had agreed define well-crafted melodies. While the teacher clearly demonstrated content knowledge in his instruction about the characteristics of melodies, and pedagogical knowledge in his lesson design, his technological knowledge—the third component of the TPACK model described in chapter 3—of GarageBand perhaps led him to choose the materials unwisely. He later confessed that the software was still new to him.

Direct interaction of students with technology was clearly important in this lesson, but the focus of the lesson was the musical concept of melody. The teacher spent a substantial amount of time leading students toward realizations about the characteristics of melodies, all the while relating those characteristics to melodies that most of them knew (commercial jingles, the Alphabet Song, etc.). It was clear at the end of this portion of the lesson that the students had a firm grounding in melody writing.

Arranging a Chosen Piece

Level observed: high school
Suggested tools: notation software (observed using Finale)
Prior knowledge: This lesson is predicated on a set of lessons about standard band and orchestra instruments, their ranges, and transpositions.
Observed procedures:

1. Students select a piece of music they are interested in arranging for an instrumental chamber group of their choosing.
2. Students obtain this music from their personal collection or through Internet download. They submit a proposal to the teacher, who approves it and provides initial guidance.
3. Students work independently to arrange the music for the selected instrumental group. The teacher provides support and guidance as necessary.

Analysis/commentary:

This project obviously holds sophisticated expectations for the students. In addition to the knowledge gained through previous lessons in this class, all of the students in the class I observed had substantial musical experience. Several of them played in ensembles, and some of them had successfully completed AP Music Theory. They were well equipped to complete this kind of project, and the teacher recognized that he could elevate expectations based on the students' developmental levels.

Projects that involve arranging are often more restrictive than this one was. In this case, the teacher consciously decided to allow the students to choose the music they would arrange. Students' selections varied from Stevie Wonder to the Beach Boys, from video game music to jazz standards. The teacher felt that giving the students the opportunity to select their own music to arrange provided them with a sense of ownership and would encourage construction of knowledge based on their prior experiences with the music they selected.

Throughout the course of the students' project work, the teacher noticed that the one musical aspect for which he had to offer students the most help was instrumental range. Prior lessons had focused on range and transposition, but having little experience with performing on standard instruments, some students quickly violated rules of performance range. Individual coaching that the teacher provided often focused on this aspect of arranging and helped to remedy the students' content knowledge shortcomings.

Soundscapes

Level observed: high school
Suggested tools: sequencing software for developing the final project; audio editors and external capture devices for capturing and manipulating sounds
Observed procedures:

1. The teacher provides a definition of "soundscape" and plays several examples.
2. The teacher provides directions for students to complete their own soundscape. The students are to
   a. Brainstorm
   b. Write out a list of sound effects they will need for their project
   c. Write a "score" that shows what the project will be like
3. Over several lessons, the students use many resources to create their soundscape.

Analysis/commentary:

Soundscape projects are quite common in TBMI classes, especially at the secondary level, possibly because they enable students to use many different technologies in concert with each other. Soundscapes also provide creative opportunities in a scenario that does not necessarily require music performance experience. Modifications of this project that I observed, or have done with my own classes, are electronic compositions that are based on a poem or short story and use sound effects to enhance recorded text.

The teacher I observed conducting this lesson provided a definition of soundscape: "A real or imaginary environment represented through music." The teacher had taken graduate composition classes, which turned out to be the root of this definition. This also helped explain the teacher's choice to have the students create a "score" for their soundscape. This score, or visual depiction of the project, was to be detailed enough that the project could reasonably be re-created from it. The choice to have the students do this shows a connection between the soundscape genre and more traditional notated music. The soundscape project, as assigned, was also to contain a substantial amount of composed music, although the proportion of music to sound effects was still to be determined.

Soundscape projects are also an excellent way to get students involved in recording. Through projects like this one, students can engage in recording their own voices, instruments, or found sounds. Using recording and editing software, they can edit these sound captures for use in their projects. Many teachers I observed said that they do lessons on recording techniques prior to any type of creative work so that the students have these tools at the ready.

Movie Trailer Project

Level observed: high school
Suggested tools: downloaded movie trailers with sound removed, sequencing software capable of displaying video, internal and external sound capture devices
Observed procedures:

1. The teacher downloads several movie trailers from the Internet and uses video editing software to remove the soundtracks.
2. Students select from the group of muted trailers.
3. Students use a variety of software and hardware tools to create soundtracks for the trailers.

Analysis/commentary:

Setting up an assignment for students to create sound for a movie trailer allows them to compose for a medium with which they are familiar. Also, because of the very nature of movie trailers, the projects will be short—typically about one or two minutes. Therefore, the teacher need not impose time limits on the project as might be necessary in a less clearly defined assignment, and need not evaluate appropriateness of time. This project demonstrates Mayer's principles of multimedia learning in that students learn to align visual cues with auditory cues.

This project requires a bit of advanced planning on the part of the teacher. Students will usually want to compose soundtracks for trailers for the latest movies, so simply stockpiling a collection of trailers will not always work. Teachers can use any of a number of websites that allow for downloading videos from online video depositories such as YouTube. Then, a bit of technological savvy is necessary for extracting sound from the videos. Teachers should also be aware of the copyright implications of projects like this and should be sure to make students aware of the potential for infringing copyright law. The project was assessed according to minimum guidelines that the teacher established, and the students shared their projects with each other for informal assessment.

Adding a Bassline

Level observed: elementary general music
Suggested tools: MIDI keyboards, sequencing software
Observed procedures:[2]

1. Students sing a familiar song, such as "Twinkle, Twinkle Little Star."
2. The teacher plays a simple accompaniment along with the singing.
3. The teacher demonstrates a bass line, using quarter notes, prepared in advance. Teacher can do several different bass lines to show variety.
4. Students discuss what they heard, and teacher can talk about notes used in the chords.
5. Students then sing another familiar song in the same key, such as "Hot Cross Buns." Teacher again plays accompaniment.
6. Students discuss which chords they heard in "Hot Cross Buns." Teacher writes the notes of the chord on the whiteboard to which students can refer while creating their own bass line.
7. The teacher passes out keyboard cards and the students begin to experiment making a bass line of their own. Paper and pencil can be available for those students who wish to write their notes down.
8. Students are paired to share their bass lines.
9. Once students have added their bass lines, play back and do peer evaluations to see if their lines are successful. As the students get more comfortable with simple songs, the teacher can add songs that have more chord changes.

Analysis/commentary:

This lesson demonstrates a great way to integrate technology into a traditional lesson on singing familiar songs and creating accompaniments. Without the aid of technology, it is likely that creating accompanying lines would be a far more difficult task for students; however, the technology provides instant aural feedback so that students can tell immediately if they have chosen chord tones appropriately.

The lesson plan was written for a classroom that has one computer. Notice that the teacher used supplemental, "low-tech" materials such as paper, pencils, and keyboard cards. This is an excellent way to engage

2.   This lesson is used by permission of its author Carol Carstensen of Safety Harbor Elementary School, Pinellas County (FL) School District.

students with the creative process even when technological resources are limited and shows thoughtfulness on the part of the teacher in terms of varying the complexity of materials.

Role #2: Performing

As TBMI has been defined in this book, a distinction has been drawn between performance-based classes and classes in which technology is the major means of music instruction. While the majority of the strategies involved in TBMI are designed to take place in a computer lab, musical performance can still exist in that environment, and foundations of TBMI can also guide integration of technology into traditional performance classes. Reimer (2003) defined performing as "bringing previously composed and variously notated musical events to completion in actual sounds" (p. 222). Some of the strategies in this section extend that definition quite liberally; however, performance remains at the heart of musical activity, and TBMI teachers should make efforts to include some types of performance in their curricula.

Drum Machine Programming

Level observed: high school
Suggested tools: printed drum machine patterns, sequencing software
Observed procedures:

1. The teacher instructs students as a group on procedures for operating a virtual drum machine within a complex sequencing software package.
2. Students follow teacher's instructions carefully; they all produce the same drum pattern at their individual stations.
3. The teacher distributes printed drum machine patterns and explains the notation; students are to select a pattern from those that appear on the handout.
4. Students take independent time to program the drum machine according to the printed pattern they selected.

Analysis/commentary:

Recall the definition of music performance stated earlier that characterized performance as conversion of notated music into sound. While the drum machine lesson described here does not imply that the students are actually creating the sound through some physical manipulation of an instrument, it does result in sound produced through decoding of notation.

The drum machine is an important tool in electronic music, both historically and in current practice. Exposing students to the process of creating rhythmic tracks with a virtual drum machine introduces elements of the use of virtual instruments, rhythmic alignment (quantizing), patch selection, and many other aspects of digital music production. It is important that the teacher has well-developed technological knowledge and content knowledge—as suggested by the TPACK model—in order to convey good use of the drum machine tool.

The notation material used in this lesson came from a book of drum machine patterns; there are many such books available. Using this type of printed material is advantageous because it provides a performance experience that does not rely on standard music notation and all the intricacies associated with that notation. The type of notation used in drum machine pattern books is simple and easily accessible by students who do not have traditional notation experience.

Podcast Creation

Level observed: high school
Prior knowledge: The class has already gone through a series of lessons on recording techniques using external microphones, cables, pre-amps, and other necessary equipment.
Suggested tools: sequencing software (observed with GarageBand), internal and external recording/capture devices
Observed procedures:

1. The teacher reviews previous lessons on microphones, cables, and other equipment. He draws the students' attention to the USB interfaces at each of their stations and points out that these are the connection points between computers and external microphones.
2. The teacher introduces podcasting unit by going over the following information:
   a. Distinction between audio and video podcasts
   b. "Rules of podcasting"
3. The teacher explains the specific features of the podcasting template within the GarageBand.
4. The teacher further explains the typical structures of podcasts by playing some examples he has pre-loaded on his own computer.

Over the next several classes, the students created podcasts using the techniques they learned in this introductory session. The enhanced podcasts that they created featured images that they took using their computers' internal cameras, and the topic of the podcast is the work that they have completed throughout their time in the music technology course. A unit followed in which the students developed simple web pages on which they posted their podcasts.

Analysis/commentary:

Podcasting is a widespread and popular form of media, so integrating it into TBMI courses makes good sense. This teacher used it as a way for students to create "showcases" featuring brief clips of the work they had done throughout their time in his class. Creating and publishing podcasts is also a good way to introduce students to popular technologies such as web page development, RSS feeds, and reader/aggregator software. Podcasts are yet another way to allow students creative freedom without placing expectations of traditional musical performance on them. Since many students in TBMI classes, especially at the secondary level, do not have extensive experience in traditional instrumental or vocal performance, teachers must always have this consideration in mind.

As mentioned in step 2, this teacher chose to give his students some "rules of podcasting." There were only two rules, but he spent a good amount of time discussing them. The first rule was that the students should not use their last names or other identifying information in their podcasts. Since the recordings would ultimately be posted on publically accessible websites, the teacher made sure the students protected their own identities by withholding identifying information. This is an important security measure and, in the case of this teacher, one that was mandated by his school's administration. The second rule was to avoid copyright infringement. The teacher used some general rules he had picked up throughout his career to help students maintain safety from copyright violation, and also referred to *The Teacher's Guide to Music, Media, and Copyright Law* (Frankel, 2009).

Teachers who use podcasting as a mechanism for learning production techniques in their classes have indicated that they find GarageBand to be among the best tools for doing so. Recent versions of this software integrate video and audio seamlessly and allow for quick and easy export of finished recordings in digital formats appropriate for podcasts, such as MP3 and .mov. The podcast template, built in to GarageBand, offers a feature called "ducking," which allows the user to select particular tracks that are prioritized over others; volume is automatically decreased for tracks that are "ducked" when sound is recorded onto tracks that have higher priority. For podcasts, this is an essential tool, and one that students find very helpful. The teacher in this lesson made sure to point out this feature and demonstrate its use.

Teachers who use podcasts in their classes might consider having students do a "scavenger hunt" of sorts to provide examples for the class to listen to. This teacher chose to provide all the examples, but students are certainly capable of searching for them and sharing them with their classmates. This is another way in which students can feel a sense of ownership of the lesson.

Live Sound Reinforcement

Level observed: high school
Suggested tools: sound reinforcement equipment (mixer, amp, speakers, cables, microphones); any equipment necessary for performance
Observed procedures:

1. Teacher and students engage in a series of lessons that introduce the various components of live sound reinforcement systems as listed under "tools."
2. Students are arranged into small groups to organize some sort of performance that can be amplified using the equipment they have learned to use.
3. Over as many class meetings as are necessary, students set up the equipment, do the performance, and disassemble the equipment.
4. While each group performs the tasks in step 3, the rest of the class completes an evaluation of the performing group's work. Following each performance, the class discusses the performance(s).

Analysis/commentary:

Live sound reinforcement is a topic that many teachers avoid in their TBMI classes, often because they are not familiar enough with it to feel comfortable teaching it. This is an area in which teachers should pursue training so that they can help their students to learn how to amplify their own performances. Many of the students who take secondary level TBMI classes are in rock bands or other types of popular music groups outside of school, so sound reinforcement is important to them.

As discussed, however, many of those same students might not have much traditional performance experience. Yet, if students are going to learn to reinforce live sound, there has to be something to amplify. Assembling students into small groups allows them to invent some type of performance with which they are all comfortable. Observed performances have included rock bands, amplified acoustic instruments, beat poetry readings, a cappella vocal performances, and many others, all with the purpose of producing something that can be amplified.

In this lesson, students were given the responsibility for selecting sound reinforcement equipment. Teachers might consider having students create an inventory list of equipment their performance requires. The students set up the equipment with the guidance of the teacher and, just as important, they tear down the equipment and store it in ways that are safe and secure. This series of lessons should emphasize good habits of storing and maintaining equipment.

Engaging the rest of the students who are not involved in the performance happening during a particular class meeting accomplishes several things: (1) it keeps the rest of the class involved in the happenings of the performance; (2) it allows the students to be involved in the critical feedback process; and (3) it provides students with advice on how to improve their own performances. The evaluations that students complete of other groups can be on a pre-printed evaluation form, or they can be less formal. They can also become part of a grade for this project.

PROFILE OF PRACTICE 6.1

The SmartMusic accompaniment system has become one of the most popular forms of technology integration in music performance classrooms. It is an enormously useful tool that works on a software subscription model so that it connects in-class learning to at-home practice. It enables real-time assessment of pitch and rhythm accuracy, and it facilitates online submission of recordings to teachers for grading. It also works seamlessly with Finale so that teachers can build their own exercises to add to the impressive library of content available in the system.

Mrs. D has been making expert use of SmartMusic in her middle school band program for five years. She said, "SmartMusic is the basis of our curriculum. Our kids have one lesson every six school days.... I pick out exact exercises that we want them to practice because of the skill involved.... It's assigned that it has to be done by Sunday night." She recognizes that there are appropriate uses for SmartMusic at all levels of instrumental music instruction, including some outstanding possible uses for learning jazz improvisation.

A criticism of SmartMusic is that while it does an admirable job of providing feedback regarding accuracy of pitches and rhythms, it does not do much in terms of other musical elements. Mrs. D has come up with a great way to overcome that: Once students submit their work electronically, they are then required to listen to it and take notes about elements such as articulation, breathing, and "those kinds of real musical issues that you really can't hit in a group lesson."

Mrs. D uses SmartMusic in conjunction with an interactive whiteboard in her classroom. She typically has students standing during lessons and recognizes the motivation it provides when she lets them go to the board to indicate elements within the notated exercises. She also pointed out that she is able to provide concrete data on student achievement, in both audio and visual form, whenever she is asked to do so, and she is keenly aware of every student's individual level. She has seen vast improvement in the performance level of her students in the past few years, and she attributes it directly to SmartMusic. She told me that her bands play more advanced music now and said, "The only thing I have changed in the way that I work is having this as a part of our curriculum."

Using SmartMusic as a foundation of music performance classes is not necessarily the type of technology-based music instruction that is the focus of this book, mostly because it is usually situated in ensemble classes as opposed to a computer lab. However, SmartMusic engages students directly with technology, and it furthers the musical goals that teachers set in a fashion mediated by technology. SmartMusic is a welcome addition to performance classes because it helps students and teachers achieve musical goals, and we should continue to embrace this type of technology integration. Mrs. D encouraged anyone interested in SmartMusic to try not to worry about technical difficulties and give it a shot. As a veteran teacher, without a lot of technological savvy, she said, "If I can do it, you can do it."

Role #3: Improvising

According to Reimer (2003), improvising is much like performing, but "performers as improvisers must supply the ... ideas themselves ... those ideas must be generated *during the act of performing*" (p. 223, emphasis in original). Very few of the teachers observed for this book engaged their students in activities involving improvising. When improvisation was observed, it was done within the context of a musical-theoretical construct such as progression. Improvisation is an area that needs to be explored more within TBMI.

Blues Improvisation

Level observed: high school
Suggested tools: Band-in-a-Box software, MIDI keyboard
Prior knowledge: Students have done several lessons on construction of the minor blues scale in a variety of keys.
Observed procedures:

1. The teacher displays a Band-in-a-Box file containing a simple 12-bar c minor blues progression, on an interactive whiteboard.
2. The teacher verbally reviews with the students the structure of the 12-bar blues progression.
3. The teacher points out the controls within Band-in-a-Box for playback and recording. She circulates around the room to make sure the students see these controls.
4. The teacher instructs students to record improvised melodies from their MIDI keyboards into Band-in-a-Box, one 4-bar phrase at a time.
5. The students take independent time to accomplish the improvising/recording tasks.

Analysis/commentary:

The teacher I observed teaching this lesson, in addition to her TBMI classes, teaches group piano classes. She told me several times during our discussions that she tries to keep the musical-theoretical concepts somewhat parallel or consistent between the two classes. Doing so helps her to know that she is covering musical ideas in her TBMI classes and keeping music at the core of her curriculum. Presumably, blues scales and improvisation are ideas that she also covers in her keyboard classes. The activity described in this lesson is an advanced one that would most logically be characterized in Bloom's Taxonomy as an application exercise, since students are using existing knowledge in a new context. This is also similar to activities suggested in many of the music pedagogies explained in chapter 2; here, however, technology is used to provide accompaniment rather than the teacher or students performing the accompaniment.

Band-in-a-Box is automatic accompaniment software that has been on the market for at least 20 years. Although its interface is strikingly similar in its current version to its original appearance, the functionality of the program has grown more sophisticated with each new version. Many teachers in TBMI classes use Band-in-a-Box for purposes similar to that which was demonstrated in this lesson: for providing accompaniment for students to practice performance. Here, the teacher expected the students to improvise melodies; however, the students knew that if they were not happy with the melodies they recorded, they could simply try again. This is one of the powerful elements of recording into software—it allows for nearly infinite takes and retakes.

Role #4: Listening

Listening is certainly embedded into other musical roles. Reimer (2003) described active, engaged listening as: "That musical role, the most widespread of all, is, as much as any other, the manifestation of a genuine way to be musically intelligent—a way in which musical discriminations and interconnections are the basis for the experience gained" (p. 224). As described in chapter 4, many listening activities are designed to "feed" students' creativity, while others have a less specific goal of exposing students to new types of music.

Technology-enhanced Listening Journal

Level observed: high school
Suggested tools: audio system, word processor at each student station
Observed procedures:

1. At the beginning of the semester, students are told to bring in music (as MP3, on CD, etc.) that they would like to play for the class. The teacher collects this music and assembles it in a playlist on an iPod.
2. Each day, the teacher selects one piece of music from the students' contributions and occasionally uses something from his own collection, to serve as the listening example for the day.
3. The teacher connects the iPod to the group audio controller, which serves as the classroom's audio system, and plays an example for the students.
4. The students open a word processing program at their stations and write about what they hear.
5. Every few weeks, the students submit their listening journals to the teacher via a common network folder.

Analysis/commentary:

Listening should be a core activity of TBMI classes. Students engaged in technology-based music often have diverse tastes in music and can often awaken each other to new types of music. Researchers have shown that the high school years (roughly ages 14–18) are the time in students' lives when they are least likely to seek out new music and when they are least tolerant of music that they do not consider "their own" (Hargreaves, 1982; LeBlanc, Simms, Siivola, & Olbert, 1996). TBMI classes are opportunities to expand the range of listening students do; this teacher valued that opportunity.

The technological techniques that the teacher used—collecting music from various formats onto his iPod, using the group audio controller, using the word processor and shared network folder—are all examples of streamlining workflow. Because the techniques actually engage students with technology, they go beyond the simplistic uses of technology suggested by the Technical Basin and the Practical Plane, approaching the Pedagogical Summit of the topographical model described in chapter 1. These examples are important to model for students. This teacher demonstrated how consumer electronics and software could be adapted for the needs of the class and in doing so provided an excellent model of efficiency. Teachers of other subjects who use journaling could learn from this teacher regarding strong uses of technology.

A difficult issue related to this activity is that of assessment, a key component in the TBMI framework. What elements of a listening journal can and should be assessed? Or is it important to place any type of assessment on the students' journal entries? If students are asked to spend time on a listening journal every day, they should certainly receive some kind of credit for their work. Before each listening exercise begins in this teacher's class, he prompts the students about what specific elements of the music he wants them to try to focus on while they listen. The teacher chose to focus assessment of the journals on completeness; that is, he checks to make sure that the students addressed the elements about which he prompted them and that they did so in a thorough way. His concern, more important than any specific criteria for the journal entries, is that the students are demonstrating an understanding of the musical concepts they study and can relate those concepts to the listening examples.

Cover Project

Level observed: high school
Prior knowledge: This is a series of lessons that takes place over about one or two weeks of daily classes. Each step in the following procedures represents approximately one

class of instructional time. Students already have some familiarity with sequencing software, and all students have some background in music performance.

Suggested tools: sequencing software, external microphones/audio interfaces, various instruments

Observed procedures:

1. The teacher instructs students on the uses of pre-packaged loops in the sequencing software and guides them through the creation of a simple composition using the loops.
2. The teacher distributes and explains the rubric that will be used for project assessment.
3. The teacher instructs students on the uses of effects, panning, and fading within the software. Students apply these techniques to the loop-based composition they have already created.
4. Students choose a song they know well and of which they would like to create a cover version. They are given time to practice performing the instrumental and vocal parts of the song.
5. The teacher instructs students on the uses of external audio interfaces and microphones for the purpose of recording instruments and their voice.
6. Students use both loops and recorded material to create a cover version of their chosen song.
7. Students share work with each other to receive feedback.

Analysis/commentary:

The idea of creating a cover song was, in this case, the musical means to familiarize students with the complex features of sequencing software. The teacher provided a minimal amount of instruction in the software—just enough for students to find their way around and accomplish some basic tasks. From that point, the students were essentially set free to work on their own project. Throughout the observation, students asked many questions about the uses of the software. Most of the questions were unique to software-based tasks that the students needed to accomplish for their own project, as opposed to general concerns that might be shared by other members of the class. This is an example of the Cycle of Mastery working in many layers and of the teacher recognizing that each student would have unique needs.

A particularly important element of this lesson was the way the teacher chose to assess. Two forms of assessment were used, both of which will be discussed in detail in chapter 7, the chapter on assessment. First, the teacher had the students share their project work with each other—a technique that is quite common in TBMI. Second, the teacher used a form to evaluate the students' achievement regarding required elements of the project. The form contained the following criteria:

- Faithful representation of the melody and rhythm of the original so that it is recognizable
- Minimum of three layers (example: rhythm, bass/harmony, and "lead")
- One layer recorded in "live"
- One segment with "vocals"
- Good fit between melody and accompaniment
- Creativity/originality/finesse

The teacher was careful to distribute this form toward the beginning of the project so that the students would understand her expectations.

Mixing

Level observed: high school
Prior knowledge: This lesson occurred at the end of series of lessons in which students were creating original compositions in sequencing software. The lesson could be conducted at the end of nearly any type of composition project in the sequencing environment.
Suggested tools: monitor speakers, sequencing software, students' projects
Observed procedures:

1. The teacher collects rough versions of students' sequencing projects and displays one through a projector and monitor speakers.
2. The teacher distributes a handout that contains a list of seven elements to listen for when mixing a project.
3. The teacher instructs students to listen to the project and take notes regarding elements of the project they might mix differently.
4. Students share their thoughts about changes in the mix with the project's (student) composer.

Analysis/commentary:

Mixing music well is inextricably linked to good listening skills. Mixing engineers develop, over years of practice, the ability to identify the need for very fine adjustments to recordings. Only through practice, and through exposure to many types of compositions and recordings, can budding mixers develop their listening skills. While this lesson was part of a larger project of original composition, the day I observed was dedicated time for the students to listen to one another's work and provide critical feedback.

I observed many classes in which students were sharing the work they had done on a particular project. This one was different for several reasons. First, this sharing session was being done prior to the completion of the project. The purpose of this sharing session was for the students to provide each other with feedback on a specific element of the project's workflow (mixing), with the understanding that the feedback they received from each other would then be implemented into later versions of their compositions.

Second, the teacher in this scenario went to some lengths to set up an additional pair of high-quality monitoring speakers. He wanted the students to know that music can sound different when it is heard from various sources. The students commented during the observation about the relatively quiet bass sounds from the monitors, compared to the sound in the headphones they had been using while composing. In terms of real-world music production models, this is an important lesson for students to learn.

Third, the use of a structured advanced organizer made this sharing session focused and efficient. The teacher had obtained a simple guide to mixing from an audio manufacturer's website and had adapted it to the class's needs. This simple preparation paid dividends in helping to narrow the students' attention so that they would concentrate on the element of mixing rather than being distracted by compositional issues. While there were some comments that were not related to mixing, the majority of the feedback students received was about issues of blend, balance, and effects, all techniques that are accomplished during the mixing process. This type of organizer was an excellent technique for keeping the sharing session focused and making it effective.

Role #5: Music Theory

Similar to listening, music theory is embedded into other musical roles. Much composition, performance, and improvisation relies upon music theory. Describing the work of music theorists, Reimer (2003) wrote: "Recognizing the necessary interdependence of process and product, theorists explore, articulate, and to the extent it is possible and useful to do so, hypothesize processual/structural principles for, the operations by which sound-gestures and their organizations ... produce their expressive effects" (p. 226). The lessons I observed involve musical roles other than that of a theorist but rely heavily on theoretical concepts, so they are categorized in this section.

Theme and Variation

Level observed: middle school

Prior knowledge: The teacher has led several lessons on theme and variation. The students have engaged in identifying themes and in identifying compositional devices used to produce variations. The students are also familiar with the capabilities of audio editing software, particularly the effects and process functions available within the software for manipulating sound.

Suggested tools: audio editing software (observed using Audacity), microphone

Observed procedures:

1. The teacher assigns students to small groups (3–4 students in each). Students decide on a sound they would like to use as their theme.
2. Students produce a written list, based on their knowledge of the capabilities of the software, of the types of variations they intend to create.
3. Once students have produced a list of a required number of variations (here, 15), the teacher approves their written work and the groups move to a computer.
4. Students use the microphone to record the sound for their theme.
5. Students use the devices within the software to create variations of the theme sound.

Analysis/commentary:

Theme and variation form is a common theoretical concept for music classes to address. Rather than approaching it using purely listening-based pedagogy, this teacher engaged the students in creating their own themes and variations using technology, a teaching strategy that appeals to the philosophical bases of TBMI. While the strict definitions of "theme" and of "variation" were stretched in this lesson—the sounds the students recorded were short, often percussive, and did not necessarily have to be melodic—the idea that composers create variations by manipulating original material was conveyed through the course of the lesson.

The middle school general music class in which this lesson was taught was not a fully fleshed-out computer lab. I observed this lesson over two class periods. In the first, the students assembled in groups in front of the four desktop computers in the classroom. While the students appeared to be accustomed to this arrangement, doing so was not comfortable, nor did it engage more than one student at a time in direct contact with a computer; rather, one student was responsible for all the direct interaction while the others watched and gave input. The teacher and students made the best of this situation; the students were generally cooperative and attentive. The teacher also periodically gave instructions for the groups to rotate so that different students were responsible for interacting with the computers. For the second observation, the teacher was able to obtain a cart of laptops so students were able to work on their own more easily.

The arrangement of the classroom also influenced the teacher's decisions about the steps that the lessons followed. Since she knew that students would be working in groups, the teacher decided that the planning stages of the project would be done on paper, away from the computers. This allowed the students more room to interact with each other. It also allowed the teacher to monitor the students' process of assembling their plan. A drawback to this procedure is that it does not truly capitalize on the power of software to provide a consequence-free environment, where students can make changes and edits without destroying their work completely.

While the software the students were using tends to feature technological terminology in its various menus and commands, the teacher was insistent that she and the students use musical terminology as much as possible. For example, when students would refer to the *speed* of their recorded sample, the teacher was quick to point out that this equated to its *tempo* in musical parlance. When they would use the software to change the sound so that it was of higher or lower frequency, she would remind them that in musical terms they were shifting *pitch*. This placed an important emphasis on the musical aspect of the lesson, which could easily have been lost in the technological shuffle.

Scale Construction

Level observed: high school
Suggested tools: listening example in any minor key, piano keyboards, notation software or staff paper, MusicTheory.net website
Observed procedures:

1. The teacher provides, and students listen to, an example piece in a minor key.
2. The teacher and students discuss characteristic sounds of pieces in minor keys.
3. The teacher displays the section of Musictheory.net on an interactive whiteboard. Students and teacher work together to (key of listening example).
4. The teacher uses the software to play the scale back and reviews the construction of natural minor scales.

5. The teacher assigns each student a root note on which they are to construct a natural minor scale. Students may use keyboards for help if they wish. Students are to notate the scale using notation software and save it.

Analysis/commentary:

The goal of this lesson was a fairly common one: to review the "formula" by which scales—here, natural minor scales—can be constructed. This is fairly low-level work in terms of the cognitive taxonomy, but the teacher maintained the students' interest by integrating technological means to deliver and review the content and by providing a technological interaction with which the students could practice the concept. Using a listening example was a good way to put students in the "headspace" of minor tonality. The teacher chose a piece of music by the metal band Godsmack (the song was "Keep Away") so that the students would be familiar with the style of the example. Choosing a less familiar genre might have distracted the students from the purpose of the lesson.

MusicTheory.net, a free online tool, served in this lesson as a technological replacement for a more traditional approach such as drawing notation on a chalkboard. The major advantage to this strategy is that, as the students and the teacher constructed the scale together, the website played back the pitches in the scale. This provided instant feedback, and the students immediately knew if their answers were correct. Since the website was projected onto an interactive whiteboard, it did not provide students with direct interaction with the technology. Therefore, the lesson could be seen as situated in the practical plane of the topological model.

The students were provided with a final technological interaction when the teacher instructed them to work on their own to construct a natural minor scale on a given pitch. While the students could easily have done this step on staff paper, using notation software allowed for practice with an additional technology and provided immediate feedback as they worked.

Transposition

Level observed: high school
Suggested tools: keyboards, notation software, playing example

1. The teacher introduces a simple melodic song (observed using "Ode to Joy"). Students take time to practice playing the song on the keyboards.

2. The teacher introduces the concept of transposition as "shifting an entire piece from one key to another."
3. The teacher uses notation software on the interactive whiteboard to demonstrate how the notation for "Ode to Joy" can be transposed to a new key.
4. The teacher plays the transposed version of the piece and leads students in a brief discussion about the process of transposing.
5. The teacher assigns students a major key signature to which they are to transpose "Ode to Joy" and notate it using the notation software at their own stations.

Analysis/commentary:

The non-traditional music students in this class had varying levels of keyboard proficiency, but none were experienced keyboard performers, which made this lesson challenging for them and for the teacher. While the teacher is to be commended for attempting to teach the important concept of transposition to this class, in line with his commitment to teach music theory fundamentals, it is always important to assess students' readiness for all aspects of lessons. While the students were intellectually ready to understand transposition, application of the concept to the keyboard and to written notation proved difficult tasks.

Those with experience with notation software will question its use in the context of this lesson because the software is itself capable of performing the transposition the students were asked to complete. The students had not learned that function of the software when they were engaged in this lesson. The teacher could have ensured that the students would not take advantage of that function by giving the students time to practice, then listening to each of them perform the song in the assigned key.

Pop Song Chord Progressions

Level observed: high school
Prior knowledge: Students are familiar with the construction of scales and chords and have a basic understanding of the functions of chords in progressions.
Suggested tools: YouTube, group instruments (either keyboards or guitars)
Observed procedures:

1. The teacher explains that many pop songs share as their foundation a common chord progression: I-V-vi-IV in a major key.

2. The teacher shows students a YouTube video that demonstrates the use of the progression in many songs.[3]
3. The teacher and students use the knowledge they have been developing of scales and chords to determine what chords were used in the video.
4. Students take time to practice playing the progression on the instruments.

Analysis/commentary:

The goals for this lesson were to apply a music theory idea and to show students that the theoretical knowledge they had gained was indeed related to the types of music they listen to on their own. The video the teacher used quickly conveyed that by showing students how many popular songs are based on the progression.

One important difference between this lesson and many of the others analyzed in this chapter is that in this lesson the students were not necessarily engaged with the technology themselves. The teacher chose to show the YouTube video on a screen from a projector and have the students watch it as a group. One possible modification to this choice would be to have the students watch the video at their individual stations in the lab. This is an immediate way to engage students with web video technology. Later in the lesson, when the students were practicing the progression, they did so on keyboards, a natural way to engage them with electronic instruments.

No evaluation was planned for this lesson. Not every lesson needs to be evaluated, and in this case, the teacher chose to focus on concept and skill development without tying that development to an evaluation. A possible extension of the lesson is to have the students compose a song that uses the progression. In doing so, the teacher might have been able to assess students' uses of the progression in the creative sense, and their ability to perform the progression. This type of assessment would instantly demonstrate understanding of the theoretical concept.

3. The video used in this lesson was found at http://youtu.be/oOlDewpCfZQ. It is one of several videos by the Australian comedy-rock band Axis of Awesome. This video contains some material that would be deemed inappropriate for many classrooms. Teachers should always preview online videos for their classroom appropriateness.

Orchestration

Level observed: high school
Suggested tools: notation software, materials for teaching about instruments (timbres, ranges, etc.)
Observed procedures:

1. The teacher leads several lessons about a particular family of instruments (observed using brass instruments).
2. The teacher distributes a 4-bar chorale style composition, both as an audio file and as a printed score.
3. Students use their knowledge of instrument sounds and ranges to orchestrate the chorale in the notation software.
4. Students play orchestrated arrangements for each other and provide critique.

Analysis/commentary:

This is an example of an advanced lesson for a TBMI class. The students in this class were performing musicians, most with experience in their school's band or choir, and many had taken an AP Music Theory class. Much of the theoretical knowledge, such as fundamental part-writing and voice-leading, was taken care of in their prior experiences, so the teacher was able to focus this lesson on the technological aspects of the tasks at hand. The focus of the lesson was on orchestration; as such, the teacher expressed to his students that they should pay careful attention to the ranges of the instruments for which they were writing and that they should consider how their writing would effect the blend of the ensemble.

Similar to the model followed in traditional college-level arranging or orchestration classes, the teacher made sure that the students understood the instruments they would be writing for, how they sounded and behaved. Between the school's other music teachers, some students, and himself, the teacher was able to provide live examples of each instrument. Some teachers who do not have resources as extensive as this engage students in seeking out examples of instrument sounds prior to beginning an orchestration project. Many fine example are available free online; teachers also use their own collections or borrow examples from local libraries to accomplish this preliminary step.

Having done this lesson previously, the teacher knew that while the compositions would be similar, each student would bring his or her own "spin" to it. For this reason, the teacher felt it important to include the sharing component of the lesson. This allowed the students to hear one another's arrangements and comment on the ideas their classmates had used. Sharing project work makes the experience feel more real to the students; rather than letting their work exist only between themselves and their teacher, they are able to experience feedback from their peers, and the task becomes situated in an environment they might experience outside of class. This also created an opportunity for students to speak using musical language and aesthetic terms, which is an underlying goal for the music department in this school.

Role #6: Musicology

Reimer (2003) defined musicology as the study of "the forces that cause or help to determine why and how music became what it was, or becomes what it is, at various times, in various places, and among particular people" (p. 227). In lessons that address the role of musicologist, students are engaged in activities about the unique historical contexts of music. Most often, these lessons focus on a particular musical period or style. A subrole of the musicologist is that of the music critic, who provides commentary on music and its craftsmanship of composition or performance. In TBMI environments, students examine music in historical or cultural contexts, and do so with the support of technological tools.

Critiquing

Level observed: middle school
Prior knowledge: The class has engaged in several sessions in which they provided feedback about one another's work but have not done so for quite some time.
Suggested tools: a collaborative website such as a wiki
Observed procedures:

1. The teacher instructs students to log on to networked computers and open the wiki they created in a prior lesson. He also instructs the students to add the URL to their list of "favorites" so that they can access it more easily during subsequent lessons.
2. The teacher connects his iPod to the classroom audio system. He tells the students he is going to play a song, and he wants them to think while they listen about what they like about the song, and what they do not like.

3. When the song ends, students write comments on the wiki related to their critiques. The teacher reminds them about the techniques for providing critique that they have discussed during previous lessons.
4. The teacher displays the wiki site on the screen and points out some of the comments that contain the kinds of feedback that he is looking for.

Analysis/commentary:

Part of the role of the musicologist is to provide critique. In this lesson, the teacher led the students through an activity designed to structure critique and to help them understand the kinds of feedback that he considered to be acceptable and helpful in the particular setting of this class. In some schools and districts, the process of peer critique is commonplace and students develop very sophisticated skills on both ends of this process; this was not the case in the particular classroom where this observation took place. These middle school students needed to be taught how to provide appropriate feedback, and this teacher did an excellent job of leading them through the experience.

Step 1 of this set of procedures featured the process of "bookmarking" the wiki site the students were using; several comments are necessary to explain this. First, the choice to use a wiki was an outstanding one for this activity. Wikis allow for collaborative, near-real-time posting and can be secured so that only the members of a particular group (here, the class) can have access to it. Wikis have become very popular in educational settings and can be set up very simply, usually for free. Second, having the students bookmark the site's address was a clever way to expedite the process for subsequent lessons. This simple step would eliminate the need to have the students type a lengthy URL into their browsers. This is an example of using technological infrastructure that will surely make future lessons run more efficiently.

Asking students to provide commentary on each other's work is a relatively common technique in TBMI classes. In another observation, sixth grade students commented on each other's video soundtrack projects. The videos were posted to the teacher's website, and students provided comments using a blog forum. This presented some technical issues because the server where the teacher's website was hosted did not allow the video to be viewed by more than one user at a time. The students simply had to be patient and wait for the video to be available. In the particular classroom where the lesson took place, the students were involved in several simultaneous projects, so they were able to wait without losing valuable time. Using wikis or teacher websites for project sharing also facilitates direct student interaction with technology, a hallmark of TBMI.

Creating Compilations

Level observed: high school
Prior knowledge: This lesson was done at the end of a semester of music technology class.
Suggested tools: iTunes or other software capable of burning CDs, CD labels, and label design software
Observed procedures:

1. The teacher instructs students on procedures for exporting various projects from throughout the semester into universal audio formats.
2. Students export all of their project work from composition programs and import into iTunes.
3. Students record a short (voice) description of the pieces in their compilation and export it to iTunes.
4. The teacher instructs students on procedures for burning a CD of all of their project work.
5. The teacher instructs students on use of CD labeling software.
6. Students create a label, including a title, capturing the spirit of the contents.

Analysis/commentary:

The role of musicologist is present in this set of lessons in that the students are learning to analyze an entire body of work—which happens to be their own—and find a fitting label for it. Often, students' bodies of work are not considered as a whole; rather, they are thought of, both by teachers and students, as individual projects that appeal to particular guidelines. Viewing projects as a body of work helps students to analyze their own stylistic tendencies and also helps them to notice growth in their own creative products.

In addition to the musicological aspect of this project, collecting all of the projects that students produce in a given period allows them to produce a portfolio of their creative work. Evaluation of a portfolio can be a valuable form of feedback for students' development. Even if a formal assessment of a portfolio is not the goal of this type of compilation, students who do this activity will have a reasonably permanent record of their work that they can bring with them when they finish the class.

Role #7: Music Teaching

Reimer (2003) suggests that music teaching is a distinct type of musical intelligence. During the observations for this text, at no time were students engaged in teaching each other in structured, sequential ways. Students often had opportunities to listen to or view one another's work and provide feedback, but that hardly qualifies as the type of planned, intentional instruction that is associated with the music-teaching role.

At this point in the development of TBMI, it is quite possible that examples of lessons in which elementary and secondary students are teaching each other do not exist; none were observed during the preparation of this book. Development of the music teacher role typically occurs in teacher preparation programs. It is within this context that pre-service teachers should develop technology-based music pedagogy. Future projects are necessary to determine how TBMI skills are being developed in teacher preparation programs.

PROFILE OF PRACTICE 6.2

Differentiated instruction is a "hot topic" in all fields of education because it helps students to achieve at a rate that is developmentally appropriate by recognizing and accounting for individual differences. The music technology lab is not immune to the demands of differentiated instruction; in fact, it can serve as an excellent environment for the strategies that make this kind of teaching work.

Mrs. M teaches in a public high school where the arts and technology are highly valued by school administrators. The music department in which she works is successful by any measure, and her technology classes receive excellent support. Though she is "largely self-taught" in terms of her technology skills, Mrs. M has a sophisticated knowledge of hardware and software. Her background is in piano, and she spent the initial years of her teaching career in an elementary music teaching position. She says she learned a lot about addressing students' individual needs there, and her amazing ability to sequence educational material comes from her experience as an Orff-centered general music teacher.

The environment of Mrs. M's music technology classes is one of high expectations, but it allows students the freedom to work at their own pace. She said, "I think, in a creativity-based class, you need to be comfortable as an instructor relinquishing control. You cannot control the students' outcomes. All that you can do is set parameters and guide them while they're in the middle of their creative phase. Check their work, make sure they're on target, remind them of what the expectations are."

Mrs. M recognized some time ago that requiring students to have some experience in music prior to taking her class would be beneficial, so she instituted a "music reading prerequisite." Therefore, students can register for her class only if they have music reading skills. This does not, however, mean that the students are able to perform musically—only that they can recognize notes on a staff. She expressed several times that she wishes there was a keyboard performance prerequisite. To accommodate the students' widely varying performance skills, Mrs. M recognizes the importance of allowing students to work at a comfortable pace. She said, "I have a picture in my mind going into any given lesson about how things might go, and then I have to monitor the progress that my students are making. So, I had a couple of students that I told to just go [because they] seem to totally get the hang of how it works, [they are] very comfortable with the notation, [they] move right ahead at whatever pace is comfortable for [them]. And then there are other students who are very fine musicians but aren't as comfortable with the music notation, and that seemed to be slowing them down a bit. So I try to find some semblance of a happy medium. And often, as happened with the lessons subsequent to [the observed one], some of my students were nearly finished, and others needed considerable help. So we had two tracks going: the kids who were far ahead and they needed instructions on how to do things with formatting before they went ahead and printed, things like deleting all the blank measures at the end and changing staff size. Meanwhile there are other kids that are still working on basic note entry kind of techniques. And that's OK, that happens all the time in these sorts of classes. So as a teacher, you have to be ready to roll with that, and have another project on tap for those kids who are finished."

Mrs. M's classroom is an excellent example of Cycles of Mastery running simultaneously. And since she has developed a disposition of openness, her pedagogical choices encourage her students to be creative and to approach their work with care at a comfortable pace.

SUMMARY OF CHAPTER 6

In this chapter we saw some models of TBMI lessons including the Cycle of Mastery and the spectrum of lesson content. In the lesson plans explained in this chapter, we saw how these and other theoretical ideas are present in actual lessons. In chapter 7, we will examine the role and practices of assessment in TBMI.

ITEMS FOR DISCUSSION

1. Think about a lesson you have taught or observed in a technology-based music class. Now consider the TBMI Lesson Content Spectrum described at the beginning of chapter 6. Draw the spectrum and decide where along the continuum the lesson might fall. Do you think the location along the spectrum was the same for both the teacher and the students?
2. Have you seen the Cycle of Mastery in action? Try to observe a technology-based music class. What examples of the cycle can you see occurring?
3. Chapter 6 included many examples of lessons that were categorized according to Reimer's Musical Roles. Choose a role that interests you. Design a lesson that appeals to that role. Be sure to articulate the goals, materials needed, prior knowledge, procedures, and means of evaluation.

CHAPTER 7

Assessment and Technology-Based Music Instruction

Assessment is such an important cornerstone of the current educational landscape that it must be a part of discussion about any educational topic, including TBMI. To paraphrase Duke (2005), rather than thinking about assessment as the culmination of an educational cycle, teachers should embed assessment into every lesson, every activity, and our plans for everything that comes next. Duke stated, "The distinction between the assessments and the substance of instruction day to day should be diminished to the point that the day-to-day activities of instruction closely resemble the assessments themselves" (2005, p. 71). In a TBMI class, this is the scenario for which teachers should strive. Still, assessment remains a thorny issue for TBMI teachers because they are often unaccustomed to assessing the types of work that students do in TBMI classes, examples of which were seen in the sample lessons in chapter 6.

Assessing what students do informs us about the extent to which they retain information and achieve learning objectives, the quality of that learning, and students' abilities to apply conceptual understanding to both familiar and novel situations. If we do it for no other reason, assessing students tells us when they are ready to go on to the next bit of information, the next activity, or the next level of complexity of work.

PROFILE OF PRACTICE 7.1

I observed Mr. U during a day trip to his school in a suburb in the northeast United States. Mr. U has been teaching music technology classes at the high school level for about 15 years—perhaps the longest of any teacher profiled in this book—and has been nationally recognized for his excellence in doing so. Over that time, he has gone through many changes of equipment, software, and course designs. He has developed a vast and sophisticated set of projects for his students, who can take level 1 and 2 music technology classes. Most of the assignments and requirements are housed on a website that Mr. U developed as part of a professional development project. His students clearly enjoy the music technology classes he teaches. He calls himself a "pretty easy guy to deal with" and characterizes the environment of his classes as "pretty informal."

Given the informality of Mr. U's classes, I wondered about how he assesses his students' work. Mr. U quickly confessed, "My biggest weakness is creating the rubrics to assess.... And I've gone through many books and I've looked at how different teachers do things. I try not to just blatantly steal what other teachers do, but from my teaching, I know that's my weakest part ... how to come up with the formal rubric."

We talked a bit about how important assessment is and agreed that, in his teaching situation, Mr. U benefits from having hard data, just to prove the worth of his class. Given the importance of assessment for the betterment of the TBMI environment, why does he avoid it? What would make this a more integral part of his teaching?

"From my perspective," he said, "I just need more time. More time developing [the evaluations]. We have some for the [level] 2 projects; I have some for the [level] 1 projects, but not all of them. I switch projects a lot from year to year. So, I'm not consistent on doing the exact same class every year. I'll throw some things in, pull some things out, things that worked better and things that didn't. But I need to know more on how to do that. That's my issue as a teacher."

Mr. U is careful to make sure that his students know what he is looking for when he assesses their projects—what makes a more or less successful student project. He puts criteria on his website, usually in the form of a checklist. He talked about his involvement in what his district calls "job targets," or professional development goals, and that creating evaluation tools for the music technology class projects was his job target for this year, and probably the next year as well. The school district had been pushing all of its teachers to develop clear assessments and measures for student work that would ultimately be linked to the school's website. I commented on the serendipity of the school's goal aligning with his personal goal of making assessment of student work function better.

Even experienced, accomplished teachers can struggle with the idea and practices of evaluating or assessing student work. To lend validity to what we do, it is time we put some of these ideas into common practice.

In this chapter we will explore assessment as it relates to technology-based music instruction. I will suggest the possibility that, in addition to assessing students' work, there are other elements of TBMI itself that need to be examined critically. Perhaps because TBMI is relatively young, or perhaps because it breaks with some traditions, we need to test whether teaching music by technological means in a particular setting is the smartest choice.

In this chapter, *assessment* is used as a "catch-all" term for the many types of related activities. In its simplest form, assessment occurs when teachers look at, listen to, or otherwise observe students' work and provide any kind of feedback about it. Assessment need not be teacher-to-student; many effective assessments happen when students provide feedback for one another. Feedback could be written or verbal and can serve functions of guidance for improvement or can render a judgment of the quality of the work. When a *value* is attached to the assessment, then it takes the form of an *evaluation*. Teachers, in almost all circumstances, are required to draw evaluative conclusions through the mechanism of grading. The discussion herein is intended to provide suggestions for how teachers might assess students' work in several ways including formative feedback that provides guidance along the way and summative evaluation.

It is important at this point to recall the learning objectives related to TBMI because they form the basis of what can be assessed. This is based on a (perhaps not entirely trustworthy) assumption that students learn what we expect them to when we teach or set up learning activities. In general, as stated in chapter 1, the goals of TBMI are the same as in other types of music teaching and learning scenarios. Teachers should teach, and students should learn, skills and concepts in performance (vocal and instrumental), listening, improvising, composing, analyzing, connecting music to other disciplines, and recognizing the roles of music in cultures. In addition to these foundational objectives, however, teachers should teach, and students should learn concepts and skills in the software and hardware used for music making. The specific skills and concepts—both musical and technological—are determined by individual teachers, as governed by their local requirements and according to what they believe is right for their students. Assuming teachers make smart, informed decisions about these learning objectives, what follow are suggestions for methods by which those objectives might be assessed.

TESTS AND QUIZZES

There are no standard tests that appeal directly to the types of goals that teachers typically set in TBMI classes. Tests and quizzes are rarely used as forms of assessment in technology-based music classes where educational experiences tend to emphasize and value creativity over factual or procedural knowledge. Most of the teachers observed for this book stated clearly that whenever possible, they avoid tests in TBMI classes in favor of assessing students' creative work, or other forms of engagement with music and technology. Those teachers who do use tests or quizzes favor the strategy because (1) testing provides a concrete means by which students can be assessed; (2) testing allows teachers to grade their students on a standard scale and offers them evidence to support the grades they are responsible for assigning; (3) testing generally addresses knowledge students may acquire, and that content—such as vocabulary—may otherwise be difficult to assess.

Teachers who do use tests and quizzes in TBMI classes tend to do so only as it relates to *information*, not to assess students' skills or creative imagination. Common types of information that teachers report testing are constructs such as types and uses of microphones, cables, and other components of music workstations. Also, teachers who include substantial amounts of music theory or performance training in their TBMI classes might test those skills.

One teacher, who uses written tests in her class, told me about her justifications for doing so. She said that the school where she teaches requires that students take a written final exam in every one of their classes. Her final exam includes both music theory concepts and questions about basic music technology knowledge. This teacher mentioned her belief in using a variety of assessments, and that using written tests are only one component of grading. She uses tests and quizzes partially because of her belief that development of literacy is the job of every teacher. Her students write about their own work and the work of their peers in order to develop writing skills. She said:

> [The students] may be very, very successful as far as the projects are concerned. And then you see a big drop-off when it comes to quiz grades and writing. But those are important too. You have to be able to write a sentence, and you have to be able to read, and I feel like that has to be part of it. I can't just have projects after projects and not expect them to be able to explain it or say, "This is the reason why I did this in a certain spot." I want them to explain themselves.

This teacher's choices require students to participate in many kinds of assessment opportunities; while the emphasis remains on their project work, she includes tests and quizzes as ways to check for understanding and to expand the students' responsibilities.

One possible way to engage students with technology while using traditional testing techniques is by using student response devices, commonly known as "clickers." These devices, which typically connect to a central computer through Bluetooth or infrared signals, allow teachers to create prompting questions that students respond to individually. The accompanying software typically generates reports of performance, which can be used as assessment data. Alternatively, online services are available for creating polls that can substitute for clickers, and students can respond to polls with devices such as smart phones and tablets. I observed an elementary music teacher use clickers to give an informal quiz in a TBMI class, and it was very engaging and effective for the students. I have also used the devices in my college music technology classes with similar results.

The de facto sets of standards that relate to TBMI, which will be discussed later, do not specifically call for any type of testing. It is reasonable to assume that as technology-based music classes become more prevalent, a standard body of knowledge may emerge, both for students and teachers. This may eventually lead to the creation of standardized testing instruments, and the profession will need to think carefully about the value of using those tests given the constantly changing landscape of available technologies.

ASSESSING STUDENTS' PROGRAMMED WORK

Perhaps the simplest, most user-friendly type of assessment teachers can do in TBMI is to use assessments that are provided for them by software in the style of programmed instruction. This scenario is most commonly found in software designed to help students learn music theory concepts and aural skills. Developers of this type of software realize that in most cases, there are correct and incorrect answers, and computers are capable of providing students with feedback in such "black-and-white" settings, and of keeping track of students' performance.

Examples of this type of software include popular packages such as MusicAce, Auralia, Musition, Practica Musica, Alfred's Essentials of Music Theory, and MacGAMUT. These software packages, to varying extents, offer exercises in notated music theory and aural skills. Each is designed for a particular age level, though most are flexible enough to be used across several grades. These pieces of software harken back to behaviorist methods of learning in that the students using them start at a particular level of complexity and must demonstrate mastery of that level before proceeding to the next level. The software monitors the student's progress and, in many cases, makes a determination regarding when it is appropriate to move on.

Built in to many of these software packages is the ability to create individual student profiles or accounts, often by setting up virtual "classes," or lists of student users. Students can log in with unique credentials; as they use the software, their performance is tracked and the software retains the data in their profile. With administrative privileges, the teacher can then access the individual students' scores. Some teachers use this information to help students target specific areas of weakness, while other teachers use the simple percentage score to assign a grade.

There are both positive and negative characteristics of using programmed instruction software. Advantages of doing so are these: (1) grading criteria are clear, and because most of the software packages mentioned provide immediate feedback, students are constantly apprised of their performance; (2) students can work independently with the software, which aligns well with a lab setting or a situation in which few computers are available; (3) levels of difficulty can be tailored to match students' preparation. Some of the software packages allow teachers to customize the content to very specific detail, and (4) data are easily retrieved and provide relatively irrefutable evidence of students' performance.

Despite these benefits, there are cautions to note. First, programmed instruction software rarely allows for any student creativity. Some modules within the software might ask students to compose simple melodies or complete chord voicings, but there are rarely any open-ended tasks that would allow for original thought. Second, students who are more advanced than others, or students who are not quite as capable as others, may experience frustration when working with this type of software because it is either too easy or too difficult for them. Teachers should carefully examine the data they collect from the software and talk with students about their experiences so that difficulty levels can be adjusted. Finally, a practical obstacle is the use of this type of software in labs that work by having students login with individual network credentials. If this is the case, it might be difficult for the teacher to set up virtual class lists of students, at least in the fashion that the software developers usually intend for this function to operate. Teachers should work with IT administrators to determine solutions for overcoming this obstacle.

ASSESSING STUDENTS' CREATIVE WORK

In chapter 1, in the section on teachers' concerns, I mentioned that supporting students' creativity is a challenge for many teachers, especially those who see their role more as a traditional *music director* than as a guide, partner, or facilitator. Assessment, to the ensemble director, takes several forms including informal assessments of the ensemble's performance during rehearsal, festival-style evaluations of ensemble performance, and individual playing tests that may be tied to students' chair placement or grades. In addition, since many ensemble directors have difficulty with formal assessment, they frequently rely on assessment of non-musical characteristics such as attendance, attitude, behavior, and participation.

In the TBMI approach, students are frequently responsible for individual production of creative musical work. Evaluations in the form of tests and quizzes should be considered somewhat passé. Instead, we must examine some novel ways to assess what students do in TBMI environments. Of course, since the setting is the school classroom, attendance, participation, and behavior are important. But TBMI classes often serve as an important motivational factor for students (Dammers, 2010), and their level of focus and intensity of involvement can be quite mesmerizing, often making these other factors less necessary for assessment.

So, if behavior, attitude, participation, and attendance are less important contributors when assessing students in TBMI, how, then, can we assess the creative work they produce? The complexity of assessing this work stems from the fact that students' creative work is intended to be novel; that is, no two students will produce work that sounds the same. Comparison of one student's project to another is therefore a difficult idea, so it is probably not the best strategy to try to decide whose project is "the best." Described herein are a few strategies that I observed as those most frequently used when assessing students' creative work in TBMI classes. These strategies value the individuality of the students' work while maintaining, for the most part, the integrity of giving a grade and the responsibility of the teacher for providing that grade.

GENERAL CRITERIA FOR ASSESSING STUDENTS' ARTISTIC WORK

Before we begin examining the ways in which students' creative work in TBMI classes can be assessed, it is important to think about assessing artistic product from a broader view. It is difficult to establish criteria for assessing art in a general sense because works of art are, by nature and by necessity, individualistic. Despite the similarities that works might have due to the constraints placed on them—whether through selection of materials or media, or through teacher-made assignments—the point of engaging students in producing artistic works is for them to create something distinct and personal.

Eisner (2002) offered three general characteristics of artistic works that can be assessed. First, we can assess technical quality, which is to say that we can observe the students' mastery of the techniques employed to create the work. In the musical context, we can use this characteristic to assess whether the student has presented evidence of an understanding of musical elements and of musical thinking. Second, Eisner wrote that we can assess inventiveness, or the extent to which the student has expressed something new or different. The final criterion is aesthetic quality, meaning the extent to which the student has expressed something artistic.

The criteria Eisner offered were to be applied to arts in general; Reimer (1991) provided four elements of assessment that can be applied specifically to musical examples. Reimer did not write precisely that these criteria were to be used in judgments of students' creative work; rather, he wrote that we should apply them to evaluating "high quality examples for study and performance" (p. 331). So, while the extension of these criteria may represent something of a stretch from their original intention, they are certainly applicable as general guidelines for evaluating music. The criteria are listed here:

- *Craftsmanship*—Reimer defines craftsmanship as "the expertness by which the materials of art are molded into expressiveness" (p. 332).
- *Sensitivity*—This criterion refers to the ways in which artists express feelingful elements of their art form.
- *Imagination*—This criterion refers to the distinctness of a work of art. Works that are imaginative, Reimer wrote, "do not follow through in a straight, undeviating line of expectation but reach for the original solution, the unexpected event, the novel twist and turn, the unfolding events that pull us, as we follow them, to feel more deeply because we cannot entirely predict the outcome" (p. 335).
- *Authenticity*—Reimer wrote that authenticity has to do with "the genuineness of the artist's interaction with his materials" (p. 336).

There are parallels between the sets of criteria offered by Eisner and Reimer, and they are useful to a point. While they can serve as key guidelines for evaluating art, they do not contextualize evaluation in the setting of student musical creation, nor do they consider the technology-assisted element introduced in TBMI settings. The Eisner and Reimer suggestions, while useful broadly, do not include elements that are measurable. If we choose to assess students' creative work in TBMI, then that assessment must be based on the learning objectives for the particular lesson or project, and on the learning goals of the unit or course. Overarching goals have been stated in previous chapters, and teachers determine specific objectives relative to individual lessons.

SPECIFIC TYPES OF ASSESSMENT FOR TBMI

This section will offer suggestions for ways teachers might assess students' work in the TBMI setting. While the suggestions are not necessarily comprehensive, they are a reasonable overview of the assessment techniques teachers tend to use most commonly.

Checklists

Perhaps the most frequently reported strategy is the use of a checklist. When teachers provide assignments for their students, they typically do so with a set of minimum requirements that the students are expected to fulfill based on the objectives of the lesson or project. For example, several teachers I observed created assignments in which students were to produce a soundtrack for a movie trailer using sequencing software such as ProTools, Logic, or GarageBand. The teachers provided minimum requirements such as these:

- A certain portion of the soundtrack—often given as a percentage—must be original, composed music;
- A minimum number of sound effects must be used throughout the soundtrack;
- The project must be of a minimum length of time;
- The project must include at least one recorded speaking voice;
- The project must be exported from the software in use as a particular file type.

As students work, they can look to these guidelines to make sure they are meeting the objectives. Students' projects are considered satisfactory if they meet all of the expectations that the teacher sets. In most cases, students exceed the minimum expectations. Some teachers develop these expectations with the input of their students, providing students with a sense of ownership over the assessment of their work.

Checklists are a simple, quick way to assess whether students' work meets or does not meet minimum requirements. They are particularly appropriate or useful for assignments in which teachers have provided step-by-step instructions, and where those instructions may lead all students to achieve a similar (if not identical) result.

Some teachers I have observed are tempted to use checklists for every project or assignment they create for their students, perhaps because checklists are so convenient. However, a danger associated with checklists is that they can often be used inappropriately for projects or assignments in which teachers expect students to be creative. If teachers structure assignments well, students can create complex projects, even though those projects may not exactly address the type of minimum criteria that checklists tend to establish. Teachers should avoid turning creative assignments into assignments that adapt to a particular checklist. Good assessments address the reality of an assignment rather than the inverse.

How does this translate to an evaluation? In order to give students more targeted, detailed feedback on their work, it may be necessary to make assessments more complex.

Rubrics

Rubrics represent a more sophisticated level of assessment and are capable of providing more detailed feedback about students' work. Several teachers I interviewed stated plainly that they oppose the use of rubrics because they felt that rubrics were too restrictive or rigid to be used in assessing creative work. However, other teachers felt that rubrics were an effective means by which to provide feedback and a convenient way to produce data from which they could formulate a students' grade. There is no right or wrong approach to the use (or non-use) of rubrics; it is a determination that teachers can make on their own.

A rubric is a checklist in which the responses to each of the items may contain more variability than is typically found in a checklist. Those listed earlier are simply "yes/no" responses—either the student meets the criteria or not. Consider the same movie trailer project described previously and how a rubric might be constructed to assess it. In the checklist form, the first criterion read: A certain portion of the soundtrack must be original, composed music. Note that, in this assignment, creating original music of a certain length is a learning objective. In a rubric, this element would be reformed into a response with greater variation, as in Table 7.1.

In Table 7.1, the teacher can select the box that is appropriate for the project and in doing so assign a particular number of points. Notice that this element does not ask the teacher to draw judgments on the *quality* of the music that the student composed, only to acknowledge that it is present. Another element of the rubric may focus on the quality or some other characteristic of the music, as in Table 7.2.

Here, the teacher can evaluate both the mood of the original music and the techniques the student used to achieve that mood. Since these

Table 7.1 A RUBRIC ELEMENT

The project contains evidence of original, composed music.

4	3	2	1
60% or more of the music is original, composed by the student	40–60% of the music is original, composed by the student	20–40% of the music is original, composed by the student	Less than 20% of the music is original

Table 7.2 A RUBRIC ELEMENT WITH QUALITY JUDGMENTS

Musical mood and instrumentation/orchestration

4	3	2	1
Mood of the original music reflects the video; instrumentation/ orchestration techniques are appropriate throughout the trailer.	Mood of the original music usually reflects the video; instrumentation/ orchestration techniques are usually appropriate.	Mood of the original music sometimes reflects the video; instrumentation/ orchestration techniques are sometimes appropriate.	Mood of the original music rarely or never reflects the video; instrumentation/orchestration techniques are not appropriate.

elements are often somewhat linked, it might be appropriate to evaluate them together.

As you can tell, some types of objectives are more easily assessed with rubrics than others. The elements I have described here have a logical variability, but not all elements can be laid out so neatly. For example, some teachers like to impose a minimum number of tracks that students should use in a sequencing project. Doing so might represent the effort that a student puts into a project, as in Table 7.3.

Table 7.3 A RUBRIC ELEMENT REFLECTING EFFORT TOWARD A PARTICULAR CRITERION

Minimum number of tracks.

4	3	2	1
The student has used a minimum of 6 tracks in the project.	The student has used 4 or 5 tracks in the project.	The student has used 2 or 3 tracks in the project.	The student has used only 1 track, or has not completed the project.

Does this seem a reasonable way to evaluate the minimum criteria of using six tracks in a project? Yes and no. This rubric element awards the student *maximum* credit for putting forth *only the required* amount of work. Some teachers who use rubrics design them so that students who do the required amount of work receive acceptable credit, but then allow additional credit for students who exceed the minimum expectation, as in Table 7.4.

Table 7.4 REVISED CRITERION RUBRIC ELEMENT

Minimum number of tracks.

4	3	2	1
The student has used more than 6 tracks in the project.	The student has used exactly 6 tracks in the project.	The student has used 3 to 5 tracks in the project.	The student has used 1 or 2 tracks, or has not completed the project.

Here are steps teachers should take if they decide they want to use a rubric to assess students' project work:

1. Determine the elements of the project to be assessed;
2. Determine the scale by which these elements will be assessed (the examples given use a four-point scale, but other options are certainly possible);
3. Determine the descriptors for each element of the rubric, and for each point value;
4. Create a printed or electronic version of the rubric (spreadsheet programs such as Excel and Numbers are particularly useful for this);
5. Distribute the rubric to the students prior to the beginning of work on the project. This will help the students understand how their work will be assessed.
6. When grading, stick carefully to the rubric you have designed. Note any flaws that make it difficult to use so that you can modify it for the next time you use it.

Electronic Portfolios

Many projects that students produce in TBMI classes result in some sort of digital artifact. Compositions may take the form of notated scores, digital audio, or MIDI files; soundtrack projects might be completed videos with original music; improvisations may be recorded. Regardless of the type of project students are engaged in, there is usually some logical and efficient way to capture the project as a digital artifact or set of artifacts.

As students progress through their work in TBMI classes, and perhaps in other classes, artifacts represent their development. Artifacts provide a view of their growth as musicians, as students, and as people. Electronic portfolios can be assembled to provide evidence of the progress that students have made and to create a place for them to reflect on past work. Depending on the purpose of the portfolio, students may include only their best work, or they might include all of the work they have done.

Electronic portfolios can be created in many ways. In their simplest form, a portfolio can be a CD or DVD that contains students' project work. In more complex forms, students can develop websites that feature their work. Online systems for portfolio creation are also available. The method of electronic portfolio creation you choose for your student should reflect the level of importance you place on portability of the portfolio, storage capacity, technical knowledge (which can be part of the TBMI curriculum), and financial expense.

Project Sharing

Another very common technique for assessing student creative work is engaging students in providing feedback for each other. Project sharing is most frequently done at a point in time when all or most of the students have finished a project, although it is also possible to hold a session like this during the process of completing a project, in which case peer critique would be used to inform the completion of the project. The members of the class "take a break" from the intensity of creative project work to listen to or watch each other's work and provide critical commentary about what their peers have produced.

Two kinds of project sharing were seen most frequently during my observations. First and most frequent was in-class project sharing. As described previously, this is a group activity during which students present their work to the rest of the class. Often, teachers will give students a chance to talk about their work before they play it for the class; this gives the student the opportunity to discuss points of inspiration, challenges, and how those challenges were overcome. Students appreciate hearing about clever techniques their classmates may have discovered to move past obstacles.

The second kind of project sharing I observed was online sharing. Several teachers hosted websites where students were able to post their work. Students could listen to or watch one another's projects on their own or outside of class time. Many teachers prefer the discussions that are generated by sharing projects in class, but some prefer the level of detail and attention students bring to feedback when they can listen to their peers' work several times outside of class.

While teachers should provide feedback for the student presenting work, students should be engaged in constructively providing critical feedback for their peers. This represents an evaluation activity, which, according to Bloom's Taxonomy, is the highest order learning activity in which students can engage. For several reasons, however, this is where the process becomes challenging. Students may feel threatened by critical feedback from their peers, and they may feel hurt or insulted if that feedback is negative. Students may not feel comfortable providing feedback for their friends. They may also not be willing to engage deeply in this kind of discussion because it is not the normal kind of activity they do in other educational experiences.

An excellent set of guidelines for project sharing sessions was offered by the noted dance and choreography pedagogue Liz Lerman and her partner John Borstel in their short book *Critical Response Process: A Method for Getting Useful Feedback on Anything You Make, from Dance to Dessert* (2003). According to Lerman and Borstel, the feedback process involves three primary roles: (1) the artist is the person responsible for the creation of the work (although in collaborative work, it would be possible for several people to qualify as "the artist"); (2) the responders are the people who listen to, watch, read, or otherwise engage with the work for the purpose of providing feedback; and (3) the facilitator is the person responsible for "initiating each step and managing the transition to the next, keeping the Process on track, and assuring that the artist and responders all understand the guidelines and get the most out of them" (p. 15). Following the presentation of the work, the Process itself includes four steps, described here:

1. Statements of Meaning—the facilitator asks the responders to address ways in which the work is meaningful to them. She asks questions about how the work is unique, distinctive, or compelling. This step is intended to set the stage for the artist and to help the responders convey the aesthetic power of the work.
2. Artist as Questioner—here the artist asks specific questions of the responders as to their thoughts about the work. It is important that the artist's questions are designed to focus the work rather than to facilitate general opinions.
3. Neutral Questions from Responders—in step three, the responders question the artist about the work. Lerman and Borstel provide extensive instructions about the formation of "neutral" questions—those that do not contain veiled opinions or judgments—to gain "informational

or factual" (p. 20) understanding of the work. They provide an applicable example: the question "Do you really understand what this song is about?" contains an embedded opinion that the composer, in fact, does not comprehend the meaning of the song. An alternate form of the question, stated in neutral fashion, would be "How did you prepare your interpretation of the song?" (p. 23).

4. Permissioned Opinions—in the final stage of the Process, respondents provide opinions about the work; however, they are permitted to do so only after the artist agrees to it. Responders are to introduce their opinions with language such as, "I have a thought about the chord structure. Can I offer that opinion?" The artist has the right to disallow the opinion but usually agrees to hear it.

In the project sharing sessions I observed for this book, many of the intricacies of the Lerman and Borstel's Process were left out. Specifically, the idea behind Step 2, in which the artist is able to question the responders, is noticeably absent from most sessions. Also, the notion that opinions expressed by the responders should be somehow *permissioned* by the artist is a distinguishing characteristic of this process that is often missing from sharing sessions in TBMI classes.

Analytical discussions such as those that happen when teachers ask students to provide critical feedback are cognitively and socially demanding. In order to make these types of discussions productive, teachers should model appropriate behavior and acceptable language. It is up to the teacher to set the mood of the conversation. Some schools and districts place tremendous value on the process of critical peer feedback and train their students in ways to contribute to such conversations. Here are some techniques that arose from observations of teachers who lead sharing sessions particularly well:

- Train students in providing "warm" and "cool" feedback. Warm feedback is a positive comment. Cool feedback is more critical without being harsh.
- Ask students to frame their comments from a personal perspective. A comment might start, "If I were writing this piece, I would ..."
- Use your own work as a project example and let students make comments about it. This will allow them to practice providing feedback without involving the elements of peer pressure that come along with assessing their classmates' work.
- Encourage *specific* comments. Discourage students from making comments that are too general or apply to an entire project. Focus comments on a specific moment or element within a project.

- Make electronic comments identifiable rather than allowing anonymous comments. This helps students remember that they are accountable for the content of their comments.
- Encourage students to comment on each other's work right from the start. Young students are capable of voicing their opinion, what they like and do not like. Even though they may not have the tact of older students or feel the same intensity of social pressures, young students should practice providing feedback, as it is a learned skill.
- The length of comments will vary. Some teachers are frustrated when students provide comments that are not long or substantive enough. Each teacher has to determine how to handle this. Some teachers who set up online discussions for project sharing simply do not give students credit for comments that do not meet certain minimum standards. Students who are given opportunities to comment repeatedly and who are shown that their comments are valued will ultimately provide substantial feedback.

ASSESSING STUDENT WORK—CONCLUSION

Assessment is an important part of the role of teachers in any educational scenario, but we should be cautious about letting assessment drive our pedagogical decisions. Consider that, especially in the TBMI context where student creativity is paramount, it may not be necessary to assess every piece of student work. Students need to feel comfortable experimenting, revising, and revising again, and sometimes they need to do so without the threat of a formal assessment looming over them. The notion that subjects and assignments that are assessed are somehow more important or valuable than those that are not is an antiquated view that, evidence has shown (Pederson, 2007), is simply not reality. When we provide students with opportunities to work creatively without impending formal assessments, their creativity may flourish.

Furthermore, the nature of formal assessment may not match well with the types of creative work we ask of students in TBMI contexts. Informal assessments, or what Eisner (1985) called "qualitative assessments" can be equally as effective in guiding students toward their own brand of success. Eisner stated:

> Educators working in schools have become increasingly conscious of something that football coaches, teachers of violin, and voice coaches have known for a long time: if you want to improve the way people perform, paying attention to the final score or to the performance on opening night is insufficient; it is important

to see how the game is played during practice sessions and how rehearsals go before the curtain rises. Qualitative methods of evaluation are in large measure designed to focus upon the processes of educational practice in order to provide practitioners and others with information that cannot be secured from the scores that standardized achievement tests and other forms of summative evaluation provide. (Eisner, 1985, p. 179)

It is possible that the only valid way to evaluate the creative work of a student is to compare it to work that student has done previously. This idea accounts for differences between individual students and may provide us with the truest measure of progress from one creative work to the next (Eisner, 1966).

If we view the student's work form a long-term perspective, it becomes clear that what we now regard as the products of that work are really a part of a larger process. They are markers along a journey; the end is also the beginning. The point here is that what counts as process and what counts as product depends on how we look at it. (Eisner, 2002, p. 181)

This section has discussed a few techniques for assessing students' creative work: checklists, rubrics, and peer feedback. Each of these has its advantages and disadvantages, appropriate and inappropriate uses. In reality, most teachers I have observed use many kinds of assessments and move fluidly between them. Students are assessed in so many ways throughout their school day that they are typically comfortable with whatever type of assessment teachers decide to use. Bauer (2010) provided interesting ideas for using technological tools to assess students' musical skills and for helping teachers to manage musical assessment. Providing students with multiple types of feedback will make more likely the possibility that that feedback proves to be helpful and contribute to their progress.

ASSESSING TEACHERS' TPACK AND WORK

Recall the concept of Technological, Pedagogical, and Content Knowledge (TPACK) introduced in chapter 3. TPACK can be viewed both as a way to make teachers aware of the complexity of technology-based teaching and as a means of assessing their achievement when doing so. Its validity as a way to measure teachers' readiness to teach in technology-based settings is still under review. Lux (2010) conducted a thorough review of the concepts that compose TPACK and found that in most cases, it is a fairly reliable way to measure the ways in which teachers understand what is involved with technology-based instruction. If we rely on the measurement instruments that have been developed (Archambault & Crippen, 2009; Lux, 2010; Schmidt et al., 2009), then we can reasonably accept that some teachers are better prepared to teach technology-based music classes than others. It is important to know where potential TBMI teachers stand and how prepared they are, just as it is important to know the level of preparation of music teachers in other settings.

Coursework in which teachers are prepared for the TBMI environment is inadequate because it rarely includes a pedagogical emphasis. Caution should therefore be taken against placing too much weight on tests of preparation or of "TPACK aptitude." Instead, we should focus our efforts on assessing the work of teachers in the TBMI context, and doing so in a way that may help them to improve their teaching.

The conundrum that exists is a product mostly of the newness of TBMI. Even in circumstances where the mode of musical instruction is more traditional, such as an ensemble or a general music class, supervisors and administrators often are unprepared to assess teachers' work. Add to that the complex layer of basing music instruction on technology, and teacher assessment becomes a much thornier task.

We can look to the TPACK model for guidance as to what comprises an excellent TBMI teacher. The model demonstrates that there is overlap between technological knowledge, content knowledge, and pedagogical knowledge. While the distinct forms of knowledge are necessary for teachers' development, it is the intersections of these types of knowledge that are most intriguing. In a sense, the amount or extent of overlap of these three elements yields a measure of preparation. Consider a revision of the model as shown in Figure 7.1, in which the three types of knowledge exist, but do not intersect.

In Figure 7.1, we see a depiction of a teacher who possesses all of the requisite types of knowledge to be assessed, but has not drawn connections between them. The teacher who possesses technological knowledge and content knowledge, but has not yet wholly integrated them into her teaching would not be considered one who has mastered technology-based music instruction. Recall the "topography" of technological integration discussed in chapter 1; this teacher has likely not progressed past the technical basin of integration.

In Figure 7.2, the teacher in question has begun to connect the three distinct types of knowledge to create more closely related sets of knowledge. This movement toward developing the intersections depicted in the original model suggests that the teacher is more advanced, recognizes the

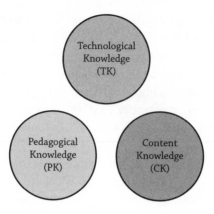

Figure 7.1
TPACK Elements without Intersections

power and sophistication of technology-based instruction, and adapts her processes to it. As teachers grow more accustomed to and recognize the influence of the components of the TPACK model on each other, their level of mastery improves. Eventually, the three components of the model will overlap, indicating full awareness of their relationships.

Assessment of TBMI teachers should be considered in at least two ways, both suggested in previous research (Fenstermacher & Richardson, 2005). First, *successful* teaching is teaching in which students learn what the teacher intends for them to learn. Second, *good* teaching implies success but also encompasses teaching that is "morally defensible, and grounded in shared conceptions of reasonableness" (Fenstermacher & Richardson, 2005, p. 189). *Good* teaching means that students are achieving the intended outcomes and are doing so in ways that lead to skills generally accepted as important

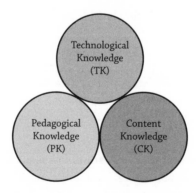

Figure 7.2
TPACK Elements with Recognition of Relationships

and that will be useful in the future, and the teaching methods are positive, harmless, and promote a sense of connectedness to the world.

These concepts of *successful* teaching and *good* teaching can be extrapolated to TBMI. *Successful* teaching in the technology-based music setting will lead students to know the functions of software and hardware. Students who are the product of *successful* TBMI understand how to function in the music technology ecosystem and will be enthusiastic consumers of technology-based music. *Good* TBMI moves the students' experiences several steps beyond this description. *Good* TBMI provides students with opportunities to engage deeply with the technologies and to explore their creative potential when doing so. Providing students with a creative outlet and enabling them to explore their abilities to produce creative work appeals to the vast capabilities of music software and hardware, and is, I would suggest, the "morally defensible" way to approach technology-based music instruction.

TEACHER ASSESSMENT GUIDELINES

Neither the TPACK model nor the topographical model from chapter 1 provides us with quantitative means to measure TBMI teachers' work. Quantification must, by necessity, be left to the various instruments and forms that state and local boards of education use to assess teachers. The role of the TBMI teacher should be to work cooperatively with the administrator or supervisor responsible for assessing their performance to establish reasonable and clear criteria for doing so. In a sense, TBMI teachers must educate their supervisors so that they can recognize the characteristics of good and successful teaching in the TBMI context. These characteristics may include, but are certainly not limited to the following:

- Demonstrated knowledge of musical content in the technological arena
- Demonstrated knowledge of technological content and processes
- Appropriate support of students' creative processes
- Appropriate balance between direct instruction and student exploration
- Effectiveness of lesson/unit planning, including selection of musical and technological materials and effective pacing of lesson implementation
- Appropriate communication with students as to promote an understanding of expectations (for project work)

If we view students' creative products as one of the end-states of TBMI, then it is extremely difficult to tie the assessment of teachers' work to the achievement of their students. As stated previously, the truest form of assessment of creative work is comparison of an individual student's work to her prior work. This suggests that there are few normative means of assessing student work, and it is therefore very difficult to use student work as an accurate depiction of teachers' successes or failures. While several states are currently relying on students' achievement scores to provide measurement of music teachers' work, *proxy measurement is inappropriate for music teachers in general, and even more so for TBMI teachers who hold among their primary responsibilities the encouragement of students' diversity of thinking.*

When teachers and their supervisors can form a shared understanding of the characteristics of good and successful teaching within the TBMI context, assessments of teaching are more likely to result in useful information that will help improve the teaching and learning process.

ASSESSING PROGRAM FIT AND NEEDS

Teachers must constantly assess the fit of technology in their programs. We should frequently ask ourselves several questions when making technology a substantial part of our curriculum:

1. What are the traditions of the school environment, and do they support TBMI?
2. Is the music curriculum robust enough to make TBMI a significant part of students' musical experiences?
3. Do faculty have enough technological and pedagogical knowledge to ensure that technology-based music classes will be done well?

SCHOOL TRADITION AND SUPPORT

Band, chorus, orchestra, and elementary general music have been the traditional means by which students engage with music in schools for many decades. In school environments where these traditional modes of musical activity are dominant, it may be difficult to venture into the world of TBMI. While some teachers and some students might have an interest in technology-based music, the school environment might not support it. Teachers should ask themselves whether expansion of the music department to include technology is the smartest choice for their circumstance. Unfortunately, in some cases it might not be. While music departments should aim to be as comprehensive as possible, they should do so within the limits of what they can do well. If the support for expansion into, or reliance on technology does not exist in the school tradition, teachers can either fight to change the tradition or they can focus on tried and true methods of music teaching.

Larger Curriculum Issues

In speaking with secondary teachers who are engaged in TBMI, perhaps the single greatest obstacle they expressed relates to the musical skills that their students bring to their classes. In most cases, these classes do not have requirements that students have musical experience, nor do they have listed prerequisite classes that would provide formal musical training. If the larger curriculum does not create a situation in which all students are required to take music classes, TBMI teachers might be "stuck" with circumstances in which the students in their classes are not adequately prepared for the kinds of musical activities they plan for their students.

I observed several remedies to this situation:

- Some TBMI teachers build time into their technology-based classes to teach basic musical skills. Many teachers include some form of keyboard training in their classes, especially for those students who have no performance experience. While most teachers feel that time to do this is limited, they typically say that the benefits of including experiences in piano, percussion instruments, and vocal training provide their students with the performance experiences they need to be creative in the technological world.
- Some TBMI teachers work closely with guidance counselors to make sure that students who want to take technology-based music classes have some musical background. While this is not possible in all schools, it is a successful strategy in others.
- Some TBMI teachers do require previous formal music classes as prerequisites. These classes may or may not be performance classes; some teachers, for example, require a semester of music theory.

Faculty Readiness

Perhaps the greatest obstacle, and the issue we must assess with the greatest integrity and truthfulness, is the readiness of teachers who intend to teach TBMI classes. As stated earlier in this book, most sophisticated teachers believe that their technological knowledge (knowledge of the software, hardware, and techniques related to music technology) needs to be relatively advanced in order to plan effective, meaningful lessons for their students. Teachers should be cautioned against diving into full-scale TBMI classes before they are prepared to do so. They will need knowledge of several pieces of software, comfort in the lab environment, and a well-developed, sequential curriculum.

If teachers are eager to make technology-based music part of their repertoire immediately, before they are fully prepared to do so, perhaps the best strategy is to use technology for a particular unit or set of lessons within a traditional music class. I have observed several teachers in the general music setting who have adopted this strategy quite successfully. This is also a way to integrate technology into performance classes where it might not otherwise exist.

Testing in schools dominates public and political discourse. Measuring the success of individual students and schools—not to mention the success of teachers using those measures as an inappropriate proxy—determines the current course of educational decisions. It is possible that technology-based music suggests a "canon" of knowledge that could be tested. Much of this knowledge would relate to software terms and functionality. Certainly there is nothing wrong with measuring what our students retain from TBMI classes in terms of procedural knowledge. In fact, in the professional music production world, successful careers often depend on deep knowledge of software and hardware that is accessible "on the fly." However, in professional music production, the ultimate test of success is the sound of the product created by applying that knowledge.

Chapter 7 has included ideas and strategies for assessment of students' work in TBMI, for assessment of teachers' work, and for general program issues. Embedded in the idea of assessment is the need for accountability, typically related to standards. This will be the subject of chapter 8.

ITEMS FOR DISCUSSION

1. Undergraduate and graduate level classes often use several types of assessment. What are some outstanding assessments you have seen in music technology classes? In other music education classes? How do those assessments help students improve?
2. Chapter 7 included some discussion about tests and quizzes in TBMI classes. Do you think tests and quizzes are appropriate in the TBMI context? Why or why not?
3. With a colleague or small group, develop an assignment for a composition that might be expected of a seventh grade student in a TBMI class. Then, use the guidelines discussed in chapter 7 to develop a rubric for grading that assignment. When you have finished, discuss the most challenging aspects of creating the rubric.
4. Most students, at one point or another in their school career, have been involved in a sharing session. Think about your experiences in a sharing session. What was the context of the session? How did the teacher structure the session? Was it helpful? How might you have done it differently if you had been the teacher?
5. If you become responsible for teaching a TBMI class, on what criteria would you want your teaching assessed? Do you think current teacher

evaluation practices are fair when applied to TBMI teachers? Why or why not?

6. In previous chapters, we have seen examples of teachers using listening activities in TBMI. Do you think listening should be assessed? If so, how might you do it?

CHAPTER 8

Accountability Concerns

With the advent of technology-based music instruction, we are at an important juncture in terms of standards and accountability. To date, there are no sets of standards that directly address the ways in which TBMI teachers and students work, and therefore there is a lack of clarity as to how we are accountable to the larger educational culture. Several sets of standards exist that come close; they address either the musical *or* the technological portions of TBMI, but not both. Others address teachers' roles *or* students' roles, but not both. In this chapter, we will examine relevant sets of standards and explore how they imply accountability for TBMI teachers and students.

NAFME STANDARDS

In 1994, the Music Educators National Conference (now the National Association for Music Education) released a document outlining the National Standards for Music Education, in coordination with similar standards in theater, art, and dance. The nine music standards from 1994 were the following:

1. Singing, alone and with others, a varied repertoire of music.
2. Performing on instruments, alone and with others, a varied repertoire of music.
3. Improvising melodies, variations, and accompaniments.
4. Composing and arranging music within specified guidelines.
5. Reading and notating music.
6. Listening to, analyzing, and describing music.
7. Evaluating music and music performances.

8. Understanding relationships between music, the other arts, and disciplines outside the arts.
9. Understanding music in relation to history and culture.

The NAfME standards suggest curricula that are distributed among performance, musical creativity, and connections between music and context. These are noble goals for which teachers should strive. The NAfME standards are widely accepted, and many teachers refer to them as benchmarks to assess the completeness of curriculum. In no way do the NAfME standards suggest that musical learning should be achieved through technology, nor do they contain suggestions about *how* students should meet *any* of them. In this way, the shapers of the NAfME standards are to be commended because the standards are flexible enough that they can be addressed in ways teachers see fit. Therefore, the standards passively suggest that technology-based music instruction is as valid a means of music learning as are other forms.

Traditional music teaching and learning environments, particularly ensembles, are well suited to address several of the NAfME standards. In most ensemble experiences, lessons are focused on singing, playing instruments, improvising, reading and notating, listening to, and evaluating music. Ensemble directors learn to support these skills through their teaching, and they often do so very well. The other standards are addressed less often and with less proficiency. Technology lends itself to processes of composing and to studying information about the connections between music, media, history, and culture, and helps to facilitate students' experiences in the roles of composer, improviser, and musicologist.

TI:ME AREAS OF TECHNOLOGY COMPETENCY

The Technology Institute for Music Educators (TI:ME) was founded in the mid-1990s by a group of music education technology experts. The mission of the organization is to assist music educators in applying technology to improve teaching and learning in music.[1] TI:ME operationalizes this mission through workshop classes for teachers and with professional conferences that feature presentations by teachers and industry representatives.

Among the important efforts from TI:ME is the development of the "Areas of Technology Competency" listed here. More detail about these

1. For more information, see ti-me.org.

areas is available from TI:ME's website and from several books the organization has published (e.g., Watson, 2005; Rudolph et al., 2005).

1. Electronic Musical Instruments
   a. Keyboards
   b. Controllers
   c. Synthesizers and Samplers
   d. Ensemble Performance
2. Music Production
   a. Data Types
   b. MIDI
   c. Digital Audio
   d. Processes
   e. Looping
   f. Sequencing
   g. Signal Processing
   h. Sound Design
3. Music Notation Software
4. Technology-Assisted Learning
   a. Instructional Software
   b. Accompaniment/Practice Tools
   c. Internet-based Learning
5. Multimedia
   a. Multimedia Authoring
   b. Web Pages
   c. Presentations
   d. Movie/DVD
   e. Digital Image Capturing
   f. Internet
   g. Electronic Portfolios
6. Productivity Tools, Classroom and Lab Management
   a. Productivity Tools
   b. Computer Systems
   c. Lab Management Systems
   d. Networks

TI:ME instructors provide training for teachers in how to use technology applications. Historically the organization has only marginally considered helping teachers translate their own knowledge of technology into strong pedagogical technique for use with their students. Also, little attention has been paid to how to engage students with the technology directly, as opposed to reserving technology primarily for teachers' uses (as suggested by the topographical model in chapter 1). In the past few years, however, the organization has begun to rewrite its curriculum materials to reflect the emerging importance of pedagogical technique. This shift recognizes the increasing sophistication of teachers in using technology and the timeliness of the study of music technology pedagogy.

ISTE/NETS

The International Society for Technology in Education (ISTE) promotes the importance of technology use across all school disciplines. The Society has a massive conference each summer for teachers, administrators, and IT professionals who work in education. The research and practitioner components of ISTE have become very closely tied to the notion of TPACK as a means to recognize the distinct yet overlapping types of knowledge teachers must have to effectively teach with technology across all subjects.

The National Educational Technology Standards (NETS) were developed in 2007. ISTE is one of the few organizations to recognize that technology standards and the skills and knowledge they imply are quite different for teachers and for students. Therefore, ISTE maintains both the NETS for Students (NETS•S) and the NETS for Teachers (NETS•T). These two sets of standards are listed below.

NETS for Students (NETS•S)

1. Creativity and Innovation[2]

   Students demonstrate creative thinking, construct knowledge, and develop innovative products and processes using technology. Students:

   a. apply existing knowledge to generate new ideas, products, or processes.

   b. create original works as a means of personal or group expression.

   c. use models and simulations to explore complex systems and issues.

   d. identify trends and forecast possibilities.

---

2. These standards are from National Educational Technology Standards for Students, Second Edition © 2007 ISTE ® (International Society for Technology in Education), www.iste.org. All rights reserved. Reprinted with permission.

2. Communication and Collaboration

   Students use digital media and environments to communicate and work collaboratively, including at a distance, to support individual learning and contribute to the learning of others. Students:

   a. interact, collaborate, and publish with peers, experts, or others employing a variety of digital environments and media.

   b. communicate information and ideas effectively to multiple audiences using a variety of media and formats.

   c. develop cultural understanding and global awareness by engaging with learners of other cultures.

   d. contribute to project teams to produce original works or solve problems.

3. Research and Information Fluency

   Students apply digital tools to gather, evaluate, and use information. Students:

   a. plan strategies to guide inquiry.

   b. locate, organize, analyze, evaluate, synthesize, and ethically use information from a variety of sources and media.

   c. evaluate and select information sources and digital tools based on the appropriateness to specific tasks.

   d. process data and report results.

4. Critical Thinking, Problem Solving, and Decision Making

   Students use critical thinking skills to plan and conduct research, manage projects, solve problems, and make informed decisions using appropriate digital tools and resources. Students:

   a. identify and define authentic problems and significant questions for investigation.

   b. plan and manage activities to develop a solution or complete a project.

   c. collect and analyze data to identify solutions and/or make informed decisions.

   d. use multiple processes and diverse perspectives to explore alternative solutions.

5. Digital Citizenship

   Students understand human, cultural, and societal issues related to technology and practice legal and ethical behavior. Students:

   a. advocate and practice safe, legal, and responsible use of information and technology.

   b. exhibit a positive attitude toward using technology that supports collaboration, learning, and productivity.

   c. demonstrate personal responsibility for lifelong learning.

   d. exhibit leadership for digital citizenship.

6. Technology Operations and Concepts
Students demonstrate a sound understanding of technology concepts, systems, and operations. Students:
a. understand and use technology systems.
b. select and use applications effectively and productively.
c. troubleshoot systems and applications.
d. transfer current knowledge to learning of new technologies.

NETS for Teachers (NETS•T)

1. Facilitate and Inspire Student Learning and Creativity[3]
Teachers use their knowledge of subject matter, teaching and learning, and technology to facilitate experiences that advance student learning, creativity, and innovation in both face-to-face and virtual environments. Teachers:
a. promote, support, and model creative and innovative thinking and inventiveness.
b. engage students in exploring real-world issues and solving authentic problems using digital tools and resources.
c. promote student reflection using collaborative tools to reveal and clarify students' conceptual understanding and thinking, planning, and creative processes.
d. model collaborative knowledge construction by engaging in learning with students, colleagues, and others in face-to-face and virtual environments.
2. Design and Develop Digital-Age Learning Experiences and Assessments
Teachers design, develop, and evaluate authentic learning experiences and assessments incorporating contemporary tools and resources to maximize content learning in context and to develop the knowledge, skills, and attitudes identified in the NETS•S. Teachers:
a. design or adapt relevant learning experiences that incorporate digital tools and resources to promote student learning and creativity.
b. develop technology-enriched learning environments that enable all students to pursue their individual curiosities and become active participants in setting their own educational goals, managing their own learning, and assessing their own progress.

3. These standards are from National Educational Technology Standards for Teachers, Second Edition © 2008 ISTE ® (International Society for Technology in Education), www.iste.org. All rights reserved. Reprinted with permission.

c. customize and personalize learning activities to address students' diverse learning styles, working strategies, and abilities using digital tools and resources.

d. provide students with multiple and varied formative and summative assessments aligned with content and technology standards and use resulting data to inform learning and teaching.

3. Model Digital-Age Work and Learning

   Teachers exhibit knowledge, skills, and work processes representative of an innovative professional in a global and digital society. Teachers:

   a. demonstrate fluency in technology systems and the transfer of current knowledge to new technologies and situations.

   b. collaborate with students, peers, parents, and community members using digital tools and resources to support student success and innovation.

   c. communicate relevant information and ideas effectively to students, parents, and peers using a variety of digital-age media and formats.

   d. model and facilitate effective use of current and emerging digital tools to locate, analyze, evaluate, and use information resources to support research and learning.

4. Promote and Model Digital Citizenship and Responsibility

   Teachers understand local and global societal issues and responsibilities in an evolving digital culture and exhibit legal and ethical behavior in their professional practices. Teachers:

   a. advocate, model, and teach safe, legal, and ethical use of digital information and technology, including respect for copyright, intellectual property, and the appropriate documentation of sources.

   b. address the diverse needs of all learners by using learner-centered strategies and providing equitable access to appropriate digital tools and resources.

   c. promote and model digital etiquette and responsible social interactions related to the use of technology and information.

   d. develop and model cultural understanding and global awareness by engaging with colleagues and students of other cultures using digital-age communication and collaboration tools.

5. Engage in Professional Growth and Leadership

   Teachers continuously improve their professional practice, model lifelong learning, and exhibit leadership in their school and professional community by promoting and demonstrating the effective use of digital tools and resources. Teachers:

   a. participate in local and global learning communities to explore creative applications of technology to improve student learning.

b. exhibit leadership by demonstrating a vision of technology infusion, participating in shared decision making and community building, and developing the leadership and technology skills of others.

c. evaluate and reflect on current research and professional practice on a regular basis to make effective use of existing and emerging digital tools and resources in support of student learning.

d. contribute to the effectiveness, vitality, and self-renewal of the teaching profession and of their school and community.

An additional, recent development from ISTE is the NETS for Administrators (NETS•A), which addresses issues of digital leadership and citizenship, and improvement of the digital learning systems for that group of educational stakeholders.

Clearly, the NETS•T and NETS•S are not tied to a specific subject matter. In fact, awareness of these sets of standards is quite limited in the music community. Adoption of these standards is more commonplace in disciplines such as mathematics, science, social studies, and technology education. The lack of direct reference within the standards to music or the arts makes it difficult for music teachers to recognize their value. However, the NETS imply that technological means of educating students can cut across disciplinary boundaries, and that students and teachers should adopt certain dispositions toward the uses of technology for learning regardless of discipline.

Among the most important elements of the NETS are references to digital citizenship. This term implies the safe and ethical uses of technology. In the NETS•S, the expressed expectation that students should "use multiple processes and diverse perspectives to explore alternative solutions" relates quite directly to the creative uses of technology for music composition and analysis. The entire first NETS•S standard implies the importance of creative uses of technologies for the generation of new and innovative works of thought. So, while the NETS might not be directly related to music or the arts, they clearly support the larger goals we hold for our students and provide additional justification for those goals.

As the music education community moves more toward technology-based methods of instruction, it is important that we begin to weave the NETS into our thinking. They are widely accepted standards that appropriately address the roles of both teachers and students engaged in technology-based teaching and learning; their adoption in music education will lend legitimacy to our practice. Music teaching that acknowledges the NETS will allow our students to connect the technology-based work they do in music class to that which they do in other subject areas, and it will allow TBMI teachers to craft lessons and curricula that are viewed as valid by those who are less informed about music as a discipline of study.

21ST CENTURY SKILLS MAP

A recent entry to the field of standards is the 21st Century Skills Map, a product of the Partnership for 21st Century Skills.[4] Embedded among the documents and frameworks created by this organization is the Map for learning in the arts. The Map contains a group of 13 statements of arts-related outcomes and suggestions for strategies at the fourth, eighth, and twelfth grade levels that might help students to achieve those outcomes, many of which reference technology. Unlike the other sets of standards that have been discussed in this chapter, the 21st Century Skills Map includes those specific strategies, that might facilitate, or at least suggest, specific means by which teachers can design learning experiences. A particular strength of the Map document is that the outcomes it includes leave room for students to be creative and to achieve open-ended goals; this encouragement of creative work, of course, is a hallmark of the type of freedom students should be given in technology-based music classes.

The risk of including specific strategies in a document like this is that teachers might feel limited to those types of strategies. The Map does not include suggestions for assessing students' achievement. Also, much of the justification for the document's creation, provided within the document itself, is based on students' future participation in business and global communications rather than future participation in the arts themselves. The 21st Century Skills Map in the arts is still new, and the impact it will have remains to be seen.

IMPLICATIONS OF THE NAFME, TI:ME, AND ISTE STANDARDS FOR TBMI

If we examine these sets of standards individually, we can establish a few short summary statements:

1. The NAfME Standards, while widely relied upon for evaluation and curriculum design purposes, are viewed with skepticism by critics and do not imply any specific type of music learning environment.

---

4. Further information about the Partnership for 21st Century Skills, as well as the full Map document, are available at the organization's website: www.p21.org.

2. The TI:ME Areas of Technology Competency, while the most directly related to TBMI, are focused on skill development for teachers and do not fully form any sort of pedagogical approach.
3. The ISTE Standards (NETS•S and NETS•T) are accepted in many disciplines and address both teacher and student roles, but they are not directly related to music. Certain elements of the NETS are more applicable in musical contexts than others, but their general approach to ideas such as creativity and digital citizenship are undoubtedly important.

A true synthesis of these standards is not possible, nor is it appropriate, because the standards address different—though overlapping—constituents. No set of standards exists that truly encapsulates all of the implications of TBMI, in terms of the teacher knowledge, content knowledge (both musical and technological), and digital citizenship issues that are critical to successful technology-based music instruction. The question that naturally follows is this: Are TBMI teachers and their curricula therefore subject to assessment according to all three sets of standards? The unfortunate, short answer is yes. Until a set of standards is established that accurately depicts what TBMI teachers do, these sets of standards are the de facto instruments for defining our roles and guiding our curricular designs. While teachers might be tempted to pick and choose which standards they want to address, the truth is that curricula should account for as many of them as possible in order to increase our accountability to the expectations of the field.

SUMMARY OF CHAPTER 8

While no particular set of standards exists that fully encapsulates the ideas or outcomes of TBMI, music teachers should be aware of the dangers that would accompany creating one. In subjects and disciplines outside of the arts, the relationship between the development of standards and standardized testing is undeniable. Standardized curricula establish an environment in which every student can be tested on the same information and processes. This book certainly does not advocate "cookie cutter" technology-based music classes. On the contrary, technology-based music classes should address a reasonably similar set of skills while allowing students maximum room to apply those skills in creative ways.

In this chapter we have explored the standards that exist that may be applicable to TBMI and may govern some of the lesson design and assessment that occurs in TBMI classrooms. In chapter 9, we will move toward the implications of all of these practices on the preparation of teachers to work in TBMI environments.

ITEMS FOR DISCUSSION

1. The NAfME standards have been in use for some time now and have had impact on many areas of music education. Do you think the NAfME standards have changed the ways you have taught or learned music? In what ways?
2. Professional organizations can be important resources for development throughout one's career. Examine the TI:ME (www.ti-me.org) and ISTE (www.iste.org) websites, and also the website for the Association for Technology in Music Instruction (www.atmionline.org). What are the major activities of these organizations? What benefits might you find from becoming a member of each?

CHAPTER 9
Teacher Preparation Considerations

In order to accommodate the growth of technology-based music classes in schools, institutions that educate music teachers—both prior to their service and during—must begin to implement structures for inclusion of TBMI in their curricula. In this chapter, I will examine some of the models of inclusion of TBMI in teacher education. I will do so with the understanding that teacher education in music is a constant work in progress, and that adding TBMI in already crowded curricula is a very difficult task.

TRADITIONS OF PRE-SERVICE TRAINING

Students working toward music teacher certification typically take a course focused on the uses of technology. Music teacher education faculty members generally agree that it is necessary for the skills embedded in these classes to be developed. In addition, the accrediting bodies that enable teacher preparation programs to grant licensure credentials suggest inclusion of such a course.

Courses in teacher preparation programs frequently address many of the standards delineated in the previous chapter, specifically the types of skills suggested by the TI:ME standards. An emphasis of some of these courses lies in the area of information management and communication. Students are often engaged—though sometimes unnecessarily so—in activities such as database creation and management, email communication, simple website development, and the uses of general education software. This is often the case when pre-service teachers are required to take courses in information technology or education departments of the university other than the music department in which the focus of the courses is general educational technology, devoid of a content area emphasis. Requiring these types of classes denies the existence of the critical intersections built into the TPACK model, which suggests that content, technology, and pedagogy influence each other. Music teacher educators should carefully consider whether such non-specific courses are advantageous for their students; perhaps there are better ways for future music teachers to gain proficiency with technologies that will be more meaningful for them in their careers.

Courses that are music-specific have also fallen victim to some flaws in their design. Interestingly, though music education technology courses have been required for only a relatively short time (in comparison to courses in more traditional areas of music teaching), patterns and traditions related to the design of these classes have emerged. Courses in technology for music education majors often include some of these elements:

- Fundamental computing exercises that develop proficiency with operating systems, file management, and networks
- A unit based on office-type software for communication and student/record management
- A unit based on notation software
- A unit based on fairly traditional sequencing software, including exploration of concepts related to MIDI
- A unit based on the uses of computer-assisted instruction
- A unit based on digital audio concepts and editing software

The purpose of this list is not to be critical of the inclusion of any of these topics in the teacher preparation curriculum. On the contrary, they all suggest important concepts and skills with which future teachers should be familiar. The controversial issue is the approach faculty members take to introduce the concepts and to develop the implied skills. Rather than be married to a traditional, structured course that focuses on these types of units, the profession should consider some alternative approaches.

TECHNOLOGY INTEGRATION IN TEACHER PREPARATION CURRICULA

In order to encourage music teacher educators to reconsider the integration of technology into their curricula, following are some models of integration that currently exist or might be implemented. These three suggestions are, of course, governed by situational realities, but they may be effective ways to prepare future music teachers to use technology in their own classrooms.

Technology Blended into Existing Courses

Music education students typically take a series of courses designed to prepare them for many types of music teaching including elementary, middle school, high school, choral, instrumental, and general settings. Each of these settings suggests uses of particular technologies. One approach, then, to including technology in the teacher preparation curriculum is to focus on particular technologies during existing classes that are appropriate for the content area and level. For example, a course in secondary general music methods might benefit from the study of uses of software for composing without notation. Students in elementary general music methods might focus on computer-assisted instruction software. The difficulty with this approach is that faculty must become familiar with technologies that are well matched to the content of each course, or they must collaborate with colleagues who have greater expertise in technology than they do.

Technology as a Methods Course

In many music teacher preparation programs, the requisite technology course lives in an isolated state of limbo. It is treated neither as a *techniques* course, in which students learn the technique of an instrument or their voice, nor as a *methods* course in which students gain experience in the pedagogy of a particular type of music teaching. Most music education technology courses lean more toward the *techniques* model, in which proficiency is gained with particular pieces of software without much regard for related teaching concepts. When compared to the depth of experiences involved in coursework in traditional types of music teaching, it is clear that the present structures do not adequately prepare music education students to handle TBMI when they enter the workforce.

As redesigns of music education technology courses occur in the near future, consider a structural shift toward treating them as *methods* courses. In such courses, students are often engaged in activities such as peer teaching, fieldwork or observations of experienced teachers, and development of a reflective and philosophical stance about teaching within the particular subdiscipline. Current music education technology courses rarely include these activities. The methods approach would force future teachers to think about the possibility that, in the near future, they might teach music in a technology-based setting and to consider all that such a role would imply.

Instead of developing music education technology coursework around software units as described earlier, technology methods courses might examine technologies organized by age appropriateness, types of musical tasks, or musical roles. Such an approach would also serve to better align instruction in the technology methods courses with other methods courses and create a more cohesive feel to the teacher education program.

Independent/Self-Guided Demonstration of Competencies

Finally, consider the possibility that teacher education programs need not train their students in technology; that technology is so robust and user-friendly, and students so adept with its uses, that students should be able to demonstrate competencies in technology on their own. Such an approach would imply that no technology-specific coursework is included in the curriculum and that students would have certain technology experiences embedded into their coursework throughout their music degree. This could be the case for all students majoring in music, not just for music education students. Williams and Webster (2011) suggested that there is an emerging core set of competencies that faculty expect of all music majors, but the training associated with the development of those competencies does not necessarily need to happen in formal coursework.

The idea of independent development of technology competencies should not be quickly dismissed. One need only look at the expectation that music students develop their performance skills with some level of independent practice to understand that such an approach would be possible. However, two obstacles prevent this comparison from being a perfect parallel. First, when students come to study music at a university, they have probably been practicing their instrument with relative independence for many years and have already developed habits of independent learning. This may not be the case with technology skills. Second, students receive guidance from applied faculty, usually on a weekly basis, in order to develop technique and musicianship under the tutelage of a master. Perhaps if a similar applied structure were instituted with technology skills, independent development of competency could be more reasonably expected. Such a structure could even make use of a formal evaluation of technology skills, just as music performance programs typically require jury exams.

TPACK-BASED TEACHER PREPARATION

Teacher training in technology integration can also be aligned with the TPACK model. TPACK-based training is being conducted and researched at both the pre-service teacher preparation level and at the in-service teacher training level.

Several examples of TPACK-based pre-service training have been examined in the recent literature. Jaipal and Figg (2010) studied the technology integration practices of 25 undergraduates who were engaged in field experiences. The researchers observed their participants teaching technology-based lessons in middle school math, science, and social studies classes, and they tracked examples of the components of TPACK (TPK, TCK, etc.). They provided a framework so that future observers would be able to recognize examples of the various TPACK components in action. Of concern with this study was the way in which the researchers determined that a student teacher had been successful: Success of the teacher was measured according to the achievement of the middle school students. This type of measurement stands in direct opposition of the principles of TBMI and indicates that the lessons taught as part of this study were not focused on student creativity.

Pamuk (2011) conducted a similar study in which pre-service teachers were observed while teaching mini-units in middle schools (again, not in music or arts classes but in academic subjects). Observation data were organized according to the components of TPACK. The conclusions of the study support the ideas of the chapter in this text regarding assessing teachers' work. The researcher concluded, "while students demonstrated a certain level of knowledge in technology, pedagogy, and content, their ability to use knowledge based on their attempts to create new knowledge bases, like TPK, were limited, principally due to lack of teaching experience" (Pamuk, 2011, p. 11). The assumption is that as new teachers gain more experience, the level of sophistication they bring to the "overlaps" of the TPACK model will grow.

Chai, Koh, and Tsai (2010) provided another example of this type of research with their students in Singapore. In this study, pre-service teachers completed a questionnaire about their understanding of TPACK-related skills and knowledge. They then took a course called "ICT [Information Communications Technology] for Meaningful Learning" which was designed to target the components of TPACK. At the end of the course, the students again completed the questionnaire. A comparison of the pre-test and post-test revealed statistically significant gains in the students' understanding of content, technology, pedagogy, and the overlapping constructs.

These three examples from research literature demonstrate the possibilities for teacher preparation that is based on the TPACK model. As yet, no research has been completed regarding this idea as it relates to music teacher preparation. The model mentioned earlier in which technology is taught to pre-service music teachers in the fashion of a methods course would seem an ideal environment in which to investigate the feasibility of TPACK-based music teacher preparation. Pre-service teachers can best demonstrate their understanding of the intersections of technology, pedagogy, and music content when they are afforded time with students to do so. Methods courses typically contain a component of fieldwork and would provide an opportunity for researchers to observe the development of TPACK in the pre-service teachers.

TPACK-Based In-Service Education

In-service experiences in the development of sophisticated intersections between technology, pedagogy, and content is just as important as pre-service education. TPACK is a recent idea, and though the constructs have always existed in isolation, it is possible that in-service teachers have not considered the model in the same way that those on the cutting edge of the research have. Bos (2011) conducted a study with experienced teachers that provided evidence of their ability to recognize the power of technology integration. In this study, practicing teachers designed lessons using websites that they deemed appropriate for their classrooms. The teachers assessed their own work and the work of their peers. Bos concluded:

> The results of this study suggest that experienced teachers can see the importance of knowledge about pedagogical and mathematical content through their interactions with technology and that they also can find value in the creative and problem-solving capacity of technology. Teachers realized that the instructional choices they make are not easy, and inequities in technology exist in schools that may limit their ability to commit to TPACK. They all concurred, however, that TPACK provides a theoretical foundation for the 21st-century teacher. The transition from a casual relationship with technology to a more connected bond built on an understanding of appropriate student-oriented pedagogy, conceptualized mathematical content, and cognitive complexity can lead to more teachable moments with technology as the manipulated medium and arm of instruction rather than as a glitzy add-on. (p. 178)

Experienced teachers have a more acute understanding of their students than do new teachers. By allowing the participants in this study to use their well-developed senses of content and pedagogy, and guiding them through selection of technological tools that were appropriate for their students, the researcher helped the teachers realize that the three components of TPACK are intrinsically linked. This type of experience seems to be extremely valuable for practicing teachers and could serve as a model for future investigations and in-service learning activities. In the Profile of Practice below, we learn about a veteran teacher with a healthy view of the importance of in-service professional development.

PROFILE OF PRACTICE 9.1

Experienced teachers can really fall into a "groove" with what they teach and how they teach it. In some cases, teachers have been using the same curricula, methods, and materials for their whole careers, and they see no need to change something that works. They have a good point.

Mrs. C is a veteran teacher—in fact, she was considering retirement when I interviewed her—who has seen success in several schools and with several types of music teaching. She is well known in music education circles as a bright, innovative, enthusiastic, energetic teacher, and she has the accolades to show for it. I knew her well even before our formal interview. We had spent time together at conferences, and several years before, she took a summer workshop class I taught. Since then I had come to know her reputation as a skilled technology-based music teacher. But I also knew that she was not of the "generation" of teachers that might have had coursework in their degree programs that would prepare her for that role.

Regarding her formal preparation with technology, she said, "I really don't have any formal training. I have this personal learning network that is totally incredible. Obviously I love to learn so I've gone to a lot of conferences in technology. A lot of people think that I'm a technology teacher, which is sort of funny, you know? But you have to learn something about it before you can really play. So I haven't really had that much formal training. I try to find people that I think I'm going to really learn from. I don't want to waste my time with someone who I feel knows about the same as I know. I want to be inspired and I want to learn."

With Mrs. C's tendency to search for less formal types of technology learning, I wondered why she had taken my class several years earlier, which was very much a procedural class in the uses of Sibelius notation software. It did not seem to fit with the types of learning experiences she would typically seek out for herself. She explained, "That was when

I was just starting [to work with] the Vermont MIDI project.[a] That summer I was going to have to sit in a room with 20 people who were all musicians and already knew Sibelius, and I was very intimidated. And I'm one of those people—when my sister was four, she refused to get in the little baby pool because she didn't know how to swim. Well the whole reason why she was in the baby pool was that she needed to learn how to swim. She wanted to know how to swim before she got to the lesson. And I sort of feel like that. I wanted to know the program so that I felt secure enough when I sat with all these people, I would feel like I knew what I was doing. I didn't want to be at the bottom of the class. I wanted to already come in and be at the top of my game. That year I took three Sibelius classes because I wanted to learn and be so good at it that it was going to be secondary. So the technology gets out of the way. I already know how to do all this stuff. Technology is not the problem, it's actually enhancing it."

"So many times we as teachers say, 'I don't want to teach technology, I want to teach music.' Well you know what? You better teach some basic skills because, if [the students are] so caught up in the technology, they're not going to create. So you've got to get that technology out of it."

To Mrs. C, technology is indeed second nature. She was focused on pedagogy, and on providing students with meaningful creative experiences. She had sought out training that would instill confidence in her to a point where she could concentrate on her students' needs. Despite the fact that she is of a generation in which technology was not an emphasis in music teacher training programs, she understands the potential of technology to enhance her students' knowledge and thinking processes, and she seeks professional development that can help her do that.

IMPORTANCE OF MODELING

Many models of pre-service teacher education and in-service teacher training in technology-based teaching currently exist, some of which have been detailed in the previous sections. Many more means of helping teachers integrate technology will develop in the coming years. As the literature on

a.   The Vermont MIDI Project (www.vtmidi.org) provides training for music teachers who want to teach composition to their students. The program also facilitates connections between K–12 students and professional "mentor" composers who, using notation software and online communications tools, provide feedback for students about their composition work. Mrs. C is one of several teachers I interviewed whose students are part of the program.

the TPACK model suggests, simply keeping up with the latest technological innovations can be a daunting task. For those charged with preparing teachers for the field or with providing focused training for practicing teachers, an appropriate balance must exist between the amount of time and energy one is willing to exert toward the goal of technology integration and the focus on the general concepts of good pedagogy.

The responsibility to push forward the agenda of technology-based instruction in music and in all other disciplines falls squarely on the shoulders of teacher educators. Perhaps the simplest demonstration that teacher preparation faculty can give regarding the importance of technology in pedagogy is to model its uses in their own instruction. Faculty can use relatively low-level technological tools to model good uses of digital media in their classes. Some examples of these types of technological integrations are listed here:

- Using presentation software (PowerPoint, Keynote, Prezi) to organize and facilitate lecture and discussion classes;
- Distributing reading material through electronic means such as course management systems (BlackBoard, Moodle, etc.) instead of printing and copying;
- Setting expectations that students turn in assignments electronically rather than on paper (which is both more efficient and more environmentally friendly);
- Creating assignments for which students must use technology creatively;
- Leading students in activities in which they design lessons for their future students that involve rich technology integration.

These and many other techniques will serve as good models for pre-service teachers and may increase the likelihood that they will replicate them in their own teaching.

SUMMARY OF CHAPTER 9

Chapter 9 has presented some models of inclusion of technology in the training of future music teachers. This training is done in the context of music teacher certification and, more important, preparation of those teachers to teach in TBMI contexts. Chapter 10 will examine some of the considerations of the future landscape in which those new teachers will work.

ITEMS FOR DISCUSSION

1. Some college-level music programs have technology integrated throughout their curriculum rather than isolating it to a single technology-based class. Have you seen examples of technology in your coursework, especially your music coursework, that were particularly innovative or effective? Why were they effective?
2. Similarly, some college professors can be excellent models for incorporating technology into individual courses or lessons. What models of technology integration you have seen, and how did the teacher artfully blend technology into the lesson?
3. The idea expressed in this chapter about students demonstrating individual technology competencies with little to no guidance from faculty is something of a radical notion. However, it is possible that schools of music, already overburdened with requisite courses, may begin to adopt this model. How would you feel about this expectation?
4. Many schools/districts expect their teachers to continue their education during their careers in the form of in-service training. Because it is considered "cutting edge," technology is a frequent component of in-service experiences. What types of in-service technology experiences do you feel are most important? Should this be a required part of teachers' lifelong learning?

CHAPTER 10

Future Considerations

The dominant issues that the TBMI community will face for the next 30 years and beyond are just starting to appear through the fog. In this final chapter, I will introduce some of the trends that have recently emerged that may impact the development of TBMI pedagogy, and speculate on directions they might take. These trends include, but are certainly not limited to, (1) the emergence of mobile devices such as tablets and smartphones and their potential for music making; (2) the growing popularity of alternative and electronic ensembles; (3) concerns about connections between traditional forms of music making—specifically, the critical role that singing plays in learning to be musical—and music technology; (4) the possibilities of technology-enhanced distance learning in music; and (5) the critical examination we must do regarding social and inclusion issues, and their relationships to music technology.

PROFILE OF PRACTICE 10.1

There is little doubt that mobile devices, and particularly the iPad, will revolutionize our work in TBMI. Interestingly, as I scoured the landscape for teachers in the K–12 environment who are using iPads in their classrooms as replacements for notebook or desktop computers, few examples emerged. This provides evidence that we are at a point in technological development where we are still very much a computer lab-based culture, but we see the promise of mobile devices.

Mrs. J teaches at a small independent school. Although not an official designation, the school's teachers consider it to be project-based, and much of what Mrs. J does in her music classes is designed around projects. Her fourth grade students were composing short melodies using their recorders and then using GarageBand on iPads to create accompaniments to their melodies.

My questions for Mrs. J focused on the pedagogical aspects of using iPads in her classes. First we talked about her general experiences using iPads, especially given that her students share the devices in groups of three or four. The sharing aspect seemed like it might be problematic because the iPad is designed as a personal device, usually viewed and used by one person. She said, "I find it easier to share than a computer, especially since most of our computers are laptops, because you can view it from any direction.... They have to be really careful and I don't want them to get too casual about passing it, but it's really easy to pass it back and forth. And as the novelty wears off a little, [it] makes that part a little easier.... They're not just all trying to grab the iPad. So, to my surprise, I've found that I like it better in groups than a laptop." Conversely, she expressed difficulties she has run into in terms of file naming and saving on iPads. Many of these processes are automatic, which can lead to students overwriting each other's work accidentally.

As Mrs. J allowed her students to have open time to work in small groups, the environment shifted a bit in a way that might be encouraged by the freedom the iPads promoted. Rather than raising their hands and waiting for questions to be answered, the students charged right up to her. Over the course of several lessons, Mrs. J was still negotiating within herself the right amount of direct instruction that the students required to be able to use the iPad application effectively. She said, "The first iPad project that I did this year was using [an app called] SoundSlate. It's really easy to use. Like many things on the iPad, it's very intuitive. After a couple of initial questions, pretty much all the kids could use it perfectly well." She noted that the GarageBand app, which is more complex, required more instruction, but she was not sure how much. Perhaps the complexity of the app and the complexity of the guidelines of the project are both determining factors in that equation.

Another interesting challenge for teaching with an iPad that Mrs. J mentioned has to do with projecting its image onto a large screen. She said, "Unless the program already lights up a little dot where you put your finger, it's not like the computer where you can see the cursor or the arrow moving around. So kids can't necessarily see what I'm touching. I'm hoping that that's something that will show up as people realize that it really needs to have something that shows up where my finger is to be totally effective as a teaching tool."

iPads hold promise for teaching and learning. Perhaps the most interesting possibilities are the uses of iPads as alternative performance devices, and students creating original apps that function musically. But pedagogical concerns abound. As teachers implement these devices into their practice, continual investigation for solutions to even the simplest adjustments may arise.

TABLETS AND MOBILE DEVICES

When we consider the cutting edge of consumer technology at the moment, one of the most prominent device types in the public consciousness is the tablet computer. This product category was all but non-existent five years ago (in fact, a "tablet computer" meant something very different; it referred to a notebook computer with a screen that rotated so that it could be written on like a legal pad with a stylus), but due to the emergence of Apple's iPad, it has become an important player in the technology landscape. Some teachers have suggested that devices such as the iPad are now having a similar effect on music making that digital cameras have had on photography and digital video cameras have had on movie making; those devices have made it possible for people to practice photography or filmmaking, just as the iPad has made it possible for people to engage in electronic music making.

Devices other than the iPad certainly exist in this product category; they include, but are not limited to, the Amazon Kindle Fire, the Barnes & Noble Nook Tablet, the Blackberry Playbook, and the Samsung Galaxy Tab. While each of these devices claims to rival it, the iPad holds a dominant market share. The culture of app development that has developed around the iPad, specifically in terms of apps for music making, position the device to have a profound impact on technology-based music instruction. In addition, many of the apps for music making that are designed to run on the iPad are also usable on its younger sibling, the iPod Touch, and on the iPhone. At the time of this writing, Apple has hosted more than 30 *billion* app downloads, an average of almost four apps per person in the world.

It is difficult to predict the future of these devices as they relate to music teaching and learning. Perhaps we can begin by articulating some of the positive and negative aspects of their use in the classroom.

Positive Aspects

- Tablet devices are often less expensive than laptop or desktop computers, and most apps are very inexpensive (only a few dollars each, with many great free apps available);
- Software updates are easily done, usually without a wired connection, and usually for free;
- Tablets are smaller than traditional computers, making storage and transportation less troublesome;
- The touchscreen interfaces featured in tablets are very simple to use—students need little instruction because it seems to come naturally to them;
- The culture of app development for tablets is pushing the technology quickly; app developers are creating impressive, powerful products;
- There is still novelty associated with tablets, which can be a motivating factor for students and can make learning experiences with tablets more fun and engaging.

Negative Aspects

- Because of their prevalence in society, students might tend to view tablets (as well as iPod Touches and smart phones) as toys rather than serious tools for music making;
- Network connection is completely dependent on wireless signals, which may not be available in all school environments. If Wi-Fi is not available, the process of updating and backing up data must be done while tethered to a computer;
- The development of apps moves so quickly that it is difficult for teachers and students to keep up with changes, and to explore new apps that might be useful;
- Unless a tablet can be assigned to each student, sharing a device might be difficult, perhaps more so than with computers, which are designed for viewing by more than one person at a time.

The directions these devices will lead us in, and in which users will push them, is yet to be determined. In fact, still early in the 21st century, it is not as easy as one might think to find music classes that have become as dependent on tablets as others are on computers. In short, we are a computer lab-based climate. As tablets become more powerful and developers begin to accommodate some of their shortcomings, this indeed may change. While it is easy to recognize negative implications of tablet devices, their positive possibilities far outweigh any negatives. The ease of using a tablet, especially with well-designed operating system and application interfaces, is difficult to match in a notebook or desktop computer.

Tablets also have specific implications for pedagogy. As described in Profile of Practice 10.1, teachers need to anticipate the influences of using tablets in their classrooms and make decisions that will help students to be successful when using the devices. Many of these pedagogical choices mimic what happens in a computer lab environment, but add the complex factors of novelty and mobility. The inherent ease of using most tablet apps might also modify the role of the teacher in the educational process so that students' reliance on help from the teacher is greatly diminished. The responsibility of the teacher in selecting materials—here, apps—might be enlarged, simply because of the abundance of available apps and the appearance of new apps every day.

ALTERNATIVE ENSEMBLES

Bands, choruses, and orchestras dominate the landscape of American public school music making. These ensemble types, with their traditions of performance as a goal, often-competitive nature, and teacher-centered instruction, have offered little in terms of innovation or change.

Despite their shortcomings, school bands, choruses, and orchestras achieve astounding performance levels. Students who participate in these traditional ensembles are frequently expected to perform at very high levels and to dedicate a lot of time to developing their musicianship through performance. Schools and teachers should not be faulted for maintaining a focus on these performing ensembles because it is something they can do remarkably well, and students do indeed benefit from them.

Participation in traditional school ensembles typically requires a commitment early in a student's life. American music teachers do not see band, chorus, or orchestra as experiences for which students can come and go as they please; rather, they expect sustained commitment throughout the student's school career. While there is certainly benefit that can be gained from devotion to a particular form of music making, the negative impact of this view is that students who do not "get in on the ground floor" are left with nowhere to turn when they want to be involved in making music in a school ensemble.

Electronic instruments rarely have a place in traditional school ensembles. While some technological supplements are used in traditional ensembles (such as samplers, keyboards, or electric guitars and basses), it is not often that we find a dedicated space for a performer on an electronic instrument to participate in band, chorus, or orchestra. The future of ensemble performance may see increased opportunities for participation by students who do not specialize in wind, brass, percussion, or string instruments, or in voice; students who make music using electronic instruments may begin to find a place in school where their type of performance is valid.

The term "alternative ensemble" is a non-specific one. In a broad sense, it suggests any type of ensemble that is *not* a traditional band, orchestra, or chorus. Many music educators consider a jazz ensemble to be an alternative experience, and by this broad definition, that is true. However, school jazz ensembles typically make use of the same types of instruments as do traditional concert bands (with the addition of rhythm section instruments and possibly voices), and they rehearse and perform according to the plans of their directors.

The types of ensembles I refer to here vary from traditional ensembles in three possible areas: instrumentation, rehearsal, and performance. In terms of instrumentation, alternative ensembles make use of many non-traditional instruments and often include creation of sound through electronic means. While teachers might schedule rehearsals regularly, they are often student-led, or they might meet on a more flexible schedule. Whereas traditional ensembles might have performance as an ultimate goal, alternative ensembles might perform simply so others can hear what they are doing, or they might not perform in public at all. A final point of variation from the traditional is that alternative ensembles involve students who might not be musically trained in the typical way that a student who plays trumpet or violin is trained.

None of this is to suggest that alternative ensembles will or should replace traditional ones. Bands, choruses, and orchestras have become *traditional* because they offer good learning experiences for students. Done well, they can be expressive and creative, and they can engender a strong sense of community, both within and outside the ensemble's members. But the alternative music performance culture—including students who compose their own music electronically, who perform in rock bands, who experiment with DJ-ing—is an important part of the climate outside of school. Teachers should embrace students who are making music in different ways and should welcome them into the music program (Green, 2002). Given the tremendous expense of running a band or orchestra, seeking alternatives, and therefore being more inclusive of the larger student body, may become an important move toward sustaining school music programs.

Alternative ensembles turn the traditions of bands, orchestras, and choirs on their heads. In order to gain a better understanding of the ways in which teachers view emerging types of ensembles, I interviewed two teachers who have gained some notice for their success with alternative groups at their schools. Despite the fact that they are both engaged in alternative ensemble programs, these teachers approach their groups quite differently. We talked about the history of the groups, instrumentation, their goals for performance, rehearsal routines, and repertoire.

Mr. F is a music teacher at a Midwestern high school. For the past several years he has been running an Electronic Music Group (EMG)—a small (seven or so) bunch of students who are focused on producing music that we might associate with DJ culture. Mr. F was asked to present some of what he was doing at a state technology conference, so he officially pulled together a group of what he calls his "hard-core" students with interest in this type of music. It is an extra-curricular group. Mr. F described the culture of the group: "It's very student-led. I kind of let the students who are going to do most of the programming choose who else they want in it. I don't really audition anybody because I want to keep it really informal. It's kind of under the radar in a way. I like things to happen more or less naturally. If this is what kids want to do then we'll do it. If it's not what kids want to do I'm not going to force it."

I asked Mr. F about the instrumentation, and it was a more difficult question to answer than I expected. The instrumentation for his group, which is entirely electronic, is linked to the software and hardware that the group has available. He said, "When you get into electronic groups in general, the idea of instrumentation in the sense that most people use the word goes out the window. We could run the thing with just one person. We've basically got one kid who has the drum pad, the [Akai] MPD26, and he's triggering effects on that. He's doing a lot of the stuff that sounds like DJing—the scratch kind of stuff, the pitch drops, and the beat repeat kind of things. [Another student] is triggering clips. So he's triggering the flow of it, and he's also doing the cross-fading between different channels that we have set up. [Another student] is the keyboardist, and he's doing what I would consider some pretty light keyboard work right now. So he'll get a few spots where he's really playing for a long time. And then [there is] the rapper. In its final form when we add everybody else in, there will probably be another singer, there will probably be another person on EWI [electronic wind instrument], maybe one other person. There's a visualist too this year."

The EMG does not do traditional concerts. Mr. F said that this is due mostly to the nature of the music they perform. "To me it's more similar to that Indian street music where you go to a concert of it and it lasts five hours, because it's not supposed to be played as a concert. So we kind of design it for that. Some people might stay for the whole thing, some people might see a little bit and go somewhere else. So I think this sits somewhere between a type of formal music and a type of functional music." Mr. F does seek out performance venues for the EMG. He was planning to have them perform at some of the school's basketball games, and have some short performances in the cafeteria during lunch hour, mostly to prepare for performances at professional conferences he attends.

Rehearsals for the EMG are about piecing together sections of what will eventually become the continuous music of the performance. The group has only a few rehearsals a year when they run the entire set. During rehearsals, Mr. F sees his role as the producer. He told me, "It feels less like I'm directing a rehearsal and more like I'm managing a project."

Perhaps the most interesting part of Mr. F's EMG is that they perform almost entirely original music. The students are heavily engaged in creating the music that the group performs, some of which they do at home, some during school. The music that is not original is sampled from existing material or is manipulated material from students at the school who perform it in their recording studio. Since rehearsals do not happen on a regular schedule, Mr. F seeks out students in between rehearsals and prods them to do what is necessary. He asks them to produce sections of music that sound a particular way or that serve a particular function in the overall composition.

The second alternative ensemble I investigated is housed in an Arts High School in California. The program, led by Mr. G, is called Music Media and Entertainment (MMET). Mr. G's program began when he, as a school librarian who was running a battle of the bands to raise funds for books, caught the attention of the district's Career and Technical Education department. That department became an initial funding source for the program, which now has more than 130 students. Contrary to EMG, this program is curricular—students receive academic credit for participating in it. The school also has a traditional music program with a band, orchestra, musical theater, and dance. Mr. G's program recruits students who specialize in electric guitar, electric bass, drum set, keyboards, and pop vocals. He said, "We're not like an electronic music ensemble . . . not like a MIDI ensemble. We just form regular bands, and the kids play, and they stage over-the-top rock and roll shows." The last few years have also seen extensive collaboration between the programs: many horn and string players have performed with the rock groups when the arrangements have called for them. Students in the MMET rock bands are recruited and have to audition to be a part of the program. Mr. G seems to view the program as filling a need for students who do not want to participate in traditional ensembles. He also recognizes that students view themselves as media artists—perhaps differently from the way teachers view them: "The kids nowadays, when they get the laptop with iLife, they don't say well I'm a video guy or I'm a guitar guy, or I'm a guitar girl or a video person, they just have tools. So we basically merged video and audio together, and so we have a separate pathway from the traditional music program."

Since MMET happens during the school day, the program is quite structured. Mr. G divides the students into groups. In the first block of time, half of the group is engaged in computer lab work. Mr. G teaches a Songwriting and Recording class for the freshmen and sophomores during this two hour-block. Meanwhile, the juniors and seniors are engaged in rehearsals with their rock bands. The groups then switch, and Mr. G teaches a class called Music Technology for the new group, while the others rehearse. Band rehearsals are led by college interns that Mr. G hires, many of whom are alumni of the program. Mr. G has plans to revise the curriculum in the next couple years so that there is a different class available to each grade level.

The students learn classic rock tunes, contemporary rock tunes, and sometimes compose original music. The goal of the rehearsals is to learn songs that will be played during performances. The interns help them learn to play the songs, usually by ear, by breaking them apart into chord structures and song forms. Mr. G encourages the students to use all available resources to learn the tunes they will cover: "In the modern learning environment, you're not just getting information from one source. So the first thing they'll do is they'll get the songs, they'll go to YouTube, and they'll see if someone else has broken apart the song. So they'll learn it from YouTube, they'll do a rough chart for me—I make them do a rough lead sheet—and then I look at their lead sheet...and I see if their chords are correct." Rehearsals also help the students learn to achieve authentic sounds from their instruments and equipment. Mr. G told me of an example in which the students were playing music of the British Invasion. He and friends from Rickenbacker Guitars, a company whose instruments are often associated with bands such as the Beatles and the Birds, would demonstrate ways to achieve the vintage tones of that era, which students could then emulate on stage.

Performance is very much the goal of the ensembles in the MMET program. Students produce several main stage shows each year that Mr. G says are "not just high school shows, but professional level shows that would be equivalent to a Broadway production. So with that in mind, I make sure that [they are] top notch. And the community realizes that our shows are top notch." For these main stage shows, Mr. G selects the repertoire, and he sees the shows as educational experiences, not just for the students, but for the audience as well. For example, one year the students performed a show about "break-up albums" that featured The Beatles' *Abbey Road* and Fleetwood Mac's *Rumors*. As with all of the main stage shows, the production featured documentary footage, edited and produced by students in the program, accompanying the musical performance. The students often play to a track that helps them synchronize the performance with the video tracks, just as would be done in a professional rock concert.

Both of these teachers have taken on the challenging task of forming and organizing alternative ensembles in their school. One is attached to the curriculum, the other is not; one is student-led, the other teacher-driven; one holds performance as the ultimate goal, the other is focused on creating original music and sharing it with whoever wants to listen. They are very different approaches—perhaps polar opposites—but they fill a similar need. Over the next decade, perhaps more models will emerge, some simpler and some more complex, that will cater to students interested in alternative music-making experiences.

With so few examples of strong alternative ensemble programs from which to draw, it is difficult to offer a comprehensive set of recommendations to start one of these groups. Perhaps the next several years of technology-based music instruction will help to generate best practices for alternative ensemble pedagogy. You might consider the following:

- Who are the students who will participate in the ensemble? What are their individual capabilities? Part of the draw of alternative ensembles is that students who do not have traditional music performance background, or who are socially withdrawn or distant, might become engaged in music making with a group. Think about involving students who might not otherwise be musically engaged.
- Small groups of students working together in alternative ensembles are probably more manageable than larger, class-sized ensembles. Musical texture becomes dense very quickly with electronic instruments, and quite often the music that these groups perform implies limited instrumentation.
- Try not to be intimidated by the amount of technology equipment that is apparently needed to start an ensemble. Do not hesitate to use students' personal devices (phones, iPods, etc.). Remember that laptops are quite

usable in this setting as well, and many schools have a group of laptops that circulate for students' uses.

- Sources of music for performance are a difficult issue because there is not a standard canon of music for a group, for example, that uses iPads as their primary instruments. Consider student composition as a source of music to perform. Also consider electronic arrangements or realizations of others' music.

- Consider organizing an electronic ensemble within the context of a lab-based music technology class. While some groups are extra-curricular, doing this within a class can engage students in real-time music making in ways that might not otherwise occur.

- Allow time for play and experimentation. This should be the case at all levels, not just at young ages. Since the sources of sound are new, students need time to explore the instruments, find sounds they like, and figure out good ways to perform with them.

- Try out individual instruments and sounds that students find. As the teacher, you may have to impose limitations on sounds that do not work well in the ensemble setting. This is particularly true of some drum sounds that demonstrate latency[1] and therefore interfere with the group's ability to play together.

SINGING AND TBMI

An issue of interest to the music education community is the role that singing will play in the practice of the next generation of music teachers. If TBMI becomes a dominant form of music teaching and learning, the role of singing could be substantially diminished. Especially for students at younger ages, singing is vital for the development of pitch proficiency, musical embodiment, and other musical and social abilities.

Many technologies can be adapted for use with the singing voice, but mere adaptation does not necessarily capitalize on the unique contributions of the voice to musical experience. Perhaps the answer lies in the combination of technologies designed for electronic performance along with the voice. This type of collaboration between students "playing" electronic devices, such as iPads, controller keyboards, and electric guitars and basses in support of singers, may be the key to maintaining the role of the voice in technology-enhanced music instruction. Rutkowski (2011) wisely

---

1. Latency is a small delay that occurs between the time that the user triggers a sound and when that sound is actually heard.

pointed out that students in an electronic ensemble that features the voice seem to be engaged because of the shared musical experience that an ensemble provides: "It is possible to make music by yourself with an iPad, or an instrument. But, these young adults apparently found it more musically stimulating to have a musical encounter together; we seem to seek out ways to interact with others in the music process."

As discussed in chapter 2, most of the time-tested, successful pedagogical models of music teaching rely heavily on singing. TBMI pedagogy must explore meaningful ways to include the use of the voice in music learning that is based on technology.

PROFILE OF PRACTICE 10.3

A simple Internet search of the term "virtual high school" returns an astounding number of options for students who are interested in taking secondary school classes online. These schools include university-affiliated institutions such as Indiana University High School and the University of Miami Global Academy; religious-affiliated schools such as Christian Online School; schools organized around social concerns such as the GLBTQ Online High School; or general, for-profit institutions such as Blueprint Education and the American Academy.

Among the many interesting online education options is the Florida Virtual School (FLVS), which is a Florida public school and offers free courses to students in that state—courses for those outside Florida are available for a fee. FLVS is accredited by the Southern Association of Colleges and Schools; however, it does not offer high school diplomas. Rather, credits that students earn through FLVS are transferred to their local schools and can be applied toward high school diplomas. FLVS recently added a music offering, guitar class, to its curriculum, so I sought out the opportunity to interview a teacher who is currently engaged in this kind of practice.

Kristen Styles is an experienced teacher—she taught elementary school music for several years prior to her work at FLVS—and performs as a vocalist and on a variety of instruments.[a] When we spoke she had been teaching the guitar course for only a couple of months but already had valuable insight into its structures, advantages, frustrations, and possibilities. Kristen was a self-proclaimed "perfectionist" when she was a student and told me how much she would have loved to have something like a virtual high school available to her. As an elementary general

a.   I was authorized to use Kristen's real name because I did not interact with any of her students. She was not promised confidentiality.

music teacher, Kristen had some experiences with technology including recording classes and providing classroom teachers with sing-along tracks. Another interesting experience was her use of the course management system Moodle to facilitate enrichment activities in her students' homes. She said, "The first year I used it, I just kind of piloted it with a gifted class, and we did some optional at-home activities. They could do interviews with their parents about rock and roll music. There were little videos and sound clips that they could play from home. The second year I used it with my chorus. They were able to play the accompaniment tracks and they were able to upload the lyrics to their songs so they could practice at home." She said of her experiences with Moodle, "It really piqued my interest even more, and it made me really comfortable once I came to FLVS. It made me really comfortable doing all the online aspects." Perhaps using distance tools as supplements is a reasonable way to help teachers learn to teach online while maintaining the comfort of their traditional classroom.

Kristen felt that the strongest positive aspect of teaching online through FLVS was the ability of the communication technologies to help her foster a positive learning environment. Her students submit their playing assignments by sending her videos that they record at home. She mentioned some of the students' expressions of anxiety: "Sometimes they'll say in the beginning of their video, 'Mrs. Styles, I'm really nervous about this, so I hope I don't mess up.' But then they get automatic, positive but constructive feedback from me on their performances, and then each time they make a new video I can see them getting more and more confident because they know there's nothing to be afraid of." Kristen also said that the students grow more confident throughout their time in the class, and she expects that this type of positive environment will eventually help them perform with ease in front of people. Other positive aspects of teaching this way that Kristen mentioned were the accessibility of the course for students who do not have room for an additional arts elective in their school schedule and the technique of using instructional videos that are recorded by students in order to vary the content delivery models.

Kristen articulated the two most prevalent frustrations that come along with teaching guitar through FLVS. First, since students submit videos of their performance assignments, there are bumps in the technological road. Of these difficulties she said, "Once in a while I'll get a video that's not compatible with my media player, or I'll get a video where I can see the student but there's no audio. And then I have to ask the student to do it again. Mainly, I know that's really frustrating for them because they've worked hard. Maybe they've recorded the video a couple times to get it perfect, and then I have to ask them to do it again." The school has pursued ways to conquer these difficulties such as contacting students who express interest in enrolling in the class to make sure they have the right equipment. This speaks to the importance of developing a solid technology support infrastructure to assist both students and teachers.

The second source of frustration for Kristen was just a simple adjustment of her teaching style. She referred to an example of teaching the free stroke—a classical guitar technique in which the finger strikes the string but does not make contact with the adjacent string—and students not being able to see the technique well in video tutorials. She said, "There have been some kids who have sent in their videos and their form on their free stroke isn't exactly as we would want it to be. So in that case we just call and we give them that one-on-one kind of tutorial over the phone, or Skype. So there are definitely ways to fix that, it's just a different method. Whereas in a brick-and-mortar school I might actually place their fingers and show them how to do that, this is just a different method."

Finally, we discussed the role of collaboration in the online guitar class. Kristen said that a collaborative project is a mandatory part of each section of the course. She said:

> There four different lessons that they can use as a collaboration activity . . . and there are two ways for them to do it. They can do it using recording software—one student would send their file to the other student, and the other student would play with that recording software, record over it and send it back. But actually, our preferred method is doing it live in an Illuminate lesson, where we have a bunch of students meet. We do them on Tuesday nights, we have a bunch of students meet in a live lesson, and they can use their webcam if they would like, but they can also just use audio with a headset and a microphone. I'll use the first lesson as an example—one student plays a study of E chords, while another student improvises a solo using the E pentatonic scale, and then they switch parts. So they get to play a duet. It's been a lot of fun, and that really does provide that live performance aspect that you otherwise might not think that this course has. In the little chat box before they start performing you'll see the students type, "Well, I'm really nervous, I've never played with another student before." And that's really cool because it gives it that excitement of a live performance. And then they have a lot of fun. They play together. We have it set up as a concert, so then afterwards there's a little applause icon and the students all applaud for each other. They type comments and everybody's really supportive. And then they fill out a peer collaboration form: how do you think your partner did on the accompaniment? How do

you think your partner did on the solo? What do you think they could do better? What did you learn from your partner? They turn that in for their collaboration.

Given the prevalence of distance education at the post-secondary level, and the experiences of the next generation of teachers as students in that format, it seems logical that online learning will make an even stronger push into the K–12 level soon. Options already abound. Are teachers ready to teach online? Do they have an interest in doing so? What pedagogical and professional issues are raised when we consider porting other types of music learning to the online environment?

DISTANCE LEARNING

The type of technology-enhanced learning that has been discussed in this book has been firmly situated in the context of a physical computer lab space, with students and teachers able to interact in person. As we consider the future of music education, and especially technology-based music education, we should consider the possibility that distance learning, mediated through computer technology, will become a viable form of teaching music. In the section that follows, we will consider three ways in which online learning is currently impacting music instruction and will likely continue to do so into the future.

Online Tutorials

In our current connected culture, the Internet is the place where people look for information. Students understand that if there is something they want to know how to do, there is probably useful information available online that will guide them through it. Of course, caution should be taken against referring to user-generated content as an accurate academic source, but in many cases, information found online can prove to be valuable.

This is particularly true for learning to use music software. When we learn to use new music software, someone else can teach us, we can learn by experimentation, or we can refer to sources of information. Manuals that accompany software rarely focus on how to accomplish the specific types of things users want to do, especially when the software they describe is open-ended and supportive of infinite creative applications. When an expert in the use of a particular piece of software is not available for direct instruction, online tutorials are a reasonable way for students to learn to use software.

Video tutorials for software use can be found quite easily online. A simple YouTube search for tutorials for videos about using Ableton's Live generates, currently, more than 37,000 possibilities, and a search for Acoustica's Mixcraft results in more than 15,000 returns. Some online tutorials are poorly produced, but many provide valuable, step-by-step information, often using screen capture software, that will help users to accomplish tasks in the software. Alternatively, those who are interested in professionally produced tutorial videos can visit sites such as lynda.com or macprovideo. com, sites for online training in many types of software and technology. These sites contain tutorials for several music software packages including GarageBand, iTunes, Logic, Sibelius, and ProTools. They are accessed through paid memberships with subscription plans available.

It is quite possible that online tutorials—products created by other users of software—will find growing popularity in TBMI classes. Try as they might, teachers simply cannot be experts in all aspects of every piece of music software. With information available online at students' fingertips, perhaps teachers should consider encouraging students to search for answers to their procedural software questions rather than relying on their teacher as the source of all knowledge. This would also allow teachers to focus on their roles as facilitators of their students' creativity, coaching them through creation of projects.

Collaborative Online Music Making

The promise of the Internet for collaborative music making at a distance seems to be a dream partially realized in the last few years; one can only imagine that as Internet infrastructure grows more capable and software more sophisticated, collaborative performance between people in remote locations will become more robust.

Early efforts at collaborative online music were pioneered by such large organizations as the New World Symphony, under the direction of Michael Tilson Thomas, who regularly held rehearsals and master classes online. These events made use of technology known as Internet2, a network of high-speed, high-capacity computer connections between organizations, typically universities and government facilities, which allows for such real-time collaboration online with little latency or signal loss. These experiences, however, are somewhat out of reach for typical schools or classrooms that are not part of the Internet2 network. Recent advancements have made collaboration in online music making possible for more people in more situations.

Perhaps the most popular online communications technologies are systems such as Skype, iChat, and FaceTime. These programs allow for real-time audio and video communication with astonishing sound and picture quality. In certain scenarios, multiple users can engage in online chats at the same time rather than being limited to just two-way discussions. With the speed of home and school Internet connections, Skype, iChat, and FaceTime (and other systems like them) make it possible for teachers and students to connect online and share musical experiences.

An impressive and promising enhancement to audio and video technologies for communication capitalizes on MIDI protocols and transmits data over the Internet. InternetMIDI, an application by Zenph Sound Innovations,[2] allows for connection of two MIDI-capable pianos over the Internet. Because MIDI is such an efficient form of data, the connection between the instruments is nearly instant, with little noticeable delay. The software essentially allows a user in one location to play a MIDI instrument in another location. Similar technology is used in Yamaha's Disklavier pianos, and these instruments enable capture of performance data for archiving purposes. These technologies, and products similar to them, offer great potential for collaborative music making over the Internet.

Given the difficulties of travel and the desire of music educators to involve as many people as possible in learning music, Internet technologies may be crucial to the future of music teaching and learning. The proliferation of the Internet into society makes this type of connectivity a promising possibility for collaboration in music performance.

Formal Online Learning

Trends in formal education provide evidence that online learning is increasing in popularity at the post-secondary level (Allen & Seaman, 2010). This is due, in part, to the economic climate of the United States and the advantageous cost-to-benefit ratio of online learning. As current and future teachers grow more comfortable with the formats and technologies associated with online learning and begin to understand the pedagogy of teaching online, online learning may become a bigger part of K–12 education as well.

2. For more information on this product, see www.zenph.com/zenph-software/internet-midi.

Archambault (2011) observed that current teacher preparation programs tend to focus almost exclusively on preparing people to teach in traditional classrooms; however, more than one million K–12 students in the United States are currently enrolled in online classes. Teacher preparation tends to ignore this growing wave of education, perhaps because few pedagogical frameworks for online instruction exist. Archambault found that most teachers in K–12 online classes felt comfortable with the content of their instruction and the pedagogy related to that content, but they felt less comfortable with the technological aspects of teaching online. The researcher suggested that "teacher education programs have room for improvement when it comes to preparing teachers to use technology in a meaningful, content-driven way" (p. 84).

A useful way to think about online learning as it relates to music is to consider the possibilities for collaboration through online technologies. Harasim (2012) has proposed that several types of online learning have emerged, among them Online Collaborative Learning (OCL). The author suggests that the variety of features of the discourse supported by OCL (which include place-independent, time-independent, and text-based discourse) allow people to communicate with others in ways that help them to feel comfortable. In contrast, traditional classrooms limit the types of collaborative models that teachers and students can use and typically force real-time collaboration, which may not be the optimal way in which students work.

Current theoretical ideas related to online instruction are necessarily rooted in theories that describe traditional teaching. It is difficult to draw connections between educational theories (such as those described earlier in this book) and online teaching, in part because the means of interacting with students online are different from what they are in the classroom. Over the next several years of music instruction, it will be important for the field to develop theory and practical approaches to teaching music online in ways that are as meaningful, artistically supportive, and student-centered as is the instruction that currently takes place in brick-and-mortar music classrooms. It is quite possible that technology-based music instructors can lead this charge.

COMPOSITION AS THE BASIS FOR MUSIC EDUCATION

At various points throughout this text, we have examined ideas of structuring, supporting, and assessing students' creative work. Technology-based music classes, when organized according to the principles espoused in this book, are environments that facilitate students' creative work, usually in the form of composition. Composition activities may not be the ultimate goal of all TBMI classes, but when done well, TBMI should include an emphasis on students creating novel work that they have considered carefully.

In traditional ensemble environments, few teachers use composition activities as a way for students to demonstrate musical understanding, despite the validity of doing so. The future of music education may include a shift toward more composition as part of the everyday activities of music teachers and students. Kaschub and Smith (2009) suggested that composition *should* be taught in schools as a full-fledged curriculum because of the human capacity for composing and because schools represent the best possible opportunity to learn the skills related to composing. They wrote:

> Over time, a composition curriculum should offer access to traditional compositional styles as well as computer-based composing. Many children gravitate toward one means of sound production as their preferred sounds source for periods of time. Then new sounds may cause a shift in their preferences. There should be multiple opportunities for experiencing different approaches to composing as a student progresses through formal schooling. (Kaschub & Smith, 2009, p. 263)

Clearly, these experts in composition education see the intrinsic connection between composing and technology. With both composition and technology on the rise in music education, the near future may hold a greater focus on technological tools in support of students' composing.

SOCIAL/INCLUSION ISSUES

Many of the observations conducted for this book took place in rather idyllic circumstances. These settings are often suburban, upper-middle-class communities, where access to a computer lab and a group of relatively sophisticated students is somewhat simple to find. While efforts were made to include varied demographic and socioeconomic settings in the observations, the locations were not as diverse as would have been desirable. This points to problems in the diversity of access to, and experience with, music technologies along characteristics such as socioeconomic status, gender, ethnicity, and special educational needs.

Webster (2002a) observed that the research community, particularly in the United States, has been negligent toward exploring questions of gender equity as it relates to music technology. The related studies that Webster reviewed, which were conducted in European settings, revealed differences between boys and girls in terms of preferences for, and interest in music technology. In the decade or so since Webster's assertion, little has been done to address this issue.

Armstrong (2008) proposed that "with the introduction of technology another layer of symbolic masculinity is added to an already gendered music classroom where teachers perceive boys as having greater 'natural' ability for both technology…and composition." Armstrong found differences between boys and girls in terms of dominant behaviors in technology-based discussions, confidence of technology use, and preferred methods of learning technology. Tobias (2010), in his study of secondary students in a songwriting and technology class, noted that students took on roles that reflected social norms, some of which reflected gendered perceptions of how music makers are expected to act. One of the participants in this case study even expressed her own perception of the expectations of boys and of girls in the music-making process, which were vastly different from each other.

In observations conducted for this text, technology-based music classes were dominated by male students, both in terms of numbers and in the discourse of the classes. One teacher told me that while his current class had seven boys and one girl, the previous year's class was an even split. This still suggests a longitudinal dominance of males in the class. He saw no particular pattern or reason for the gender split for enrollment in his class. The teacher mentioned, "Typically, some of the boys are a little bit more adamant with their guidance counselors that they really want to take the class and it fills up very fast."

Composition has long been male dominated as a profession, as have recording, engineering, producing, and other music-industry related jobs. There is no logical explanation for this. The future of technology-based music instruction should emphasize gender equality and should extoll the virtues that being involved in all of the experiences that technology-based music making affords to all people. A complete treatment of this issue is beyond the scope of this book, but others have begun documenting the importance of gender equity in music technology. In particular, Armstrong (2011) frames this as a sociological issue and reminds us that technologies themselves are used in predetermined gendered roles, likely advancing those roles by their very use. The profession must take steps to be more inclusive of girls in classes that boys typically dominate. Similarly, TBMI teachers should make efforts to include students of varied ethnicities in their classes, another under-examined factor.

An additional social issue that may hinder the development of TBMI is that of access to the Internet. People in urban and suburban areas often take for granted access to high-speed Internet connections, both wired and wireless. Direct, high-speed connections have been available to home consumers for just longer than a decade, and to schools and institutions perhaps a bit longer, but many homes and schools in rural and remote areas struggle with access issues. In a recent report, representatives from the Federal Communications Commission stated:

> It is clear that much more remains to be done to ensure that every American has the opportunity to participate in the broadband era. The best data available indicate that more than 20 million Americans lack access to broadband.... Significantly, approximately 73 percent of these Americans reside in rural areas. (Genachowski, 2011, p. 3)

The report provided data showing that despite some progress in the preceding two years and investment from both the public and private sectors, in rural areas, greater than 28% of people were without access to high-speed broadband access, compared to 3% in non-rural areas. Given the emergence of cloud-based applications and data storage, consistent, reliable access to high-speed Internet connections could serve as the great equalizing force in the foreseeable future of technology-based music instruction, just as it might in many facets of education.

Finally, a social issue of tremendous importance is the inclusion of students with special needs in technology-based music instruction. Special needs music teaching in general is beyond the scope of this text; however, it is necessary to recognize the multi-faceted relationship between technology and special needs education. Special needs students have creative potential that is often untapped. Technology can facilitate opportunities for students with special needs to be creative without reliance on difficult systems of notation and the like. In many circumstances, mere exposure to sound and the ability to manipulate sound can provide powerful experiences for students with special needs.

Technology can support the practice of teachers and therapists with special needs students. Hammel and Hourigan (2011) suggest that tools such as SmartMusic and notation software can supplement teachers' practice to adapt common music learning activities. Beyond those types of technology uses, interaction with technology can enhance the lives of profoundly disabled students. As the music teaching profession grows more adept in teaching students with special needs, teachers should consider new and innovative ways to enhance those students' experiences with technology.

"Lost satellite reception," barked my GPS. I hadn't expected this school, where I was going to observe a rather sophisticated use of technology in a music class, to be in such a rural locale. But there I was, passing the dairy farm and turning left into the parking lot of a modern school building, the design of which starkly contrasted its rustic surroundings. After five months of pleading for permission to enter the school and making travel arrangements, I was there to observe Mrs. O teach a small class of special needs students in an elementary general music setting. She was one of the few teachers I was able to find who makes regular use of a device called the Soundbeam for teaching music to students with severe physical, intellectual and social disabilities. I observed Mrs. O teach two students in particular: Julie, who was mobile but non-communicative and was tethered to an oxygen tank; and Michael, who was largely non-responsive, used a wheelchair, and suffered many seizures each day. The students are well cared for; in fact, a quick count including Mrs. O, the classroom teacher, and the paraprofessionals, showed that at one point there were more adults in the room than there were students.

All of the students in the school's special needs class have complex diagnoses and represent substantial challenges for music teaching and learning. Mrs. O had no training in special education other than what was required for certification, but she had been teaching special needs students for most of her eight-year career. She mentioned to me before the class began that while it was challenging, the special needs class was her favorite. She said, "I think part of it is that it's just so incredibly rewarding.... When you're teaching these kids, you work so hard to get a response that when there is *any* kind of response, especially a musical one, you're just overjoyed. I think the other part of it is, when I did my research on them, I just started to understand them and appreciate them so much more because... I just came to value them so much as people. I think that they're a population that is often overlooked by everyone. By society in general and by the music education society specifically. There's a lot to learn from them."

Soundbeam is a device that translates even the slightest body movements into manipulations of synthesized sounds. The device has sensors that look something like microphones that emit a field and sense movements. Alternatively, there are large switch-like devices that can be tapped, stomped, or otherwise pressed to trigger synthesizer sounds. Mrs. O used Soundbeam as part of her lesson. She has had the device for a few years and confessed during our interview that she wants to be much more proficient with it; she feels comfortable doing what she knows how to do but is sure that she has only scratched the surface of its capabilities. When she designs her lessons for special needs students, she is careful to create musical goals for them, but she treats each of the students individually—even more so than in a traditional class. She consults regularly with physical therapists and classroom teachers so that she can be part of the team focusing on teaching each child.

With Julie, who is very mobile, Mrs. O used a technique that she referred to as "hand-over-hand," in which she guided Julie's movements. She stood behind her, as a golf pro would do when adjusting a pupil's swing, and moved her toward and away from the Soundbeam sensor, integrating sudden stops, all of which would change the sound. Julie's face lit up with a big smile each time she came to a sudden stop. I asked Mrs. O if she thinks Julie understood that her movements actually changed the sound:

> It's hard to tell with her. She was gone from school for two months, so she hasn't had as much experience with it as the other kids. So I know when she uses the switch that she understands, but with the beams, I'm not sure that she does. And that's why I was trying to do the move-move-stop, because I felt like if I made it into sort of a game, maybe it would flick a little switch in her mind. I cannot say definitively if she knows that she's affecting the sound using the beams or not. Some of my other kids who weren't there, you can see it in their faces. But with Julie, I still feel that maybe she doesn't know. It's hard to tell because they can't tell you. So really that's been my main goal with her and the Soundbeam so far is just to try to get her to understand that she can manipulate the sound. She loves to play instruments and things, so I think that when she understands that, it will open up a world of possibilities for her.

I sensed some disappointment from Mrs. O that Michael was not more responsive during my observation, but she explained that his demeanor was pretty typical.

"Sometimes when I use the switches with him, next to his head...it seems silly, but I really believe that he's hearing it because I'll see his eyes flicker or his eyes move, and basically that's all he can really do to show you. But yesterday I didn't even see that." Still, the Soundbeam helps Michael interact with a musical instrument, which he otherwise might not be able to do.

Mrs. O has developed an impressive level of comfort in teaching special needs students. She mentioned that perhaps the most successful activity she uses with the Soundbeam is when she programs it to play back pitches from familiar songs when the students use the trigger switch. The students enjoy this and she can see the anticipation of the next note on their faces. Technology holds incredible potential for providing musical experiences for students with special needs, even in the most severe circumstances. We can hope that teachers like Mrs. O, and even those who are less comfortable with this kind of teaching, will have opportunities to develop their pedagogical skills as the profession realizes this potential.

CONCLUSION

The ideas set forth in this book, which I have referred to as TBMI, are derived from a number of places. First, I considered that technology-based music teaching is simply another form of music teaching and therefore must have substantial connection to the other ways we typically teach music. Analysis of tried-and-true pedagogies such as Orff Schulwerk, Suzuki, Gordon's Music Learning Theory, and others revealed commonalities that were used to determine the elements crucial to imagining a distinct pedagogy: theoretical and philosophical foundations, materials, teacher behaviors, and assessment. Each of these has been explained in detail throughout the chapters of this book.

The future of TBMI is difficult to predict, in part because of the rapidly changing pace of technology. For that reason, future development of TBMI pedagogy must continue to remain technology-neutral; it should focus on the technique of teaching music with technology, rather than on teaching technology for its own sake. Practices based on equity and inclusion, alternative ensembles, distance learning, and new devices and technologies will certainly influence the foreseeable future.

Throughout this text we have considered various factors that make the pursuit of sophisticated engagement of music students with technology worthy of systematic consideration:

- Teachers have many justifiable concerns about technology-based music instruction such as preparation, curriculum development, and ways to evaluate creativity that are difficult to overcome given limited support and training.
- Examples of musical-pedagogical processes abound, but none of the tried-and-true methods account for the types of experiences students can have with technology as the major means for delivering

music instruction. TBMI must include an examination of the valuable components of each of these methods as a foundation for its own development.

- Philosophical and theoretical foundations for music instruction (constructivism, active learning, stage theory, multimedia learning, TPACK, etc.) offer a strong profile for designing TBMI experiences, but they must be artfully combined to make those experiences authentic and beneficial.
- Selection of musical materials for listening and performance, and technological materials (software and hardware) can be facilitated through guiding principles, but it is ultimately governed by teacher experiences and the best fit between materials and circumstances.
- While observations of lessons in typical TBMI classrooms suggest certain patterns of interaction, as encapsulated in the Cycle of Mastery model and in the Spectrum of Lesson Content model, every classroom, every teacher, every student, and every lesson is individual, and teachers need to be confident in their lesson design and delivery to make experiences worthwhile.
- Assessment of student work with rubrics, sharing sessions, and other tactics; teacher work using the TPACK model as a guide; and technology's fit into the music classroom and program are challenging ideas that the profession still needs to work through. Assessment of student work should be directly linked to the learning objectives of TBMI as established globally and by individual teachers.
- TBMI is subject to accountability measures that are not necessarily appropriate, including recognized sets of standards (NAfME, ISTE, etc.). Future consideration should be given to reassessing accountability measures for TBMI.

As teachers grow more comfortable with the idea of integrating technology into music learning, additional factors may become apparent and will presumably make TBMI even more complex. As with all types of music instruction, possibilities are infinite, so developing strong pedagogy that allows teachers to thrive despite a rapidly changing technological landscape is of paramount importance.

ITEMS FOR DISCUSSION

1. Many students you know probably have tablet or mobile devices that use music apps. What are some of the best apps for music that you and your classmates have encountered? How might these apps be used in a classroom of K–12 students?
2. Think about your own middle school and high school music experiences. How might they have changed if an alternative ensemble had been available? What musical skills and concepts can students learn from alternative ensembles that they might not in traditional ensembles?
3. How might you integrate singing into a TBMI lesson? Design a short lesson plan that includes the use of the voice in a technology-based music setting for a fifth grade class.
4. What are the possibilities for online classes at your institution? At local K–12 schools?
5. Of the social/inclusion issues mentioned in this chapter, which do you see as the most pressing? Why? Are there other, similar issues that you see as important for the profession to consider?

Philosophies and Training Profiles of Participant Teachers

In initial formal meetings with each of the teachers who volunteered to be observed and interviewed for this book, I asked a consistent set of questions that would help to establish a profile of the participants. This served two purposes: (1) I wanted to get to know the participants on a personal level rather than merely extracting meaning from the answers they gave me during interviews; and (2) I hoped that these data would lead to some consistent pattern that would help me to establish the overall profile of the kind of person who teaches technology-based music. The dispositions described earlier were relatively common features that the individual participants shared. But the people who participated were quite diverse. This section attempts to encapsulate some of the answers I received to these, as I referred to them, "get-to-know-me" questions.

The questions I used for the initial interviews were these:

1. Can you tell me a little bit about your musical background and your teaching experiences?
2. Tell me about your training and prior experiences with music technology.
3. How would you describe your teaching philosophy?

Answers regarding music teaching philosophy proved to be an inconclusive set of data. Rather than referring to philosophical or theoretical ideas, such as those discussed in the early chapters of this book, most teachers simply referred to their approach, more than to an over-arching philosophical stance. They said:

> "I want every kid to soar."
>
> "I really feel like the students have to be actively engaged in learning something."
>
> "I make sure that I know what the curriculum is. What is my employer expecting me to deliver to these students? Then I look at the students' interests and find some middle ground in all of those.... My classroom is a very loose situation."
>
> "Every student comes in to the music classroom with a different degree of prior knowledge, so my job is to figure out what that prior knowledge is and take that to the next step for them."

These responses helped me gain insight into the dispositions of the participants and further enhanced my belief in the need for the connection of music education philosophy to the new environments suggested by TBMI.

Previous teaching experiences ran the gamut of possibilities. The majority of the participants were mid-career teachers. Some had taught at various levels and in diverse socioeconomic settings. (I tried to make the sample of participants as representative as possible of elementary, middle, and high school, but I found that technology-based music instruction, at least in the way I envision it, is much more prevalent in middle and high schools than it is in elementary schools.) Musical experiences in the teachers' backgrounds ranged from classical instrumental performance, to jazz, to marching band, to choir. There did not seem to be a clear tendency for people who specialized in certain types of musical performance, or in certain instruments, to gravitate toward technology. This, however, might be an interesting element to investigate in the future.

In most cases, the teachers started their music teaching careers as traditional music teachers—in band, choir, orchestra, or general music settings—and at some point made a "transition" to being technology-based music teachers. Few of the participants predicted during their teacher training programs that they would be teaching music in a computer lab; still some (especially the younger participants) sought out technology in their pre-service years. In almost all cases, the teachers were involved in some traditional music teaching—perhaps an ensemble or a group piano class—in addition to their responsibilities in technology-based music instruction.

Training in music technology was perhaps the one item in this set of questions that produced the most consistent answers. There were, in general, two ways that the participants had become fluent with music technologies. Many of the participants cited their involvement with formal classwork, usually in the form of professional development workshops. The majority of the participants had taken workshops offered through TI:ME. Several had taken undergraduate classes or graduate classes that focused on technology applications. None of the participants suggested that they had any type of training in technology-based pedagogy.

Even more prevalent was the suggestion that the teachers learned technology on their own. Not uncommon were phrases such as these:

> "I feel like I just learned a lot of it through playing with keyboards growing up."
>
> "...a lot of it's been self-taught."
>
> "I read a lot of blogs, and I kind of watch what other people do. A lot of YouTube informational videos."

A few conclusions can be drawn from these comments and others like them. As mentioned in the premise of this book, pedagogical approaches to technology-based music instruction simply do not exist. Perhaps a more focused conclusion from these comments, however, is that in-service teachers are in a difficult spot because the support for technology integration into their music teaching is difficult to locate. This could change with the next generation of teachers, who may gain greater exposure to technology and related pedagogical approaches in their teacher training programs.

BIBLIOGRAPHY

Adamy, P. (2001). The primary importance of experience in the evaluation of educational technology. In W. F. Heinecki & L. Blasi (Eds.), *Methods of evaluating educational technology* (pp. 201–214). Greenwhich, CT: Information Age.

Allen, I. E., & Seaman, J. (2010). Class differences: Online education in the United States, 2010. Retrieved November 2011 from http://sloanconsortium.org/publications/survey/class_differences.

Anderson, L. W., & Krathwohl, D. R. (2001). *A taxonomy for learning, teaching, and assessing: A revision of Bloom's Taxonomy of Educational Objectives.* New York: Addison Wesley Longman.

Archambault, L. (2011). The practitioner's perspective on teacher education: Preparing for the K–12 online classroom. *Journal of Technology and Teacher Education, 19*(1), 73–91.

Archambault, L., & Crippen, K. (2009). Examining TPACK among the K–12 online distance educators in the United States. *Contemporary Issues in Technology and Teacher Education, 9*(1). Retrieved from www.citejournal.org/vol9/iss1/general/article2.cfm.

Armstrong, V. (2008). Hard bargaining on the hard drive: Gender bias in the music technology classroom. *Gender and Education, 20*(4), 375–386. doi: 10.1080/09540250802190206.

Armstrong, V. (2011). *Technology and the gendering of music education.* Surrey, UK: Ashgate.

Badolato, M. J. (1995). A user assessment of workspaces in selected music education computer laboratories. *Dissertation Abstracts International: Section A. 56*(04), 5428.

Baer, J., & Garrett, T. (2010). Teaching for creativity in an era of content standards and accountability. In R. A. Beghetto & J. C. Kaufman (Eds.), *Nurturing creativity in the classroom* (pp. 6–23). New York: Cambridge University Press.

Bakia, M., Means, B., Gallagher, L., Chen, E., & Jones, K. (2009). Evaluation of the Enhancing Education through Technology program: Final report. Washington, DC: U.S. Department of Education.

Barrett, J. R., McCoy, C. W., & Veblen, K. K. (1997). *Sound ways of knowing: Music in the interdisciplinary curriculum.* New York: Schirmer.

Bauer, W. I. (2010). Technological pedagogical and content knowledge, music, and assessment. In T. S. Brophy (Ed.), *The practice of assessment in music education: Frameworks, models, and designs—Proceedings of the 2009 Florida symposium on assessment in music education* (pp. 425–434). Chicago: GIA.

Bauer, W. I., Harris, J., & Hofer, M. (2012). "Grounded" technology integration using K-12 music learning activity types. *Learning and Leading with Technology, 40*(3), 30–32.

Beghetto, R. A., & Kaufman, J. C. (2010). Broadening conceptions of creativity in the classroom. In R. A. Beghetto & J. C. Kaufman (Eds.), *Nurturing creativity in the classroom* (pp. 191–205). New York: Cambridge University Press.

Berg Rice, V. J. (2007). Ergonomics and therapy: An introduction. In K. Jacobs (Ed.), *Ergonomics for therapists* (3rd ed., pp. 1–16). Philadelphia: Mosby Elsevier.

Bloom, B. S. (1984). *Taxonomy of educational objectives: Book 1—cognitive domain.* New York: Longman.

Bos, B. (2011). Professional development for elementary teachers using TPACK. *Contemporary Issues in Technology and Teacher Education, 11*(2). Retrieved from www.citejournal.org/vol11/iss2/mathematics/article1.cfm.

Bransford, J. D., Brown, A. L., & Cocking, R. R. (Eds.). (2000). *How people learn: Brain, mind, experience, and school* (Expanded ed.). Washington, DC: National Academy Press.

Bruner, J. (1977). *The process of education.* Cambridge, MA: Harvard University Press.

Chai, C. S., Koh, J. H. L., & Tsai, C.-C. (2010). Facilitating preservice teachers' development of technological, pedagogical, and content knowledge (TPACK). *Educational Technology and Society, 13*(4), 63–73.

Choksy, L. (1999a). *The Kodály method I: Comprehensive music education* (3rd ed.). Upper Saddle River, NJ: Prentice Hall.

Choksy, L. (1999b). *The Kodály method II: Folksong to masterwork.* Upper Saddle River, NJ: Prentice Hall.

Colwell, R. (Ed.). (2006). *MENC handbook of musical cognition and development.* New York: Oxford University Press.

Colwell, R., & Richardson, C. P. (Eds.). (2002). *The new handbook of research on music teaching and learning: A project of the Music Educators National Conference.* New York: Oxford University Press.

Dammers, R. J. (2010a). A case study of the creation of a technology-based music course. *Bulletin of the Council for Research in Music Education* (186), 55–65.

Dammers, R. (2010b). *Technology based music classes in high schools in the United States.* Paper presented at the Association for Technology in Music Instruction, Minneapolis, MN.

Del Borgo, E. A. (1988). Selecting quality literature for bands and orchestras. *The Instrumentalist, 43*(4), 22, 24, 26.

Deubel, P. (2002). Selecting curriculum-based software. *Learning and Leading with Technology, 29*(5), 10–16.

Dewey, J. (1938/1969). *Experience and education.* New York: Macmillan.

Dockrell, S., Fallon, E., Kelly, M., Masterson, B., & Shields, N. (2007). School children's use of computers and teachers' education in computer ergonomics. *Ergonomics, 50*(10), 1657–1667. doi: 10.1080/00140130701585438.

Dorfman, J. (2003). *The integration of computer technology into music teacher training: An historical perspective.* Unpublished master's thesis, University of Miami, Coral Gables, FL.

Dorfman, J. (2006). Learning music with technology: The influence of learning style, prior experiences, and two learning conditions on success with a music technology task. (Doctoral dissertation, Northwestern University, 2006), Dissertation Abstracts International, 67, 2919.

Dorfman, J. (2008). Technology in Ohio's school music programs: An exploratory study of teacher use and integration. *Contributions to Music Education, 35,* 23–46.

Dorfman, J., & Jacoby, M. M. (2006). Looping software: Philosophy and practice. Paper presented at the Association for Technology in Music Instruction conference, Quebec, City, Canada.

Duke, R. A. (2005). *Intelligent music teaching: Essays on core principles of effective instruction*. Austin, TX: Learning and Behavior Resources.

Duke, R. A., Prickett, C. A., & Jellison, J. A. (1998). Empirical description of the pace of music instruction. *Journal of Research in Music Education, 46*(2), 265–280.

Einser, E. (1966). Evaluating children's art. In E. Eisner & D. W. Ecker (Eds.), *Readings in art education* (pp. 384–388). Waltham, MA: Blaisdell.

Eisner, E. (1985). *The art of educational evaluation: A personal view*. Philadelphia: Falmer Press, Taylor & Francis.

Eisner, E. W. (2002). *The arts and the creation of mind*. New Haven, CT: Yale University Press.

Erez, A. B.-H., Shenkar, O., Jacobs, K., & Gillespie, R. M. (2007). Ergonomics for children and youth in the educational environment. In K. Jacobs (Ed.), *Ergonomics for therapists* (3rd ed., pp. 246–264). Philadelphia: Mosby Elsevier.

Fenstermacher, G. D., & Richardson, V. (2005). On making determinations of quality in teaching. *Teachers College Record, 107*(1), 186–213.

Fonder, M. (2003). Ostling's criteria for choosing fine music for all ensembles. *The Instrumentalist, 57*(6), 40, 42, 44.

Frankel, J. (2009). *The teacher's guide to music, media, and copyright law*. Milwaukee, WI: Hal Leonard.

Frazee, J., & Kreuter, K. (1987). *Discovering Orff*. New York: Schott.

Frazee, J. (2006). *Orff Schulwerk today: Nurturing musical expression and understanding*. New York: Schott.

Furst, E. J. (1994). Bloom's taxonomy: Philosophical and educational issues. In L. W. Anderson & L. A. Sosniak (Eds.), *Bloom's taxonomy: A forty-year retrospective* (pp. 28–40). Chicago: University of Chicago Press/National Society for the Study of Education.

Gaines, D. A. (1988). A core repertoire of concert band music. *Journal of Band Research, 34*(1), 1–24.

Genachowski, J. (2011). *Bringing broadband to rural America: Update to report on a rural broadband strategy*. Washington, DC: Federal Communications Commission. Retrieved from http://hraunfoss.fcc.gov/edocs_public/attachmatch/DOC-307877A1.pdf.

Gibbs, W., Graves, P. R., & Bernas, R. S. (2001). Evaluation guidelines for multimedia courseware. *Journal of Research on Technology in Education, 34*(1), 2–17.

Gordon, E. E. (1980). *Learning sequences in music: Skill, content, and patterns*. Chicago: GIA.

Green, L. (2002). *How popular musicians learn*. Aldershot, UK: Ashgate.

Hammel, A. M., & Hourigan, R. M. (2011). *Teaching music to students with special needs: A label-free approach*. New York: Oxford University Press.

Harasim, L. (2012). *Learning theory and collaborative online technologies*. New York: Routledge.

Hargreaves, D. J. (1982). The development of aesthetic reaction to music. *Psychology of Music* [Special issue], 51–54.

Harms, W., & DePencier, I. (1996). Experiencing education: 100 years of learning at the University of Chicago laboratory schools. Retrieved from http://www.ucls.uchicago.edu/data/files/gallery/HistoryBookDownloadsGallery/chapter1_3.pdf.

Hoffer, C. R. (1993). *Introduction to music education* (2nd ed). Long Grove, IL: Waveland Press.

Houlahan, M., & Tacka, P. (2008). *Kodály today: A cognitive approach to elementary music education.* New York: Oxford University Press.

Howard, S. K. (2007). Teacher change: A preliminary exploration of teachers' risk-taking in the context of ICT integration. Paper presented at the Australian Association for Research in Education conference, Sydney.

Hughes, B. (1990). Survey of band repertoire. *The Instrumentalist, 45*(4), 60–65.

Jaipal, K., & Figg, C. (2010). Unpacking the "Total PACKage": Emergent TPACK characteristics from a study of preservice teachers teaching with technology. *Journal of Technology and Teacher Education, 18*(3), 415–441.

Kaschub, M., & Smith, J. P. (2009). *Minds on music: Composition for creative and critical thinking.* Lanham, MD: Rowman & Littlefield.

Kendall, J. D. (1966). *What the American music educator should know about Shinichi Suzuki: Talent education and Suzuki.* Washington, DC: Music Educators National Conference.

Kendall, J. (1978). *The Suzuki violin method in American music education.* Reston, VA: Music Educators National Conference.

Kirkman, P. (2009). Embedding digital technologies in the music classroom: An approach for the new Music National Curriculum. Retrieved from www.slide-share.net/prk24/edtmc-kirkman-09a.

Koehler, M., & Mishra, P. (2008). Introducing TPCK. In AACTE Committee on Innovation and Technology (Ed.), *Handbook of Technological Pedagogical Content Knowledge (TPCK) for educators* (pp. 3–29). New York: Routledge/American Association of Colleges for Teacher Education.

Krathwohl, D. R. (1994). Reflections on the taxonomy: Its past, present, and future. In L. W. Anderson & L. A. Sosniak (Eds.), *Bloom's taxonomy: A forty-year retrospective* (pp. 181–202). Chicago: University of Chicago Press/National Society for the Study of Education.

Labinowicz, E. (1980). *The Piaget primer: Thinking, learning, teaching.* Menlo Park, CA: Addison-Wesley.

Landis, B., & Carder, P. (1990). The Dalcroze approach. In P. Carder (Ed.), *The eclectic curriculum in American music education* (pp. 7–54). Reston, VA: MENC.

LeBlanc, A., Sims, W. L., Siivola, C., & Olbert, M. (1996). Music style preferences of different age listeners. *Journal of Research in Music Education, 44,* 49–59.

Lerman, L., & Borstel, J. (2003). *Critical response process: A method for getting useful feedback on anything you make, from dance to dessert.* Takoma Park, MD: Liz Lerman Dance Exchange.

Lever-Duffy, J., McDonald, J. B., & Mizell, A. P. (2005). *Teaching and learning with technology* (2nd ed.). Boston: Pearson.

Low, R., & Sweller, J. (2005). The modality principle in multimedia learning. In R. E. Mayer (Ed.), *The Cambridge Handbook of Multimedia Learning* (pp. 147–158). New York: Cambridge University Press.

Lux, N. J. (2010). Assessing technological pedagogical content knowledge. *Dissertation Abstracts International: Section A., 71*(12).

Mayer, R. E. (2005). Introduction to multimedia learning. In R. E. Mayer (Ed.), *The Cambridge Handbook of Multimedia Learning* (pp. 1–18). New York: Cambridge University Press.

Mayhall, B. (1994). The quest for high-quality repertoire. *Choral Journal, 35*(2), 9–16.

Mead, V. H. (1994). *Dalcroze eurhythmics in today's music classroom.* New York: Schott.

Mishra, P., & Koehler, M. (2006). Technological pedagogical content knowledge: A framework for teacher knowledge. *Teachers College Record, 108*(6), 1017–1054.

O'Toole, P. (2003). *Shaping sound musicians: An innovative approach to teaching comprehensive musicianship through performance*. Chicago: GIA.

Ostling, A. E. (1978). An evaluation of compositions for wind band according to specific criteria of serious artistic merit. *Dissertation Abstracts International: Section A., 39*(6), 325.

Papert, S. (1980). *Mindstorms: Children, computers, and powerful ideas*. New York: Basic Books.

Pearson, B. (2000). Selecting music for the young band. In T. Dvorak (Ed.), *Teaching music through performance in beginning band* (pp. 45–60). Chicago: GIA.

Pamuk, S. (2011). Understanding preservice teachers' technology use through TPACK framework. *Journal of Computer Assisted Learning*. doi: 10.1111/j.1365-2729.2011.00447.x.

Pederson, P. V. (2007). What is measured is treasured: The impact of the No Child Left Behind Act on nonassessed subjects. *Clearing House: A Journal of Educational Strategies, Issues, and Ideas, 80*(6), 287–291. doi: 10.3200.

Phillips Jr., J. L. (1981). *Piaget's theory: A primer*. San Francisco: W.H. Freeman.

Prensky, M. (2001). Digital natives, digital immigrants. *On the Horizon, 9*(5), 1–6.

Reeves, T. C., Benson, L., Elliott, D., Grant, M., Holschuh, D., Kim, B., et al. (2002). *Usability and instructional design heuristics for e-learning evaluation*. Paper presented at the ED-MEDIA World Conference on Educational Multimedia, Hypermeida & Telecommunications, Denver, CO.

Reimer, B. (1991). Criteria for quality in music. In R. A. Smith & A. Simpson (Eds.), *Aesthetics and arts education* (pp. 330–338). Urbana: University of Illinois Press.

Reimer, B. (2003). *A philosophy of music education: Advancing the vision* (3rd ed.). Upper Saddle River, NJ: Pearson Education.

Roblyer, M. D., & Doering, A. H. (2010). *Integrating educational technology into teaching* (5th ed.). Boston: Allyn & Bacon/Pearson.

Rudolph, T. E. (1999). *Finding funds for music technology: Strategies for getting your music program into the 21st century*. Wyncote, PA: SoundTree.

Rudolph, T. E. (2004). *Teaching music with technology* (2nd ed.). Chicago: GIA.

Rudolph, T. E., Richmond, F., Mash, D., Webster, P., Bauer, W. I., & Walls, K. (2005). *Technology strategies for music education* (2nd ed.). Wyncote, PA: Technology Institute for Music Education.

Rutkowski, J. (2011). *Response to "Transitioning to music education 3.0."* Paper presented at the Committee on Institutional Cooperation, East Lansing, MI.

Saliba, K. K. (1991). *Accent on Orff: An introductory approach*. Englewood Cliffs, NJ: Prentice Hall.

Schmidt, D. A., Baran, E., Thompson, A. D., Koehler, M. J., Mishra, P., and Shin, T. (2009). Survey of preservice teachers' knowledge of teaching and technology. Retrieved September, 21, 2011 from http://tpack.org.

Schmidt, D. A., Baran, E., Thompson, A. D., Mishra, P., Koehler, M. J., & Shin, T. S. (2009). Technological pedagogical and content knowledge (TPACK): The development and validation of an assessment instrument for preservice teachers. *Journal of Research on Technology in Education, 42*(2), 123–149.

Serafine, M. L. (1980). Piagetian research in music. *Bulletin of the Council for Research in Music Education, 62*, 1–21.

Shehan Campbell, P., & Scott-Kassner, C. (1995). *Music in childhood: From preschool through the elementary grades*. New York: Schirmer Books.

Shulman, L. S. (1986). Those who understand: A conception of teacher knowledge. *American Educator, 10*(1), 9–15,43–44.

Smith, L. (2009). Piaget's pedagogy. In U. Müller, J. I. M. Carpendale, & L. Smith (Eds.), *The Cambridge companion to Piaget* (pp. 324–343). Cambridge: Cambridge University Press.

Stokes, P. D. (2010). Using constraints to develop creativity in the classroom. In R. A. Beghetto & J. C. Kaufman (Eds.), *Nurturing creativity in the classroom* (pp. 88–112). New York: Cambridge University Press.

Straker, L., Malsen, B., Burgess-Limerick, R., Johnson, P., & Dennerlein, J. (2010). Evidence-based guidelines for the wise use of computers by children: Physical development guidelines. *Ergonomics, 53*(4), 458–477.

Sweller, J. (2005). The redundancy principle in multimedia learning. In R. E. Mayer (Ed.), *The Cambridge Handbook of Multimedia Learning* (pp. 159–168). New York: Cambridge University Press.

Taylor, J. A., & Deal, J. J. (2003). *The status of technology integration in college music methods courses: A survey of NASM colleges and universities.* Paper presented at the Association for Technology in Music Instruction, Santa Fe, NM.

Tobias, E. (2010). Crossfading and plugging in: Secondary students' engagement and learning in a songwriting and technology class. *Dissertation Abstracts International: Section A., 75*(5).

Watson, S. (Ed.). (2005). *Technology guide for music educators.* Boston: Thomson Course Technology.

Watson, S. (2011). *Using technology to unlock musical creativity.* New York: Oxford University Press.

Williams, D. B., & Webster, P. R. (2006). *Experiencing music technology: Software, data, and hardware* (3rd ed.). New York: Schirmer Books.

Williams, D. B., & Webster, P. R. (2011). *Music technology skills and conceptual under-standings for undergraduate music students: A national survey.* Paper presented at the annual conference of the College Music Society/Association for Technology in Music Instruction, Richmond, VA.

Williams, I. M. (2001). Elementary school teachers' working comfort while using computers at school and at home. Retrieved from www.iea.cc/ECEE/pdfs/ElementarySchoolTeachersinger.pdf.

Webster, P. R. (2002a). Computer-based technology and music teaching and learning. In R. Colwell & C. P. Richardson (Eds.), *The new handbook of research on music teaching and learning* (pp. 416–439). New York: Schirmer Books.

Webster, P. (2002b). Creative thinking in music: Advancing a model. In T. Sullivan & L. Willingham (Eds.), *Creativity and music education* (pp. 16–33). Edmonton: Canadian Music Educator's Association.

Webster, P. R. (2011). Construction of music learning. In R. Colwell & P. R. Webster (Eds.), *MENC Handbook of research on music learning* (Vol. 1: Strategies, pp. 35–83). New York: Oxford University Press.

Wheeler, L., & Raebeck, L. (1977). *Orff and Kodály adapted for the elementary school.* Dubuque, IA: Wm. C. Brown.

INDEX